Qian Mu and the
World of
Seven Mansions

Qian Mu at his home in Taiwan, April 1986.

Qian Mu and the World of Seven Mansions

Jerry Dennerline

Yale University Press
New Haven and London

Published with assistance from the Kingsley Trust
Association Publication Fund established by the
Scroll and Key Society of Yale College.

Designed by James J. Johnson
and set in Baskerville Roman types by
Delmas, Ann Arbor, Michigan.
Printed in the United States of America by
BookCrafters, Inc., Chelsea, Michigan.

Library of Congress Cataloging-in-Publication Data

Dennerline, Jerry, 1942–
Qian Mu and the world of Seven Mansions / Jerry
Dennerline.
   p. cm.
   Includes English translation of Qian Mu's Pa shih i
shuang ch' in.
   Includes index.
   ISBN 0–300–04296–5 (alk. paper)
   1. Ch'ien, Mu, 1895– .2. China—Intellectual life—
20th century. 3. Scholars—China—Biography. I.
Ch'ien, Mu, 1895– Pa shih i shuang ch' in. English.
1989. II. Title.
CT3990.C47D46 1989
951'.0072024—dc19
[B]   88–20576
                                           CIP

The paper in this book meets the guidelines for
permanence and durability of the Committee on
Production Guidelines for Book Longevity of the
Council on Library Resources.

10 9 8 7 6 5 4 3 2 1

For Sus

Contents

Illustrations

MAPS

Preface

How to explain one culture's conception of "truth" in the language of another culture without turning it into a falsehood: this may well be the primary dilemma facing intellectuals in the modern world. Whether the two cultures are scientific and popular, political and intellectual, Eastern and Western, or yours and mine, the problem of understanding remains the same. Can we create new, "modern" standards of truth that are at once universal in scope and acceptable to communities that conceive of themselves as distinct from some "other"? The degree to which we succeed in this effort depends on how well we can explain in the language of one culture what makes certain "truths" believable in the language of the other.

This book is an attempt to explain what made certain truths believable to one modern intellectual who, because of their believability, has devoted his life to teaching those truths. As a modern Chinese intellectual, Qian Mu (Ch'ien Mu) confronted the problem of cultural relativity early in life. It was forced on him, as it has been on all non-Western intellectuals, by the political and economic expansion of the West. Unlike those Chinese who turned to Western Enlightenment ideas and rejected the cultural values of the Chinese past, Qian Mu has tried consistently over the past seventy years to renew belief in traditional Chinese values. But if Qian's "other" is not the cultural past, neither is it the "modern" present. It is the culture of the West, whose standards of truth Qian deems inapplicable to China and its problems.

Understandably, Westerners tend to be preoccupied with the struggle of China's "Enlightenment" thinkers and their heirs to establish new standards of truth there, not just for intellectuals but for all the Chinese people. Yet intellectuals like Qian Mu, who see the relevance of traditional values to modern problems, have much to contribute to the common effort. These thinkers are believers not so much in the past as in those particular values that, after considerable reflection, still seem to distinguish Chinese from Western culture. In Qian Mu's case, the experience of learning and teaching in an environment where these values were still being transmitted despite political and economic change reinforced his belief and refined his understanding. I hope to explain something of this belief and understanding by juxtaposing Qian's conception of transmission, as revealed in his memoirs, with my own reconstruction of the environment in which it occurred.

In effect, there are two Seven Mansions in this book. The first is Qian Mu's, the product of many long years of reflection, finally recorded in his "Reminiscences on My Parents at the Age of Eighty." This Seven Mansions is inseparable from the truth Qian Mu wants to transmit. My translation, while it cannot convey all the nuances of the original, is designed to transmit as much of that truth as possible in English. The second Seven Mansions is a historical reconstruction based on evidence obtained from gazetteers, family histories, inscriptions, genealogies, letters, and other documents; on-site observations, interviews, and social surveys. This Seven Mansions is the product of theories and methods developed in Western historiography and applied to Qian Mu's native place. Perhaps it is only mine, but I would like to think that it partakes at least as much of some objective reality as it does of me. If the same can be said of Qian Mu's, then we might conclude that a third Seven Mansions—the real one—is the source of some significant common ground.

It is my conscious choice to let Qian Mu speak for himself as much as possible in this book. He has been identified as a "cultural conservative," part of a generation that divided over the relevance of Enlightenment ideas to China, and his differences with the Westernized academic leadership there are well documented. His perspective has been described as Neo-Confucian, and his influence among contemporary intellectuals who interpret Confucian thought is great. He has also been labeled an anti-Communist, and his association with others who have objected to Communist ideology and Soviet influence in China is real. Yet Qian Mu's own words and actions demonstrate the pointlessness of reducing him to any of these characterizations. He is primarily a child of the old culture who grew up in a world that provided the richest possible experience of that culture in the worst of times. Rather than his own arguments and their contextual justification, it is this experience I intend to reconstruct. If there is an argument in this book, it concerns the relevance of that reconstruction to the broader issues of continuity in Chinese culture as they might be understood in a language that transcends the culture itself.

This project began at Yale University in 1980, when Yü Ying-shih introduced me to Qian's "Reminiscences on My Parents at the Age of Eighty" after a conversation about my study of the New Hua Charitable Estate, which I had just completed with the generous support of the Modern China Project funded by the National Endowment for the Humanities at the University of Chicago, under the direction of Tsou Tang. It was then I discovered that Qian Mu owed his early education to that estate and that his father's life and his childhood had been greatly influenced by the very political culture I was trying to reconstruct from less vivid sources. I decided to translate the text, benefitting from the support of the American Council of Learned Societies fellowship program in Chinese Civilization, and I began using it as a source in my undergraduate teaching at Amherst College the following year. Professor Yü later put me in touch with Qian Mu, with whom I was finally able to discuss my project in 1983. The Miner Crary Fellowship at Amherst College made possible not only this discussion but also several other crucial interviews in Taiwan and Bangkok. Hsü Cho-yun introduced me to the Taiwan Wu-hsi T'ung-hsiang Hui (Wuxi Native Place Association of Taiwan), which has continued to provide me with sources and introductions that are indispensable to my research. Thomas Hung-ch'i Lee was my gracious host at New Asia College, Chinese University of Hong Kong, where Qian Mu's former students, successors, and colleagues took time off from their busy schedules to reminisce and offer much needed advice. I wish to thank all of these people and institutions for their help.

In 1985, and again in 1986, I was able to conduct field research in parts of Wuxi County not normally open to foreigners. The Wuxi County Foreign Office, the county government, the administrative townships of Dangkou, Hongshengli, Ganlu, Anzhen, and Meicun all went out of their way to facilitate my research. I also owe thanks to the Wuxi City Foreign Office, the Wuxi Public Library, and the Wuxi Light Industry Institute for facilitating this research. The Committee for Scholarly Communication with the People's Republic of China provided generous support, and Nanjing University was my supportive host. My research goals would have come to nothing without the constant assistance and superb advice of Lü Zuoxie, whose comments and discussions of historical issues—and interpretations of Wuxi dialect—during our long days together have also contributed significantly to my understanding.

My writing was completed with generous support from the John Simon Guggenheim Memorial Foundation, and the East Asian Institute of the University of Copenhagen welcomed me as a visiting research professor during a year-and-a-half leave from Amherst College, providing much needed tranquillity as well as collegiality. I am indebted to Huang Po-fei, Yao Tao-chung, and Yü Ying-shih for valuable suggestions that improved the translation; to Jonathan Spence, Yü Ying-shih, Chang Hao, Ernst Schwintzer, Birthe Anderup, Vibeke Petersen, Robert Gross, and Vera Schwarcz for reading the manuscript and offering especially helpful suggestions; to Yao Tao-chung, Hua Chung-hou, Hua Shu-ho, Tsou Ching-heng, Wang Hai-p'ing, Ch'üan Han-sheng, Yan Xuexi, Zhu Hairong, Qian Weichang, Qian Ciming, Wang Yuancai, Wang Gengtang, and Gao Zuoliang for providing important leads, documents, and information; to students and colleagues at Amherst College, the Five College Colloquium Orientologicum, the Columbia University Regional Seminar on Modern China, the Conference on Family and Kinship in Chinese History, and the University of Copenhagen Sinology Seminar for helpful discussion of various aspects of the research; to Rhea Cabin for expert production of the manuscript; to Stephanie Jones for superb editing; and to Susanne Jorn for sustaining this work with love. I am solely responsible for the outcome.

I.

Behind the Red Gate

ON THE EDGE of a narrow valley in the hills north of Taipei lies a small, displaced institution of higher learning called Soochow University. The location is marked by a bus stop on the country road, a few hundred paces below the main gate. One steamy morning in late July 1983, a historian emerged from the clattering bus in search of the big red gate bearing the placard that identified the residence known as Su Shu Lou, "Plain Book Building." It is an odd name for a residence. But oddities are common among the names chosen by Chinese scholars for their homes and studios. Such places are sacred, and behind each name is a personal story that sanctifies the place. In this case, the name was taken from the scholar's childhood home where his mother had nursed him back to life from a critical illness in 1911. The name—an obscure classical reference*— had been chosen by some forgotten ancestor in the scholar's native village of Qifangqiao, a remote island of humanity amid the rice paddies of the lower Yangtze Valley. This was the village I call Seven Mansions.

As I stood before the red gate by the lane that leads from the modern university campus to the villages in the hills beyond, I reflected on the name. The scholar who lives there, the historian Qian

*It may be one of four categories in the Han Dynasty's Imperial Library, designating the history collection, or it may refer to a Han syncretic Taoist text.

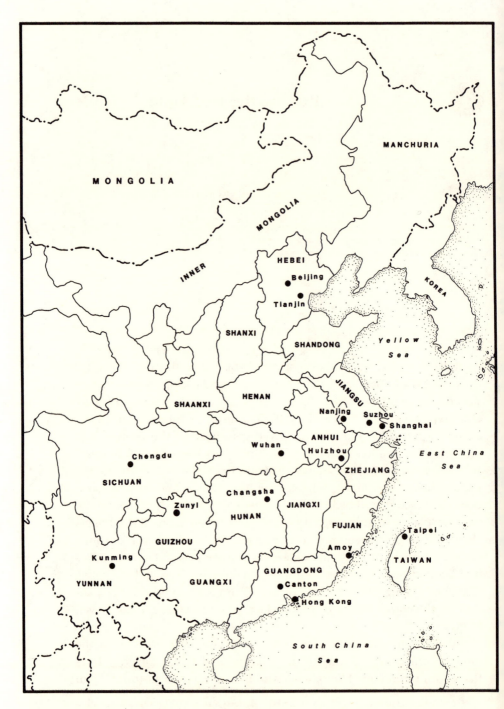

Map 1. Qian Mu's China. Drawn by Roy Doyon.

Mu (Ch'ien Mu), had been born in Seven Mansions in 1895, the year the emergent Japanese nation took Taiwan from the decrepit Qing Dynasty by force. It was this humiliating defeat more than anything else that had turned a generation of young scholars into revolutionaries, changing their perception of the Chinese past. Despite its remoteness, Seven Mansions was not immune to the influence. The village lay about two and a half hours by boat from Suzhou (Soochow), the center of scholar-official culture, and four hours from the county seat of Wuxi. The revolutionary spirit reached Seven Mansions through the country schools and the young literati who taught there; it came via family links to Wuxi, Suzhou, and Shanghai. Qian Mu's education partook of it and I had arrived at the red gate in the hope of learning more about it.[1]

My quest was not so much for the truth about the origins of the Chinese revolution as for the meaning of the Chinese past in the mind of a great historian of that generation. Like all Chinese, Qian Mu grew up with an awareness of China's great legacies. It is the world's oldest living civilization, home of some of the world's greatest empires and many of its greatest inventions and intellectual traditions. But the West had overtaken China in the nineteenth century. Most Chinese of Qian Mu's generation shared a sense that China's history had somehow betrayed the Chinese people. The history of the world was on another course, and no matter how proud China's rulers or how profound its values, history did not bear them out. In rejecting their past, Chinese revolutionaries were not worried just about standing up to the West or catching up with history as they now understood it; they were determined to find new values in the process. From the anti-Manchu movement of the 1890s through the Cultural Revolution of the 1960s and the democracy movement of the 1980s, political activists in China have thought of themselves as struggling against the burdens of their own history in order to join, perhaps to overtake, the vanguard of a more progressive and modern one.

For those who left the revolution as it unfolded, and Qian Mu was one, the role of history became less clear. Since the death of Mao in 1976 and the acceleration of reforms in the People's Republic in the 1980s, the quest for the meaning of the past has been revived. At one level, the Chinese Communist party reassessed the role of Mao officially in 1981, leaving the impression that much of what he did (the negative aspects of his career, to be sure) was determined by a history that preceded his revolutionary thoughts. Mao, it was said, was acting like a traditional Chinese emperor when he ignored the counsel of his administrative planners after 1949. On another level, reform has restored the historical role of the peasant economy. Both the rural collective economy, which is now industrializing rapidly, and the peasant family economy, which is given free rein to develop privately, are changing in unprecedented ways. Where Mao once warned that capitalist tendencies could reverse the course of history after the socialist revolution, Deng Xiaoping has announced that it matters not at all if the cat is black or white so long as it can catch a mouse. In this ideologically relaxed, postrevolutionary atmosphere, family values are being restored along with historical sites and relics. Confucius is again respected, Buddhist orders have been revived, and history, as it were, is being unwrapped again. Professional historians have begun raising from the dead the positive influences of the past, placing them alongside the negative ones. In short, a postrevolutionary critical eye is seeking new links with the past as China prepares once again for an uncertain future.

Reviving the quest for the meaning of Chinese history does not mean returning to the past. On the contrary, the study of history is, as always, the study of change. But with the passage from revolution to postrevolutionary reform, revolutionary thoughts *alone* are no longer sufficient for explaining the process of change in China. Though reform has generated enthusiasm about *how* things can change, it needs the support of *whence, why,* and *whither.* Without a broader and deeper historical context, the vision of the revolution cannot provide that support. With these thoughts in mind, I hoped to catch a glimpse of the spirit of the generation that first conceived of a China free of autocracy and the threat of foreign rule, yet unspoiled by the ideological conflict between capitalism and communism and still aware of living links to the past. Qian Mu was my source.

One of modern China's best-known historians, Qian Mu was a highly respected Beijing University professor in the 1930s. He is author of an influential comprehensive history, founder of Hong Kong's first Chinese-language college, and spokesman for cultural conservatives outside the People's Republic since 1949. Like most Chinese intellectuals of the twentieth century, he favored revolution in his youth. But unlike most he could not divorce his revolutionary ideas from his deep love for both the beauties and the quirks of his native culture. As a historian he tried to bridge the terrible chasm between China's long history and the demands of the modern world, and as a teacher he tried to instill the value of that history in the minds of a generation that he considered suspended in the void. It is easy for most of us, whose lives are much shorter and minds much shallower than his, to point out fallacies in his metaphorical arguments and dismiss them as historicist or sentimental. But there is no dismissing the effort and the insight it gives into the problem of historical meaning. The problem that preceded the revolution is not so different from the one that follows it. And Qian Mu is a living link.

From Qian Mu's first revolutionary thoughts to my arrival at the red gate, seven decades passed. The slight, bespectacled man I met, whom I expected to transmit something of the spirit of a different time and place, had lived through the disillusionment following the 1911 revolution that toppled the Qing Dynasty, the New Culture movement that sought to transform Chinese values by introducing science and democracy, the political reunification of China under the Guomindang in 1927, the radicalization of student politics, the anti-Japanese war, the war between the Guomindang and the Communists, and a long period of exile in Hong Kong and Taiwan. He had lost two wives and his eyesight. Yet his "Reminiscences on My Parents at the Age of Eighty," which I first read in 1981, is a unique expression of something—an idea, a passion, a worldview, a spirit—that transcended the doubts and conflicts of the intervening years.

As others denounced this spirit and joined in the political fray, Qian Mu remained a detached critic. Nothing captures the effect of this steadfast commitment to the cultural conservative ideal better than the tragic story of his encounter with Wen Yiduo (Wen I-to), the poet, classical scholar, and martyr. The two had been roommates briefly during the war with Japan, and Qian had great respect for Wen as a scholar. When Wen turned on Qian later, denouncing him in print as a man without a soul for his refusal to attack the Guomindang's repression of leftist students, Qian ignored the diatribe. In 1947, he found himself mourning at the spot in Kunming where Wen had been shot down after publicly blaming the Guomindang for murdering a friend. To Qian, Wen Yiduo's scholarship was a monument to the truth and beauty of Chinese culture, and his death a symbol of bad times, a trough in the eternal cycle of cultural florescence and decline.[2]

Others saw Wen Yiduo's death as a symbol of the link between the old culture and the new imperialism. Wen had only recently turned against the ideal of political detachment. His denunciation of Qian Mu was in tune with radical voices he and many others had tried to hear only in harmony with those who spoke of the old culture's values. But during the 1920s and 1930s the radicals came more and more to set the dominant theme. As they spoke in a language dominated by new words, and wrote in a new standardized vernacular that reflected the culture of the universities, the radicals produced sounds with a new rhythm, less and less compatible with the rhythms of the old China. Radical themes of political responsibility, technological progress, social justice, and civil rights, of revolution and resistance to imperialist aggression, made sense only if expressed in the new rhythms. To hold simultaneously to these new ideas and to the most deeply felt harmonies of the old culture—familial love, respect for learning, intellectual integrity, political detachment, moderation in personal and public affairs—may have been possible in the best of times. But in the worst, it threatened to split heart and mind in two.

Wen Yiduo had written some of the best poetry in the new vernacular and some of the best modern research essays on ancient poetry. He had studied at the Art Institute of Chicago and in New York. Although he had once been a Nationalist supporter, he had vowed to remain politically detached after returning to Beijing. But this delicate balance broke down in 1944, when Wen's sympathy for young army recruits he saw dying under forced march and in chains drove him to political action. His attack on Qian Mu was an attack on the language of the old culture, on Confucian "moderation" and faith in the family, on "antiquarianism" and Taoist "escapism." These were the elements of the old culture that allowed the Guomindang to lean on the United States during and after the war with Japan, while the Chinese people passively accepted a "life between hunger and death." Even Qian Mu, who was among the blindest of the school that "ignored the illness and avoided the cure," Wen argued, had to admit in his introduction to the *Outline History of the Nation* that China was sick. But by taking part in the Democratic League, the short-lived movement to offset the conflict between the Guomindang and the Communist party, Wen also identified himself with those who saw the Guomindang's dependency on the United States as an obstacle to the political unity of China. For leftist students, Wen's assassination symbolized the link between the

Guomindang's nationalistic appeals to the common cultural heritage of the Chinese people and American interference in Chinese politics.[3]

Such symbolic links could only be made in a language that was foreign to Qian Mu. For him, the murder was an episode in "a tragedy" and was symbolic of the degree to which political disharmony, *within* the only culture China had, had interrupted the communication of values that were necessary to its survival. The signs of disharmony were many. Qian has recorded them in his memoirs. At Lianda, the university of refugees in Kunming where both Qian and Wen taught during the war, a student couple were found sleeping together on a classroom table.[4] Feng Youlan (Fung Yu-lan), China's most prominent philosopher and dean of arts and letters at Lianda, publicly praised students who went off with patriotic intentions to join the Communist mobilization, rather than preparing themselves for postwar intellectual roles.[5] After the war, students associated with the Democratic League in Kunming were allowed to put up anonymous "big character posters" accepting Soviet news reports and denying Nationalist government ones. And, again and again, students went on strike. All these signs, Qian believed, pointed to a collapse of faith in Chinese culture as well as in the regime that supported the university, which was the culture's last chance for survival.[6]

Yet Qian also saw signs that the language in which shared cultural values could be communicated was still intact. Feng Youlan, whose speech in praise of the student defectors Qian had followed with one urging others not to follow their example, was still able to accept Qian's critical advice on an interpretive history of Chinese philosophy.[7] A postal official who rode with Qian from Chengdu to Chungqing for a lecture series had absorbed the message of his book on ancient Chinese thought.[8] Students filled a lecture hall in a remote academy in Sichuan to hear him discourse on the subject of state and society in Chinese history.[9] And the people of a rural town he visited, with a former student who had been born there, were so strict in their observance of ritual order that the visitors were required to stay an additional three days so that the drama could be played out.[10]

Somehow, through the worst of the crisis, Qian Mu retained his sense of what he saw as a distinctly Chinese moral vision, the spirit of the culture. What distinguishes the Chinese moral vision from all others is, first, a matter of language. The concepts that express it have no equivalents in other languages. Second, Chinese society has evolved along with these concepts. Chinese people understand moral prescriptions in reference to Chinese institutions and Chinese social practice. Third, that moral prescriptions exist in all cultures is a matter of fact, but whether they exist independently of language and society is a matter of metaphysical speculation. Moral prescriptions are also, necessarily, personal prescriptions, and Qian Mu's personal sense of his own, culturally determined obligations generated in him an unshakable commitment to national unity and an equally unshakable detachment from party politics.

The language that allows commitment to national unity and detachment from politics to coexist is the language of Seven Mansions. It was, in fact, that language that brought me to the red gate. Qian Mu's "Reminiscences on My Parents" describes the setting of his childhood, a setting that intersects with that of a study of nineteenth-century local politics I had just completed when I read Qian's essay. The weight of oral tradition in the essay is heavy, and I hoped by talking with the author about it to jog his memory for more stories and more details. As I climbed the fifty or sixty steps through the lush garden to the house, the language of the "Reminiscences" filled my head. Once we were seated in a room filled with highly polished Chinese furniture and hung with scrolls, and the author began to speak Chinese in his thick Wuxi accent and, despite his blindness, to write out characters for words I could not make out, the language of the "Reminiscences" took on a new life.

Only one new story and a very few details emerged from more than three hours of conversation. What I received, instead, was a lesson in Chinese culture. I reproduce it here, in my own words, as a preface to my English translation of the "Reminiscences":

A LESSON IN CHINESE CULTURE

There is a misconception abroad that the Chinese people are extremely parochial, because each is attached to his native place and its customs. In Chinese, we say that such a person has a *xiangtu guannian,* a "native place point of view." Although it is true that most Chinese are attached to their native place, that attachment has little to do with Chinese culture. The culture, in fact, has been shaped over the centuries by *shiren,* "literati," who were quite cosmopolitan. Unlike the literati of Europe, they shared a common culture no matter what their place of origin. For a Westerner, culture is bound to place, so that local customs and language serve to distinguish cultures. For a Chinese, culture is universal, so that languages and local customs only serve to distinguish place. To understand the difference, you need to understand the concept of *li*, "the rites" or "propriety."

There are no Western-language equivalents for the word li. It is a general concept that applies to standards of customary behavior throughout the Chinese world and distinguishes Chinese culture from all others. Because Western cultures have no li, you distinguish among them by measuring the differences between *fengsu*, "local customs," as if a culture were the sum total of the customs practiced within its area of influence. If you set out to observe local customs in China, you will find that they vary greatly from place to place. Even within Wuxi county, the fengsu of Dangkou, where I grew up, and those of Rongxiang, where I taught after the war, are different. The differences from one end of the country to the other are much greater. But the li are the same. By the same token, the li that are standards for the family—its internal relations, its external relations, birth, marriage, death—are equivalent to the li that are standards for the workings of government and state ceremonies—internal relations, relations between state and society, recruitment, treaties, successions. This is the only way to understand Chinese culture. It is different from customary practice.

There is another concept basic to Chinese culture that has no Western equivalent, and that is *zu*, "descent group." You might say that the *jia*, or "family," is the place in Chinese culture where li is transmitted. But it is important to distinguish between *jiating*, the "family living group," and *jiazu*, the "family descent group." It is through the jiazu that the standards of social relationships extend beyond the family to relatives. The descent group, which includes the relatives on both sides of the family, can only exist if the standards of li are applied. So, when the li are extended, a family descent group is made, and when they are further extended, a "people's descent group," or *minzu*, is made. The Chinese are a minzu because the li set the standards in social relations for all the people. Where practices vary from the li, it is because of local custom or economics, which are subject to change.

Now, when you study a place like Seven Mansions, you show a strong interest in local customs, in families, and in conceptions of those people's native place. But if you want to understand Chinese culture, you are off the mark. You are only looking at the fingers and toes. If you want to understand the culture, you need to raise your sights until you reach the heart and mind. The heart and mind of China is the li.[11]

The lesson betrayed a gulf that separated Qian and me. For all my hope of explaining what made this worldview believable from the perspective of Seven Mansions eighty years ago, I still needed to focus on the fingers and toes. I could only show how local customs tended to embody and legitimize certain cultural principles, whereas he could only explain the continuities as spiritually transcendent. The difference was similar to the one that in the 1920s had divided Chinese intellectuals into followers of the "Enlightenment" and cultural conservatives.[12] Enlightenment thinkers also hoped to detach themselves from politics, but they believed that reason could unify China; for the cultural conservatives the unifying factor was, and for Qian Mu it still is, moral vision.[13]

Qian Mu's nation is a people whose unity depends on the extension of shared values outward from the family. The interpreters and preservers of those values in the political world are shiren, whose cultivation raises them above the petty interests of social groups and releases them from the bonds of local custom. What they preserve are the li, and only when the li prevail does the state share the people's moral vision. When the state does not share that vision, the li can only be preserved and the truth transmitted by families, teachers, and friends. There is no room for a new vision reflecting the interests of social groups released from local custom by forces beyond the shiren's control. And it is just such interests that claim the attention of historians trained in the Enlightenment's schools.

Yet somewhere beneath these differences lies a more fundamental truth. Something made the li believable, unifying China in all its diversity. If, as a non-Chinese historian, I believe it will be possible to explain this truth someday in a language that transcends the Chinese past, I am nonetheless convinced that the first step is to understand it in the language that does not. What follows is a dialogue between two kinds of truth. The first part tells Qian Mu's story, as nearly as possible as he would have it told, based on his memoirs and entailing his experiments with the preservation and transmission of the truth. The second part describes the world of Seven Mansions, in terms that I believe are supportive both of Qian Mu's truth and of the notion that interests did change, and moral vision with them. The third part is Qian Mu's own "Reminiscences," in which his vision is applied to Seven Mansions and to his parents' place in it. The reader may wish to judge the appropriateness of the vision to the scene before turning to my own judgments in the chapter that follows. At the outset, suffice it to say that in Seven Mansions at the turn of the century, and throughout China for some time before and after that, the li did not prevail.

II.

To Practice When It Is Timely

> To learn and then to practice when it is timely,
> isn't that the meaning of pleasure?
> To have friends come from afar, isn't that the
> meaning of joy?
> Not to regret it when one's learning is not recog-
> nized, isn't that what it means to be a true scholar
> [*junzi*]?
>
> —*Analects*, 1:1

HE FIRST WORDS A SCHOOLBOY re-
cited from the *Analects of Confucius* taught that learning and communi-
cating with those who shared in the truth was sufficient to sustain one's
spirit. Qian Mu reached the prime of life in the worst of times, yet as
students and scholars split on ideological lines and died for speaking
their minds, he found occasion to invoke this passage. As a refugee in
the southwest during the war, his one passion was hiking in the mountains. For a month in the spring of 1942 he was a visiting lecturer at the
exiled Zhejiang University in Zunyi, Guizhou. In his memoir, he tells
this story:

> I was especially fond of the hills and streams at Zunyi. A former
> student of mine, Li Yan, who had just transferred from Kunming
> to take a teaching job there, accompanied me daily on a hike. We
> hiked at least half the day, and sometimes more. It was late spring,
> and the hills were ringed with blossoms. The ground was already
> cushioned with flowers but still shaded by those that remained on
> the trees. Li Yan and I would stretch out on the flower cushions
> that covered the mountain grass, enjoying the flower-shaded view,
> move on a bit, and then stretch out again. I am also especially fond
> of swallows. When as a boy I studied the *Analects of Confucius* with

Zhu Xi's commentary,* I noted that Zhu explained the word *xi* (practice), in the phrase "To learn and then to 'practice' when it is timely," with reference to the frequency of the flight of birds. Whenever I watched the swallows fly in the courtyard I thought of them as my teachers. After leaving Beiping I didn't often see swallows. But there was a place where a stream circled back on its way down from one of the hills outside Zunyi, and one could cross over a bridge on the way up. Trees encircled the clearing around the bend of the stream, and more than a hundred swallows flocked there, darting up into the sky, swirling about the enclosure and never leaving it. I flowed with the rhythm and was reluctant to leave.

Then, one day Li Yan said to me, "When I took your lecture course in Beiping I admired your erudition. All the students said you must spend all day with your head buried in the books; otherwise how could you do it? Then when I visited you in your mountain retreat outside of Kunming and you were writing your *Outline History of the Nation*, I saw that my image was not wrong. But here you spend all day hiking. I remember when I was a student we all were anxious that we couldn't study hard enough. Who would have thought that it is even harder to keep up with you at playing! Now I know there's another side to your life."

So I told him, "When studying, one should think only of studies; when wandering among hills and streams, one should think only of hills and streams. One rides on enthusiasm and abandons one's mind to it. That's why the first lesson in the *Analects* says, "To learn and then to practice when it is timely, isn't that the meaning of pleasure?" Whether it's studying or hiking in the mountains, it's the same mind that applies itself. As soon as one knows how it is that studying is like hiking in the mountains, studying itself becomes a wonderful form of recreation and proceeds rapidly. Otherwise, one considers studying painful and hiking fun, and something is lost in both."

Then Li Yan said, "I've never heard you talk about this before. And here I've been hiking with you for nearly a month! But you and I are the only ones in the hills and by the streams. Our fellow teachers and students at Zhejiang University never come with us. When the scenery is so beautiful, why don't you say something about it to our colleagues?"

*Zhu Xi was a twelfth-century philosopher whose commentaries were the orthodox intepretations of the Confucian classics and whose synthesis of Chinese thought was the core of Neo-Confucianism.

"Well, up to now, I've never heard of urging the students to go hiking, but only of urging them to study," I said. "But, then, there's already encouragement in the books for hiking. When *The Analects* says, 'the benevolent enjoy the mountains and the wise enjoy the streams,' that is teaching people to go out to the hills and streams. Zhu Xi urges people to hike in the mountains, too. Try rereading Confucius and Zhu Xi with this in mind and see for yourself. And when the Grand Historian, Sima Qian, wrote his *Records,** didn't he tell people that in his youth he made excursions among the hills and streams? If you first comprehend what it means to hike in the mountains through your studies, and then you begin really to hike in the mountains, it can be a real joy. When *The Analects* says, 'to have friends come from afar, isn't that the meaning of joy?' it's like your studying with me and then hiking in the mountains with me. That's being my friend in reality. Finding a friend in a teacher ought to be like studying and then hiking in the mountains. That's the real meaning of joy."[1]

This story, from Qian Mu's "Memories of Teachers and Friends," displays the wondrous power that language holds for him. The culture that, for him, unites the Chinese people finds expression in the classical literary language. This is the language in which he chose to write all his memoirs, linking his personal experience with that of Confucius and the twelfth-century Neo-Confucian synthesizer Zhu Xi, and giving him access to the metaphorical power of the Grand Historian of the Han, Sima Qian, and to that of the prose masters of later dynasties who renewed that power again and again. His childhood teachers had introduced him to it, and experience continued to reinforce it. Visual, auditory, and tactile images gave the classical metaphors a ring of truth.

Among Qian's childhood memories was a manuscript in the calligraphy of a grandfather he had never known. It was a complete copy of the *Five Classics,* which were believed to have been transmitted by Confucius, lightly stained with traces of tears from the calligrapher's eyes. Another memory was his grandfather's copy of the Grand Historian's *Records,* with its underscoring of certain passages based on classic commentaries by the sixteenth-century prose master Gui Youguang and his eighteenth-century admirer, Fang Bao. These tactile images

---

*Shiji (Records of the grand historian) by Sima Qian is a historical text from the first century B.C., a model for historical writing and prose writing in general.

of how the truth was transmitted were reinforced by the landscape poetry of his father, which Qian Mu chanted to recall his father's spirit to memory after his premature death.[2] The swallows that flitted about the courtyard linked the wisdom of the ancients to the living spirit that grew in Qian Mu's mind.

But if the classical literary language gave one access to the metaphorical power of the sages and prose masters of the past, the power to see and hear what they saw and heard could only grow with practice. Without the living spirit of the beholder, the texts themselves were dead, and the landscape remained a random display of hills and streams. Qian Mu's first lesson in the application of this power was his father's jocular comment to his tutor, when Qian Mu was six, that the boy's metaphorical understanding of an obscure character suggested that he had learned to read in an earlier life. Two years later, he overheard his father lecture his older brother on the art of comprehension. The lesson was, "When you study, you must also understand the meaning of what is not said. For every word written, there may be three that are not written. When you come upon such passages, you must use your native intelligence or you won't know how to read them."[3]

Qian's father's advice reflects the influence of the New Text school of interpretation, popular among reformers at the turn of the century, whose emphasis was on an ancient work of historical criticism, the *Gongyang Commentary on the Spring and Autumn Annals*. Although Qian Mu himself published in 1930 a study that undermined the historiographical basis for this school, the lesson remained valid.[4] No matter how sacred the text may be, its meaning depends on the context and on the receptivity of the reader's mind. Ancient metaphors were meaningful in Qian Mu's world only in the context of a larger narrative structure, a structure in which silence in one context evoked images of others, which conveyed truths that could not be uttered in the original context. This structure is what gave meaning to the writings of the prose masters. The form in which it was expressed, for nearly three thousand years, was the classical literary language, the language Qian chose for his narratives "Reminiscences on My Parents" and "Memories of Teachers and Friends."

Qian's narrative on wandering among hills and streams with his friend is a commentary on Confucian learning and communication, on study and play, on truth and beauty. What he does not say is what his commentary has to do with the third sentence in the *Analects,* "Not to regret it when one's learning is not recognized, isn't that what it means to be a true scholar [*junzi*]?" A junzi is a man of virtue who embodies the moral power expressed in "benevolence," "wisdom," and "the rites" (li). His learning must be widely recognized if the li are to prevail; when the times do not permit this, he can only hope to transmit his learning to friends. Time and again Qian Mu urged his students to concentrate on their studies, in the hope that once the political situation changed for the better, they would have the strength to prevail. Until that time, to practice what one has learned is to weave the wisdom of the classics into the narrative of daily life; and to practice in ways that are timely is to apply one's mind to studying and, when in exile, to apply it to things that are close at hand.

The memoirs, then, are narratives about the transmission of truth, in which the author plays a part. The people described are engaged, wittingly or unwittingly, in a struggle against the prevailing winds of political decline and moral confusion. The narrator believes that the classical language was better suited to this narrative than the vernacular. Given the very personal nature of the subject matter and the frequency of dialogue in the narrative, the choice seems odd at first. But once one reflects on the narrator's idea of culture and the common misconception that the most personal expressions are localized ones, the choice becomes obvious. Each personal struggle against the prevailing winds is also a cultural struggle—or at least it can be understood within the structure of Chinese culture, as conceived by Qian Mu, as a struggle for the preservation of shared values. Sima Qian, whose *Records* conveyed some of these values, could not have understood a vernacular essay based on the northern dialect that moderns called the "national language," and for Confucius, the classical language, in structure at least, *was* the vernacular. For Qian Mu's mother, who also transmitted these values, the "national language" was as incomprehensible as the literary one, since the native tongue of Seven Mansions was a variant of the southern Wu dialect. What, then, is the language best suited to a narrative that would transcend the limits of these, the worst of times, and still communicate feelings about values the author believes are broadly shared?

By now it should be clear that, differences of gender, class, local custom, and dialect aside, there are, for Qian Mu, shared values in

Chinese culture that transcend time. Never did he accept the arguments of friends, teachers, and colleagues in the 1920s and 1930s that a "new culture" must replace the old. But neither did he believe that the world his parents grew up in was a model for the future—he abhorred all attempts to look for utopian modes and frustrated modernistic trends in the more distant past. Rather, the shape of Chinese culture and of local custom was a product of China's own peculiar history. There was a logic to it, and a feeling, just as there is to Qian's memoirs. And the central problem in Chinese culture, as in the memoirs, is the divergence and reconvergence of history and value.

Four months before Qian Mu's birth in 1895, the Qing statesman Li Hongzhang signed the Treaty of Shimonoseki, giving up tributary rights in Korea and ceding Taiwan and southern Manchuria to Japan. More than fifty years had passed since the British had won the right to colonize Hong Kong and to apply British law to British subjects in Shanghai and other ports forced open by the Opium War. The Taiping Revolution had shaken the empire for fifteen years in the meantime, and the Beiyang navy that had just been sunk by the Japanese was the best the Qing could produce in a thirty-year effort to restore relative strength. Yet nine more years would pass before Qian Mu learned that the emperor of China was not a Han Chinese.

The nine-year-old schoolboy who suffered the shock of this news had already committed to memory many, if not all, of the 120 chapters of the classic fourteenth-century novel *Romance of the Three Kingdoms*. Just the previous year at an opium den in Dangkou he had acted out an episode from the novel on the demand of his father's friends.[5] The words and deeds of China's great third-century martial heroes came to life in the *Romance*. Schoolboys read it on the sly to escape from the dreary task of memorizing examination essays, and their elders, most of whom had given up the classics, took vicarious pleasure in the lives of heroes the likes of which their world did not know. In the episode Qian Mu had recently performed for his opium-besotted audience, the brilliant strategist Zhuge Liang trounces in debate the scholarly advisers of Sun Quan, one of the contenders for the empire after the collapse of the Han Dynasty. One of Sun's men has returned from a reconnaissance mission with Zhuge Liang, who serves Liu Bei, the prince to whom Sun nominally owes allegiance. The third contender,

Cao Cao, is by far the strongest, and Sun's scholarly advisers seek to persuade him to submit to an unequal alliance that will seal Liu Bei's defeat.

Xue Zong said, "Tell us your opinion of Cao Cao."

Zhuge Liang answered, "That is an uncalled for question—Cao Cao is a traitor to the House of Han."

"You are wrong there," retorted Xue Zong. "The Han Dynasty is approaching the end of its allotted time. Cao Cao has two-thirds of the empire and the people are turning to him. Your master, ignorant of Heaven's Will, is still contending with him. When you try to smash a stone with an egg, the result is certain failure."

Zhuge Liang answered sharply, "You talk like a man who bears no allegiance to either father or prince. Loyalty and filial piety are the prime duties of every man in this world. As a subject of Han it is your duty to oppose any man who turns traitor. Cao Cao's forebears lived on government stipends, but instead of showing his gratitude he is trying to usurp the throne. The whole world condemns him yet you claim that destiny is on his side. You are indeed a man who respects neither father nor prince. I shall waste no more words on you. Please say no more!"

... another protested, "Zhuge Liang simply distorts the truth without advancing proper arguments. It is no use continuing. But may I ask if he has made a special study of any of the classical canons?"

Zhuge Liang saw that it was Yan Jun. He replied, "All pedants are good for is punctuating texts. How can such men restore states or do great deeds? Yi Yin [adviser of King Tang, founder of the Shang] of old was a peasant, and Jiang Shang [adviser of King Wu, founder of Zhou] a fisherman, while men like Zhang Liang, Chen Ping, Teng Yu and Geng Yan were skilled in the administration of the empire, yet I never heard that they studied the classical canons. They would not fritter away their energies on pen and inkstone, wasting their time on literary futilities."

Yan Jun bowed his head in dejection and could not answer, but another man spoke up loudly, "You like to boast, sir, but can hardly have any real learning. I fear scholars would laugh at you."

This speaker was Cheng Deshu of Runan, and Zhuge Liang retorted, "There are two types of scholar: the noble and the mean. A true scholar is loyal to his sovereign and loves his country, abiding by the right and hating evil, eager to benefit the men of his time and leave a good name to posterity. A mean scholar, on the other hand, devotes himself to trivialities. All he can do is flourish a pen, wasting his youth writing poetry and studying the classics till his hair turns white. A thousand words flow from his pen, but there is not one sound principle in his head. Look at Yang Xiong, so noted for his writing, who stooped to serve Wang Mang [an usurper of the Han throne] and finally took his own life by throwing himself down from a pavilion. Such a man is a scholar of the mean type. Even if he writes ten thousand words a day, we have no use for him."[6]

Just which kingdoms a boy of eight had to conquer and which pedants he had to trounce in his fantasy world is not known, but once he entered the new-style school in Dangkou in 1904, the heroic challenge became clear. The spoiler of Qian Mu's political innocence was his calisthentics and drill instructor, Qian Bogui, a kinsman from the village of Hongshengli, not far from Seven Mansions. Since physical education was an innovation in the curriculum—it had appeared only in 1902—instructors were hard to come by. Qian Bogui, who was only twenty-one at the time, had studied in Shanghai at the newly opened Nanyang Public Institute, where he had also become associated with the emergent anti-Manchu revolutionary movement.[7] Qian Mu describes the shock:

> One day he took me by the hand and asked, "Is it true that you can read *Romance of the Three Kingdoms*?" I admitted I could.
> "You shouldn't read that sort of thing any more," he told me. "From the very first sentence, where it says 'When the empire has long been united it must fall apart, and when long divided, it must be reunited,' it tells what is wrong with the course of Chinese history. Now there is order, now disorder, and that's why people think this way. If we were like England, France, and the other countries of Europe today, then once we were united we wouldn't divide again. Once there was order there wouldn't be disorder again. From now on we simply have to learn from them."
> Ever since that day, Bogui's words have stuck in my mind as I study. The problem has plagued every Chinese for the last hundred years: Chinese or Western culture, which is right and which is best? My whole life has been plagued by this problem. But as a boy of ten, when Bogui opened my ears and announced it to me, face to face, it was as if a thunderbolt had struck me on the head and set off a quake in my heart. For seventy-four years since then, all my doubts and all my certainties have been encompassed by this prob-

lem, and all my efforts have been applied to this problem. In fact, it is because of this one lesson from Qian Bogui that I have devoted my life to scholarship.

My teacher Bogui also told me, "You know that our emperor is not Chinese, don't you?" I was shocked and said I didn't know. When I got home I asked my father about it. He said, "Your teacher is right. Our emperor is a Manchu, and we are Han people. That's why there are sometimes things in the shops with both Han and Man writing." So it was also because of Bogui that I embraced the concept of *minzu,* or "peoples," and sympathized with the ideas of revolution and democracy as a child.[8]

During the nine years between Qian Mu's birth and his political awakening, the Chinese revolution began. The battle between the revolutionaries and the Qing court raged on three fronts. Within the administrative structure of the empire, a small group of visionaries armed with the New Text ideology of the Cantonese scholar Kang Youwei won the emperor's ear in 1898 and tried, for one hundred days, to carry out a revolution from the top down. Such a revolution had succeeded in displacing the Tokugawa "tent government" (*bakufu* in Japanese) in Japan in 1868 while elevating the emperor to a symbolic position as head of the new nation. With the final disintegration of Li Hongzhang's "tent government" (*mufu* in Chinese) in the defeat of 1895, the time was ripe for a similar move in China. As in Japan, the top-down revolutionaries radicalized native religious ideas—Confucianism in the case of China—and avoided any reference to revolution, but their vision was one of a rapid and radical transformation of the structure of power. When the empress dowager ended the Hundred Days with a bloody coup, sending the emperor into seclusion, the front shifted to the movement for local self-government and constitutional controls.

A second front developed in the world of secret societies and Chinese emigrants. Sun Yatsen, himself an emigrant to Hawaii from a village near Canton, raised his first revolt in that city in the confusion of demobilization that followed the 1895 defeat. The uprising earned the name *revolution* in the foreign press, and Sun and others developed ideas of nationalism, republicanism, and socialism to go with it. The primary vehicle of revolution on this front was a loose confederation of groups, many claiming bonds of blood brotherhood, whose common cause was resistance against the grasping, gouging fingers of orthodox power. After the failure of the Hundred Days and the spread of the local self-government movement, the two fronts gradually joined, creating formal political party alliances by 1905.

With the collapse of Li Hongzhang's tent government, the regime turned for the first time to the problem of general education. Chinese-financed institutions of higher learning appeared for the first time in Tianjin, Wuhan, and Shanghai. Philanthropists in the lower Yangzi Valley rushed to open new-style private academies and study societies in preparation for the anticipated reform of the civil service examination system, and an Imperial University appeared in Beijing. The new schools began to send students to Japan by the hundreds, and soon the Boxer Indemnity promised scholarships that would allow students to travel to the United States. Within this rapidly developing world of new-style education, the third revolutionary front was formed.

Its vanguard was the Chinese Educational Association, organized in Shanghai in the spring of 1902. The association's purpose was to influence the curriculum in the new schools, but the issues it raised were far from academic. The new curriculum, the association believed, should do much more than prepare China's youth for scientific and technical careers. It should teach them that their people were engaged in a historic struggle for survival against a superior civilization. The purpose of education was first to inform the Chinese people of this fact and then to provide them with tools for survival. For forty years, the association argued, the Qing regime had retarded development of the educational front by teaching the people that technical education was a means of strengthening the state. The implication was that the state's weakness was only technical. According to the revolutionaries, the misguided policies of Li Hongzhang and the Manchu self-strengtheners had kept the people from learning that, in the course of the current historic struggle, the state's weakness was the weakness of its subjugated people. And the survival of the people and the survival of the state were two entirely different matters.[9]

Zhang Binglin, a well-known classical scholar who had joined Kang Youwei's movement in Shanghai in 1895, returned from Japan just in time for the founding of the Chinese Educational Association in 1902. As an organizer of Chinese students abroad, he was the only self-proclaimed political revolutionary in the group.[10] Zhang had taught at the missionary school known as Soochow University, among other places, and he had associated with several people who were leaders on the administrative and secret society fronts. But he objected to the use of New Text dogma as a reformist ideology. That objection aligned him with others who left Kang Youwei's camp after the Hundred Days, urging the Manchus' overthrow.

For Zhang Binglin, the problem with New Text dogma was twofold. First, it taught that the "old texts"—versions of the Confucian classics that medieval philosophers had used to support their worldview—were of no value. Zhang was trained in the tradition known as Han Learning, which had developed methods of empirical research over the previous two centuries in an effort to disprove the medieval interpretations.[11] For him it was the interpretations that were wrong, not the texts—the latter were nothing but sources for philological research. The New Text school, to which Kang Youwei had turned in an effort to develop an alternative Confucian vision, simply replaced one canon with another, the authority of which was no less dubious.

Second, Zhang was one of the few scholars deeply involved in contemporary affairs who believed that empirical historical research was essential for dealing with the problem Qian Mu calls the plague of every Chinese of the past hundred years. The New Text ideology that Kang Youwei had developed was explicitly antiempirical. In his eagerness to revolutionize imperial administration from the top down, Kang Youwei had seized upon the antiempirical bias of the New Text school and argued that twenty-five hundred years of history were quite irrelevant. In Kang's view, history progressed slowly through three great stages toward a utopian society in which virtually all social distinctions ceased to exist. The sage Confucius, whose teachings even the young emperor had absorbed, was in fact a visionary who saw the world progressing toward true democracy. The way to act on this vision was to create institutions that were both "timely"—appropriate to the current stage of historical evolution—and visionary, that is, reflecting not the legacies of the past but the ideals of the future. The regime that could act in this way would not only approach sageliness but would also produce a state that was as strong as the Western democracies and better suited to survive the deadly competition in which they were currently engaged. This ideological twist created the second problem Zhang Binglin had with the New Text dogma. In the course of denying the legacies of history, it threatened to produce a new religion in which faith in the moral vision of Confucius would serve as a smokescreen for the self-interested politics of an even stronger imperial regime.[12]

In 1898 Zhang's reputation as a radical with connections among the reformers forced him to flee the country. Returning in 1900, he was forced into exile once more in the wake of an abortive uprising organized by a few of his associates. It was then that he began developing an alternative to Kang Youwei's reformist approach. Like Kang's student Liang Qichao, who was emerging as the spokesman for the reformers among the younger generation, Zhang confronted Chinese students in Japan who were fifteen years his junior and whose political memories barely reached back to the Sino-Japanese war. The New Text origins of Kang Youwei's vision were a pointless blur to these young people. As students of the new-style education, they were already developing a whole new language for political discourse. The most radical among their leaders hoped to push them all the way to esperanto. The less anarchistically inclined saw the task as the mastery of concepts drawn from Western languages and translated into Japanese.[13]

Minzu (the word was borrowed from the Japanese *minzoku,* a neologism) was such a concept. The term *zu,* for which Qian Mu knows no Western equivalent, joined the term *min,* which has meant since ancient times "the people" as distinct from rulers, soldiers, or other politically privileged groups, to express the new concept of "a people." Zhang Binglin wrote a series of treatises on the subject before returning to Shanghai from Japan to join the Chinese Educational Association in 1902. A people, he argued, is more than a biological category (*zhongzu*). A people is formed through cultural adaptation to an environment. Depending on what sort of leadership a people has, it can develop greater uniformity and national strength, or it can segment and develop into separate peoples. In China, both patterns have occurred, but since ancient times development toward cultural unity has prevailed. As in the case of animals, Zhang argued, there are higher and lower forms of peoples. The higher forms have developed better ways of adapting to environments, and the more adaptable the form, the more it tends to prevail. The long history of the Chinese people and the spread of its culture is evidence of its high form.

The Manchus, on the other hand, are a people whose history shows little development. Not only have they clung to ways that distinguish them from Han Chinese, Zhang argued, they have used the distinction to political advantage. The institution of emperor is no longer a part of the Chinese people's evolutionary process, but the Manchus have used it to enslave the Chinese, who have adapted to the role of slavery. The only way the Chinese people can hope to stand up to the threats of Western and Japanese imperialism is to stop adapting to slavery.[14]

Liang Qichao, who had abandoned the New Text vision without giving up on constitutional monarchy, was also contemplating the political role of a people. While Zhang was working on the polemics of race in Shanghai, Liang was publishing treatises in Japan on the need for liberal education and a "new citizenry." Utopian visions, Confucian or otherwise, were of no use, he argued, without the prior development of a collective consciousness and political organization. These were the features that made Western democracies strong. Key to their development was self-mastery, the freedom from conventional ideas and customs as well as from physical environment and human passion that allows a people to reason and thereby control its fate. Self-mastery, Liang argued, was a mode of thought and action that linked individual behavior to collective action. It was the essential spirit of self-government, and national autonomy as well.[15] Realizing, nonetheless, that the Chinese people were not ready for democracy, Liang then modified this formula, emphasizing the differences among peoples rather than imagining a common path to self-mastery for all.[16] Turning to certain German ideas of the state, he argued that some states were stronger than others because they adapted their institutions to the character of the peoples whose needs they had to meet. Only then did self-mastery have a chance to play its political role.[17]

The refinement and subtlety of Liang's essays may well have escaped the students who rushed to join the revolutionary vanguard in 1902. Liang used the term *minzu* without distinguishing ethnically among Qing subjects, whom he wanted to become citizens, but Zhang Binglin's usage made more sense to student activists. Under the leadership of the Chinese Educational Association, the entire fifth form of the new-style Nanyang Public Institute in Shanghai bolted to found the Patriotic School, espousing both anti-Manchu and antitraditional ideas.[18] By spring 1903 the Hunanese publisher of the local journal *Subao*, which had been making Liang Qichao's reformist ideas available to readers in Shanghai, donated support to the school in return for student articles. Both the school and the journal attracted rebellious students from all over the country.

Among these radicals was Zou Rong, a seventeen-year-old from Sichuan whose stirring call to arms captured the mood of the new generation. Zou Rong met Zhang Binglin and *Subao*'s new editor in Tokyo in December 1902 and swore blood brotherhood with them. By April, the Shanghai group organized by the Chinese Educational Association had decided to launch an anti-Manchu broadside in *Subao*. Zou Rong's tract "The Revolutionary Army" appeared as a separate pamphlet with a preface by Zhang Binglin, and Zhang also published a series of revolutionary articles culminating in June in a letter to Kang Youwei. Kang, writing in Singapore, had continued to advocate constitutional monarchy and national unity in the face of imperialist threats. Zhang's letter accused him of playing the traditional game of factional politics. Before the Hundred Days, Zhang argued, Kang had wanted to protect China. Since then, he had wanted to protect the Qing. The reason was not hard to find. Kang needed the emperor as badly as the emperor needed him. Constitutional monarchy would only perpetuate the Chinese officials' slavish mentality, of which Kang's politics were a typical product. If the goal was to strengthen the Chinese people in their struggle against imperialism, Zhang concluded, it could not be accomplished by constitutional reforms; it could be accomplished only by revolution.[19]

The moment Zhang's opposition to Kang Youwei's constitutional movement and his theory of the evolution of peoples came together with the rage of the young students was a crucial one in the history of revolutionary politics. Where Zhang wrote of the slavish habits of old men, Zou Rong's voice rang with the spirit of frustrated youth:

> The autocracy of the last few thousand years must be swept away, the slavery of thousands of years abolished. The 5,000,000 barbarian Manchus adorned in their furs, lances, and horns must be destroyed, and the great shame they have inflicted in their 260 years of cruel and harsh treatment expunged, that the Chinese mainland may be purified. All of the Yellow Emperor's descendants can rise to the status of a Washington, rejuvenate themselves, successfully emerge from the 18 stages of hell and ascend to 33 heavenly halls, for their ultimate and resolute aspiration is revolution. Revolution is great! . . .
>
> If we were to make an extensive survey of religion, ethics, political science, or even of trifling matters, from the past to the present, [we would find that] all of our current ideas were sifted down to us through the process of past revolutions. This is the way. Thus, revolution is as ordinary as this.

After arguing that those who feared the colonization of China while ignoring China's enslavement by the Manchus were blind, Zou went on to blame the literati for the nation's lack of direction:

> Chinese people are customarily classified into scholars, farmers, artisans, and merchants. The scholars are at the head of these four groups and are called "literati." When I look at the Americans and Europeans, there is no one who cannot read. In other words, there is no one who is not a literate person. But we Chinese have a special classification of "scholar," or "literati." Therefore, I shall address myself to them.
>
> The Chinese scholars, or literati, are people without vitality. Why? The ordinary people are ignorant because they do not study, but the scholars are stupid and become more so because they do not study what they should. And furthermore, they are restricted, humiliated, made obfuscate, ensnared, and corrupted until they become nothing but empty shells, whipped and forced to obey.
>
> How are they restricted? They are restricted by having to learn to write in the style of the "eight-legged essay" for the examination paper, which takes years and years, leaving no time to learn about current events.
>
> How are they humiliated? They are humiliated by having to take the district, provincial, and metropolitan examinations. (While taking the examination for admission to the Hanlin Academy, they have no seats. They are treated as cows and horses.) Their behavior is like that of beggars. No longer do they know that in this world there is such a thing as human dignity.
>
> Why are their minds obfuscated? They are made obfuscate by the honors gained from the examinations and the positions in government. They are worried about whether they will pass or fail. There is no longer any sense of righteousness or of daring to risk one's life for a worthy cause.
>
> How are they ensnared? They are ensnared by country schools set up by aged scholars and by stone tablets regulating the scholars' lives. They are kept quiet and ignorant so that they dare not criticize politics or write books.
>
> How are they made corrupt? They are corrupted by power and influence which make them hesitant and spineless about doing the right or heroic thing. . . .
>
> They are literati in name, but in fact they are worth less than dead men. . . .
>
> Now if you want to establish schools, the government will say

there is no money. If you want to send students abroad, the government will say there is no money. For whatever will benefit the Chinese, the government says there is no money. But for no reason at all the government rebuilt and then visited their imperial ancestors' tombs. For that they have money. For no reason at all they had a birthday party for the Empress Dowager. For that they have money. My fellow countrymen, just think about that!

The link between politics and education could not have been more clearly put.

> Servile nature must be abolished before revolution can begin; otherwise, we will be overpowered by the laws of evolution and the principle of the survival of the fittest. If any power tries to seize our territory, then my fellow countrymen may become the slaves of slaves. From the slaves of slaves they will become monkeys, from monkeys to wild pigs, and then oysters, and there will be a wasteland and finally a desert without human beings.
>   . . . fight against your age-old public enemies, the Manchus. Then wipe out the foreign devils who have infringed upon your sovereignty. . . . Your goddess of freedom will point to the sky with her left hand and to the earth with her right hand and will appear on your behalf. Alas, the sky is blue and the earth is white. Revolution and independence, like a thunderstorm, will awaken the sleeping lion of several thousand years.[20]

Zou signed his manifesto, "a little foot soldier in the Revolutionary Army." One can imagine the ease with which the young students leaped from their childhood identification with Zhuge Liang, heroically silencing the "spineless" scholars at Sun Quan's court, to take up the blue-and-white banner of the revolutionary party. In the wake of the Qing response to the *Subao*'s open call to arms, the student movement went underground. The Patriotic School and the journal were closed. Zhang, Zou, and others were tried by the Mixed Court of Shanghai and jailed in the International Settlement, out of the Qing government's reach. The following year, Sun Yatsen's group claimed leadership of the new Revolutionary Alliance in Japan. Their manifesto linked the ideology of minzu to the nativism of the secret societies and to Sun's idea of people's rights. Zhang Binglin, who had served out his jail term, left Shanghai for Japan and joined the alliance.[21] The little foot soldier, who had died in jail at the age of twenty, joined the martyrs of 1898.

This was the year Qian Mu entered the brand new Guoyu primary school in Dangkou. His calisthentics and drill instructor, Qian Bogui, was a twenty-one-year-old veteran of the Nanyang student protests who had taught mathematics in Changsha before answering the call to help start a school in his native place. Perhaps he had attended the course in physical education instruction offered by the Chinese Educational Association and had signed the agreement to teach it in a country school, thus spreading the martial spirit.[22] Or perhaps he had joined in the plans of radical students to seize Changsha, aborted in 1904. Or perhaps he was only a sympathizer, preparing for a career in a rapidly changing political world. Whatever the case, he returned to Dangkou in autumn 1904 to help Hua Hongmo, his grandmother's brother and the town's senior gentryman, start up the school that heralded a revolution in rural education in the area.

The opening of the Guoyu School in Dangkou followed the opening of the new-style schools of Changsha and Wuhan by just one year. In addition to physical education and military drill, Qian Bogui taught mathematics and geography. He was joined by other young men from the area who had answered Hua Hongmo's call. Hua had passed the provincial examination, at age thirty-three, in 1873, the year of Liang Qichao's birth. Rather than pursuing an official career, he had chosen to devote his energy to lineage and community affairs. The school was located in the ancestral temple Hua had constructed twenty years earlier and financed by income from the lineage's charitable estate he and his father had inaugurated in 1875. Begun as a school for boys of the Hua lineage, it had become a rural academy by the time of the Hundred Days, sponsoring lectures and holding study society meetings in anticipation of the educational reforms. Hua's only son, whom he had been grooming to run the school, died in 1898. The oldest of his two grandsons entered the Guoyu School as Qian Mu's classmate. Hua Hongmo was then sixty-four years old. His sister, the only sibling and the grandmother of Qian Bogui, had already passed away.[23]

When Qian Mu entered the Guoyu School, he entered two new worlds at once. If Qian Bogui had awakened him to the cruel world of national and international politics, Hua Hongmo's refined world of literati culture hit him with no less force. The upper-level geography teacher at Guoyu was Gu Zizhong, from Wuxi City, who also taught the upper-level course in Chinese literature. Gu mixed the old with the new, history with geography, Chinese history with non-Chinese, and the students all agreed his instruction was much superior to that of the most popular geography textbook. From him, Qian Mu learned how to adapt the old literati style to the new education:

> The Guoyu School borrowed rooms from the Hua ancestral temple. There was a great hall, which was used for lectures, the walls and pillars hung with scrolls. To the right was the Lezai Study, where the teachers gathered every day after classes. Passing through the north door to the left from the study, one came to the pavilion behind the great hall. To the north were windows from ceiling to floor, and outside were shrubs and trees, an artificial mountain, a tiny pond, all laid out like a miniature garden, to ease the mind with its lush vegetation and shadowy elegance. Further to the left and south again was the great hall's left-hand side room, which served as Master Gu's sleeping quarters. The other teachers all lived in town, but since Gu Zizhong came from Wuxi, he stayed at the school. Every day at four o'clock, when classes were over and the other teachers had left, Master Gu would retire alone to the long table in the pavilion with a bottle of brew and a plate of peanuts, dried fish, or other condiments, and with book in hand, he would read and sip. My fellow students liked to slip in through the study, sit around him and ask questions about whatever was on their minds. He never refused.
>
> One day, when Master Gu had just returned from the winter holidays, the book he had on the table was a fine woodblock edition. The students, curious to see what sort of old classic it was, were surprised to learn that it was Shi Naian's novel, *The Water Margin.* They asked how it was that a book of light reading came to be done up in such a fine edition. He said, "*The Water Margin* is a great work of Chinese literature. I wonder why you mistake it for light reading?" They told him, "There is a younger student in the school by the name of Qian who has struggled through the book, and we all gathered round him in the early morning before class to listen to him recite from it. Would you be willing to call him in and question him?"
>
> Master Gu agreed, so a couple of the students came and found me, and took me back with them. Master Gu asked me, "Do you know *The Water Margin?*" I said I did, so he asked me some random questions about various episodes, and I answered them all without hesitation.

"When you read *The Water Margin,* you only read the large print and not the small print," he said. "That's why this is all you can say about it."

I was shocked when I heard him say that. How could he know my little secret? I went back and read it again from start to finish without skipping a word. That's how I learned that the small print was Jin Shengtan's critical comment, which I then studied assiduously and could not put aside. I read it again and again, until I knew the entire book inside out. From then on, whenever I read novels, I kept them at a distance and never read them a second time. I was suddenly over my childhood addiction to novels. Instead, I started reading translations of Western novels . . . a turn I owe to Master Gu's comment. From then on I, too, joined the students at his side in the pavilion.

One day a student asked him, "Why is it that you gave young Qian such a high mark for beginning an essay with the expression *wuhu,* "alas!"?

"How forgetful you are," Master Gu replied. "Didn't [the eleventh-century prose master] Ouyang Xiu begin the introductory essays to the treatises in his *Revised History of the Five Dynasties* with that expression?"

The others thought that was a good joke on me. "Your prose is an etude in the style of Ouyang Xiu!" they said. Then Master Gu said, quite seriously, "Don't you make fun! If this fellow continues at this rate, someday he will be able to study [Ouyang's model] Han Yu!"

I was deeply moved when I heard that. From then on I concentrated on Han Yu, and as I entered middle school, I was single-mindedly chanting Han Yu's work. It was first with these words of Master Gu that I learned formally that there was such a thing as "learning."[24]

"Learning," or *xuewen,* is another word for which there is no English equivalent. If "learning" or studying the style of a master seemed an empty task to schoolboys who were accustomed to memorizing and reciting things they could not understand, for a scholar it was a kind of communion of spirits. It was the difference between learning (*xue*) something and learning about it. Something more than diligence was required. As the sixteenth-century master Gui Youguang put it, "written words are part of the basic energy of heaven and earth. The energy of the man who can master them flows in the same current. . . . One cannot master something that others know if it surpasses one's own understanding. One becomes a master when that which he knows surpasses the understanding of others. Then he reaches back to the ancients over thousands of years."[25] One could not copy the ancients; but if one knew what they knew, one could revive them with one's own pen.

After three years at the Guoyu School, the twelve-year-old Qian Mu felt no conflict between the worlds of learning and politics. In Dangkou, before 1911, no distinction was drawn. Family, school, and community were the whole world, and that world was preparing rapidly for the future. When Qian Mu's father died in 1906, the family went on lineage welfare and the boys received scholarships. Mu's brother, six years his elder, prepared for a career teaching science and mathematics.[26] Perhaps for Mu the model family of the new China was that of three Hua brothers who also answered their lineage elder's call. The eldest brother, Hua Zhen, who had studied in Japan, taught Chinese and chorus. He had written a book of vernacular songs that remained popular in schools for over a decade. As Mu remembers them:

> I especially loved the autumn songs. Although I cannot remember any titles, I remember that they were songs about autumn evenings, and the lyrics were so fresh, the description so realistic, one could see it as one sang. Since the founding of the republic, there has been an outpouring of new-style vernacular verse, but most of it lacks the flavor of poetry. And as it inevitably emulates Western models, it is not real vernacular. But Hua Zhen simply replaced the stale with the fresh, keeping control of the language, making something quite different from the old poetry, but without losing what is essential to what we call a poem. Anyone who has seen both styles can compare the quality and judge for himself.

Zhen lived with his wife and his younger brothers' families at their parents' homestead on Yellow Rock Lane in Dangkou.

> The two younger brothers worked out of town and only returned for summer and winter vacations. Hua Long, the middle brother, taught English in a middle school in Soochow. The summer before I entered the upper-level third-year class, he held a special reading course exclusively for the upper-class students at the Guoyu School. He taught all the different styles of ancient prose from the *Book of Documents,* earliest of the classics, to Zeng Guofan of the late Qing. Classics, history, philosophy, and belles lettres were all included. He selected the most famous writers as representatives, but never more than a few from one period and

1. *A typical market-town house in Bashiqiao, Wuxi.*

2. *The entrance to a scholar-gentry settlement near Dangkou.*

3. *A typical house in a scholar-gentry settlement, Donggan, Wuxi.*

4. *Posthumous portrait of Hua Hongmo in Qing official regalia.*

5. *A courtyard of the Guoyu School, where Qian Mu studied as a child and later taught, now the entrance to the new primary school in Dangkou.*

6. *The face of Jiangnan University, built by Rong Desheng in 1946, where Qian Mu taught until spring 1949.*

7. *The view of Lake Taihu from Jiangnan University.*

only one selection from each writer. Over the course of the summer, we read about thirty pieces in all. I remember especially well that when we had finished the biographical essay on Mencius and Hsun Tzu in the *Records of the Grand Historian,* he had us write an essay outside of class. Hua Long liked my essay very much, and when we arrived at the Hua house early the following Monday, it was mounted on the wall. I don't recall the essay itself, but what happened was memorable because it was so embarrassing. The women—the brothers' mother and their wives—surrounded me and smothered me with their congratulations, patting my shoulders, pulling my arms, and rubbing my head. Then, suddenly, from my hair they extracted a louse.

That summer the dust burned in our eyes and Hua Long got an eye infection for which he had to wear tinted eyeglasses. Three tables were lined up end to end in a room next to the lecture hall. Master Hua circumnavigated with one hand grasping a long yellow pipe and the other tracking the tables. About half the texts he recited from memory.

Among the texts was a short one by Han Yu, whom Qian Mu began to emulate all the more for hearing his words flow with this impressive figure's voice. Other writers and other styles that he continued to rediscover and probe to new depths of understanding as his studies progressed passed with the smoke from that pipe through Hua Long's lips. Qian Mu traces his earliest awareness of the unseverable link between ancient prose and the Neo-Confucian "study of principles" (*lixue*) to the same resonant voice. It was the same link that brought to mind the Neo-Confucian philosopher Zhu Xi's gloss when the swallows swept through the courtyard.

But also this:

> The last essay Master Hua had us read was Zeng Guofan's essay "On the Origins of Talent." It begins, "What causes some customs to prevail while others subside? It all begins with the echo of one mind in the mind of another." Many years passed before I completely understood how it is that human talent grows only where custom nurtures it, and that custom can begin with an echo in a solitary mind. Yet what I needed to learn for myself was already demonstrated in the guidance Master Hua gave me as a child.[27]

Qian Mu was experiencing "learning" in practice.

Custom was soon to dictate that much human talent would be

wasted in China. The Guoyu School and its auspicious mixture of new and old, foreign and Chinese was an island paradise in a riptide of national and international conflict. It survived while he was there, Qian thinks, because only the most dedicated teacher and learner would venture so far into the country. But as the rural scholarly culture developed its peculiar blend of refinement and hominess, the newly united revolutionary front ripped like the tide at its foundations and then turned against itself. The future was lost in the maelstrom.

With the Japanese victory over Russia in Manchuria and the subsequent radicalization of anti-czarist politics in Petrograd in 1905, the face of the enemy changed for Chinese students in Tokyo. Not only were the Japanese now unopposed in the northeast, but the Qing regime itself was sponsoring sweeping military reforms. If the New Armies and the new-style education succeeded in nurturing in Qing soil the freshly planted seeds of nationalism, the revolution of the people would be stillborn. Since the formation of the Revolutionary Alliance in 1905, Liang Qichao's arguments for building a strong nation with blocks of self-governing units, rather than with the theory of the evolution of a people, had been feeding the movement for local self-government and constitutional monarchy. Since the revolutionists were committed to republicanism, they could oppose Liang's constitutionalist arguments only with an appeal to anti-Manchu nativism. For that appeal, they relied on the master theoretician Zhang Binglin.

Zhang had been chosen editor of the Revolutionary Alliance's house organ, *Minbao* (The people). Beginning late in 1907, he published a series of articles attacking Liang's position. For Liang, self-governing political units embodied the people's expression of self-mastery. The power of the people was immanent in the political bodies it produced, at each level of government. Ultimately, the power of the whole people was immanent in the state. In Liang's scheme, the monarch was only a symbol, and the constitutional movement, beginning with the formation of local self-governing bodies, was intended to reduce him to a figurehead by law. Zhang argued, to the contrary, that the emperor symbolized the *distinction* between the people and the state. Since the decline of the *fengjian* system, or feudalism, in China more than two thousand years ago, the state had ruled by law. Liang's theory of the state relied on the premise that both the state *and* its law had yet to be produced. If this had indeed been the case in Europe in more recent times, it was not now the case in China. Nor did Japan bear out Liang's theory, for the Japanese had developed the strength to overpower the Qing state before producing their constitution—suppressing the indigenous "people's rights" movement in the process. How could a people that was already subservient to the state by well-established custom express anything but a master-servant ethic in its body politic? The local self-government movement could only reinforce the bad habits of a people long accustomed to authoritarian hierarchies. The powerful authorities who would emerge to control the local units were the worst obstacles imaginable to a strong nation.[28] In effect, Zhang concluded, the only way for the people to have power was to rise up as a body and seize it.

For some student radicals, the need to seize power was so urgent that even the Revolutionary Alliance seemed too cautious. In the summer of 1907, the student world reverberated with the tragic news of student uprising, assassination, and bloody suppression in Anhui and Zhejiang provinces. The shock was intensified by the realization that Qiu Jin, a twenty-nine-year-old woman who had left her husband and child to join the student movement in Japan, had been organizing students, soldiers, and secret society members for the uprising using boys' and girls' schools as a front. Qiu Jin had written to her brother from Japan that her escape from the "good" marriage the family had arranged for her was an escape from "slavery."[29] The metaphorical link between political oppression and social authority could not have been made clearer. It was in the wake of this tragedy that Zhang Binglin published his assault on Liang Qichao. And the twelve-year-old Qian Mu, his mind resonating with the summer's readings in ancient prose, found his way to the brand-new Prefectural Middle School in Changzhou. Unaware of or unconcerned with the radical students' struggle, he read his first article by Liang Qichao, which he found in a collection of contemporary writings on his brother's shelf, scarcely a week before he left Dangkou.[30]

When the middle school held its entrance exam in midautumn, Qian Bogui and Hua Zhen took the entire Guoyu upper-level fourth-year class of eight students, including Qian Mu's brother, to Changzhou to sit for it. Mu, who had advanced rapidly to the upper third year, went with them. Some three weeks later all nine joined the school's first class. The Qian brothers went on a local scholarship for orphans, the elder entering the teachers' training class so that he could finish quickly and begin to earn a living. The other seven boys, all of them Huas, entered the regular middle school course with Mu, who was the youngest by far. En route, the boys put up in Wuxi at the rice depot of the Guoyu School's founder, Hua Hongmo, where "dinner and breakfast were feasts, the likes of which a twelve-year-old student had never before tasted." From there, the bulk of the Guoyu contingent continued on to Changzhou by boat along the Grand Canal, although two were favored with permission to take the newly opened railway.[31]

In Changzhou, Qian Mu confronted the authority against which students had been rebelling for the first time since his earliest Chinese tutor had made him wet his pants. The friendly world of Dangkou was not totally lost. There was, for example, the seemingly absent-minded math teacher who suddenly one day announced that he was making a gift of a book he had written to each of the eight boys from the Guoyu School. The boys, who thought he didn't even know their names, were the favored recipients of a book they couldn't understand simply because the teacher had studied under Hua Hengfang, China's first Western-trained mathematician, who had also been a native of Dangkou.[32] But the lighter side of the serious world of modern schooling did not obscure the differences between it and "learning." Mu's stories of his three years and three months at the middle school, up until the student protest that ended his studies there, are stories of the scramble for grades. The teachers he remembers, including the school's director, Tu Xiaokuan, were the ones from the old world of literati, who recognized his talent, made exceptions for his youthful naiveté, and protected him. But his most vivid memories are of the dean of instruction and of the student protest.

The dean of instruction was in charge of discipline. He lived at the school and served as housemaster for the students who were boarders. Liu Congbo was the first to hold the position. A congenial man, he seems to have governed the students more by example than by force. It helped that his younger brother was the campus drill instructor and much admired by the students. Liu's brother had the priceless ability to turn complaints into determination, opposition to discipline into self-discipline. In bad weather, he barked, "You're not sugar babies; why are you afraid of the sun! You're not paper dolls; why are you afraid of the wind! You're not clay figurines; why are you afraid of the rain! If you're afraid of this and afraid of that, when *can* you stand up straight?!" And he treated the students as if he were one of them.

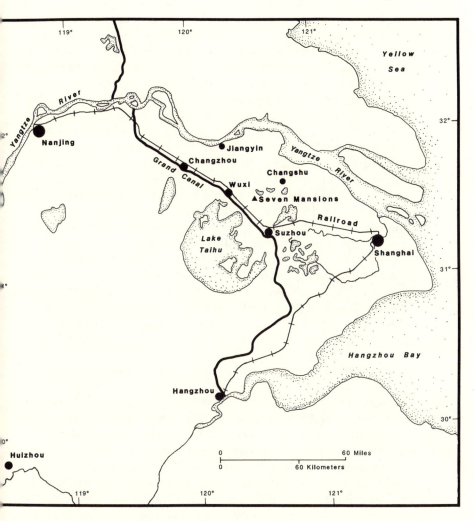

Map 2. The Lower Yangzi Region. Drawn by Roy Doyon.

But the second year brought a new dean of instruction by the name of Chen Shixin, and the climate changed:

His temperament was clearly cast in a different mold from Tu's and Liu's. They were expansive and broad-minded, combining the features of the statesman and the educator. Chen Shixin, on the other hand, was rigid and defensive, quick to close up and slow to open. He never smiled and seldom spoke. When he had an announcement, he wasted no words. It was always an order, never an instruction; or always a prohibition, never a word of guidance. The students in those days tended to be serious about their studies and respectful toward their teachers. They were eager to advance. Compared to today's students, they seem to have been more mature in that regard. But they were infected with the habits of the old-style private schools. They loved to make mischief and put on acts. Even while obeying the law, they would do something to counteract its intent, overtly defending the law but covertly making fun of it. Worrying about one's studies while despising the rules was a widespread syndrome.

Chen Shixin was never further away than one's shadow, tirelessly tracking down clues. Whenever one student or a group of students managed to show the tiniest bit of resistance it became the prime topic of conversation and the resisters became heroes. There was no great protest movement going on at the time, but still there were occasional flare-ups. Through them, Chen became a central figure in the school and an object of resistance. As his petty side got the better of him, he became stricter and more oppressive. When the word spread that he was a revolutionary, rather than increasing the students' respect for him, it heightened their fears. . . .

We had to line up before entering the classroom. There were many smokers among the students, and some would have cigarettes in their mouths until they reached the door. One day, there was an order from the housemaster's office that this would not be allowed. So the students agreed that the smokers all should light up as they stood in line and drop their cigarettes on the ground just as the drillmaster told them to march. Then when the housemaster came out to inspect, he would see the smoke rising from the live cigarette butts as if the class was still standing there in line. The students got some private satisfaction out of that.

I was quite young and naive, and so I picked up this sort of behavior. Every evening there was a two-hour study hall, after which we retired to the dormitory. Then at a certain time, the lights were to be extinguished and no talking was allowed. Chen Shixin would come around with his flashlight like a watchman to inspect. One night, I was having a conversation with the boy in the next bed, under cover of the bed curtains, when Chen came in.

"Whoever that is that likes to talk so much can come to the housemaster's office and talk to me!" he said. So I hopped out of bed and followed him down the stairs like a little tail. He didn't notice me until he got to the office, where the light was on; then he turned and saw me and asked why I had come downstairs.

"I came to chat, like you told me to," I said.

He shouted, "Get back up and sleep! Get back up and sleep!" From then on I was targeted. At the end of the year my score for deportment was 25 percent. My classmates held me and three others who also got 25 percent in considerable esteem as the four heroes whose total score was 100.

All the students were boarders, but those who lived in the city could go home on weekends. One day there came another order from the housemaster's office, that the students had to get permission before they could leave. There was a student two classes behind me by the name of Qu Qiubai, a slight, intellectual sort whom everyone admired for his brilliance. That Friday after supper, he took it upon himself to charge into the housemaster's office and carry out the board with the students' name tags on his shoulder, yelling that everyone had permission to leave. Outside, dozens of boys joined in the riot and there was nothing Chen Shixin could do to stop it. The crowd went out the gate, dumped the board, and went their separate ways with their heads in the air.

I never heard whether or not Qu Qiubai received any special punishment. He was unable to finish school because of his family's poverty. Under the republic, he entered the Russian Language School of the Foreign Ministry, which was tuition-free, and studied in Russia. Eventually he became head of the Chinese Communist Party.

Chen Shixin was also the instructor in a course on "self-cultivation," or ethical culture, which met just one hour per week. He would stand there and tell us, over and over again, "A scholar values actions, not words. If you do not remain simple and silent, you will be a petty person. If you do not become loquacious and disputatious, you can be a true scholar (*junzi*)." One day there was a mid-term exam and the students all agreed to use no more than twenty words on any single topic, to write all the answers without pausing, and to be finished within thirty minutes. I sat in the first row, and as soon as Chen Shixin had finished writing the fourth topic on the blackboard, I handed my paper in. My classmates all followed suit and filed out of the classroom in a line, reassembled in the study hall, and roared with laughter. Two classmates who were found to have written more than two lines on one of the topics were punished by the crowd. A peddler of steamed buns passed by the school each morning about an hour before lunchtime, and the two offenders were made to buy two baskets of buns and bring them up for us. Everyone was standing around the baskets and chomping on buns when Chen Shixin arrived and saw what was going on, but there was no way he could fix the blame and he left in a rage. This sort of incident occurred all the time.

Just before the winter term final examinations for the fourth-year class, the entire class agreed to demand some curricular reforms for the spring term. The demands were to eliminate the course on "self-cultivation," to add a course in Greek, and the like. Five representatives were chosen to take the case to the director, Tu Xiaokuan, and I was among them. The director told us that the curriculum was a matter for the school to decide, and that the students' opinions would be taken into consideration. We told him we wanted a concrete response. Then he turned to me.

"I understand you are not all that enthusiastic about your English class; how is it you want to add Greek?" he asked.

"That is the will of the class as a whole," I said; "not just my own."

"The self-cultivation class only meets once a week," the director said. "Why do you need to eliminate that?" We explained that, according to Chen Shixin, self-cultivation could not be transmitted in words, so there was nothing to gain from discussing it. After three meetings, we had not reached an agreement, and the class agreed to let the five representatives present the director with a letter of withdrawal from the whole class, to use for leverage. The director then told us that withdrawal was an individual matter, and that there was no procedure for collective withdrawal. So the class agreed to file in and fill out withdrawal forms one by one. The director received us in a large meeting room. He started instructing us, continuing for about an hour. I had led the students in and was seated farthest from the director. In a loud voice, I said that we had heard everything the director had to say by now, and would he please distribute the withdrawal forms for us to sign. He handed me a form and told me to fill it out. When I had done so, he looked it over and said that I hadn't done it properly and he couldn't accept it. By then the students were getting restless and telling me we should go away and discuss it some more. I was suddenly exasperated and shouted at the director, demanding that he explain how I should fill out the form. The students were waffling. The director told me how I should fill it out. I completed it and stepped outside, waiting for the next student, but the next student did not appear, and then the whole class walked out.

The examination was scheduled for the following day, and some said we should resume the discussion when it was over. Nothing more was said. But I had already submitted my withdrawal form, and since I could not take the exam and did not want to return home alone, I went to the infirmary.

There was only one other student in the infirmary, and he left to take the exam. Under his pillow I found a book. It was *Humanitarian Studies* by Tan Sitong [a martyr of the Hundred Days]. I read it with such delight that I forgot all about my withdrawal. I read all day and on into the evening. That night I kept reflecting on one point I had read, that there were four basic hairstyles for men in the world. To let it grow and cap it was Chinese; to shave it off was Indian; to clip it was Western; to shave the front and arrange the rest to hang like a pig's tail was Manchu. Next morning I went to a barber and had him cut off my queue. I was quite satisfied with myself and happy to be independent. The exam being over, I returned to Wuxi with my Guoyu classmates. Someone said, "If you take the train without a queue, the police will take you for a revolutionary." They persuaded me to sew the queue into my cap to avoid detection before we left. The following year, after the revolution, everyone got rid of their queues, but mine had been gone for a year already.[33]

By the age of fifteen, six years after learning that the emperor was not Chinese, Qian Mu had launched his own revolution. As with so many other young students, it began with rebellion against the discipline and empty formalism of the new-style schools. "Spinelessness" in a student protest translated readily into spinelessness in national and international politics. Rebellion did the same. Yet for a youth who had already been exposed to literati "learning," the rebellion did not lead inevitably to a rejection of the values transmitted from the world of the literati. The school did not embody these values, nor did they inhere in the body of students that stopped at injuring their career chances in favor of strengthening their spines. Ironically, it was the director, Tu Xiaokuan, who showed what a mastery of that learning could achieve in practice. This "statesman" and "educator" avoided factionalizing his faculty, got the students through their exams, and bent over backwards to allow the most spirited of the students to speak out without hanging themselves. It was Tu who arranged for Qian to transfer to the Chongying Upper Middle School in Nanjing, by sending an application with his personal endorsement, when Chen Shixin opposed Tu's attempt to readmit him.[34]

In Nanjing in 1911, the newborn rebel took up cavalry training and entertained dreams of fighting Russians and Japanese in the northeast. When the Wuhan uprising set off the revolution in October, he took up with another rebel who had transferred from Changzhou in the hope of joining the republican army when it arrived. The plan was foiled when the friend's family called him home on the false pretext of his father's illness. The school closed, and Qian had nowhere to hide.[35] Soon the revolution was over. The new-style schools, of course, hardly changed. To a student, the new republic looked much like the old regime. The rebels graduated and went their separate ways.

The republican revolution of 1911 accomplished three things. It ended Manchu rule of China. It removed the last Son of Heaven from his position as cosmic pivot. And it undermined the revolutionary front. By autumn 1913, the republic's modernizing president, Yuan Shikai, had destroyed the National Assembly and established dictatorial control. Reformers like Liang Qichao tried to stem the tide of militarization while revolutionaries like Sun Yatsen returned to underground organization.[36] The surviving foot soldiers on the educational front, if they had not already joined the ranks of party politicians, civil servants, or private professionals, divided into New Culture revolutionists and old culture evolutionists. With the death of Yuan Shikai in 1916, the stage was set for a decade of warlord competition for power and intellectual alienation from politics.

When Cai Yuanpei, a veteran of the Patriotic School in Shanghai, became chancellor of Beijing University in 1917, he vowed to remove the university from the world of politics altogether. In his inaugural address, he charged the student body with the dual obligation of intellectual rigor and political abstinence:

> You who come here to study should have a firm purpose in mind. In order to know whether your aim is appropriate, you must first understand the nature of the university.... A university is a place dedicated to the pursuit of scholarship. Outsiders like to point to the decadence of this school. Those who study here, they say, think only about official appointment, or getting rich.... Now there is no shortage of special schools in Beijing for those whose aim is to secure a bureaucratic appointment, or to make money ...

and they have no business coming to this university. Your aim in coming here should be to seek learning.[37]

Cai then invited students to join a campus society in which members pledged neither to accept bureaucratic appointments nor to run for elective office. Half the student body, nearly a thousand students, accepted. And Cai set about hiring a faculty that was both diverse and argumentative. His dean of the School of Letters was Chen Duxiu, another veteran of the revolutionary student movement, whose journal *New Youth* had inaugurated the New Culture movement. Another new appointee was Hu Shi, a prodigy who had studied with John Dewey at Columbia University and who brought to the New Culture movement the flavor of American pragmatism. Together with his own students at Beijing University, most notably the historian Gu Jiegang and the philologist Fu Sinian, Hu hoped to find the roots of a modern culture deep in the Chinese past. For this, the Chinese "renaissance" school, the task was to explore native traditions of vernacular literature and folk traditions, science and philosophy, that would support a modern national culture. Like Qian Mu's primary school teacher, the poet Hua Zhen, the proponents of the renaissance school would replace the stale with the fresh, but first they would distinguish the culture of the people from that of the literati. As was the case with the nations of Europe, as the people's cultural identity emerged, the culture of the literati could be assigned to museums.[38]

Ironically, Cai Yuanpei and Chen Duxiu both made their way back into the political arena, the former as a tamer of student movements for the Guomindang and the latter as secretary-general of the Communist party. The catalyst for their reentry into politics was the wave of student demonstrations that swept China after May 4, 1919, in protest against the Chinese government's acquiescence in concessions made to Japan at the Versailles Peace Conference. But renaissance scholars held fast to the principle of political detachment. Lest they be accused of abandoning the New Culture for dusty academic pursuits, they carefully distinguished their work from the concerns of cultural conservatives like Zhang Binglin and his students, who believed in an unchanging "essence" of Chinese culture, in deeper meanings imbedded in its structure that transcended the peculiar issues of this or any other age.

Those who remained in the mainstream of academic discussion thus divided themselves into "national essence" and "national studies" advocates. The national essence emphasized by cultural conservatives was expressed in the structures of the language, the meanings elaborated in arts and letters, and in religious beliefs. Hu Shi and his protégés argued, to the contrary, that it was the age that determined which structures survived. The laws of evolution, discovered by Darwin, demonstrated that what cultural conservatives called essence was only the structure of another age; what they called culture was already dead. Qian Xuantong, a former student of Zhang Binglin, joined the issue with bell-like clarity in the pages of *New Youth:*

> [Chen Duxiu has] urged that Confucianism be discarded. . . . I would carry it a step further: if we wish to destroy Confucianism, we must get rid of the Chinese language; if we wish to eradicate the childish, uncivilized and reactionary thought prevalent among our people, we must first dispose of the Chinese language. . . . In regard to its application to modern learning, it contains no terms to describe new ideas, new facts, new things; in regard to its past history, it has served, to the virtual exclusion of anything else, as the repository for Confucian morality and Taoist superstition. Such a language is utterly unsuited to this new era, to the twentieth century.[39]

And the scholars of what came to be known as National Studies would develop a new language, the language of modern science, with which they would dissect the carcass of the Chinese past and explain the cause of death to the survivors.

Despite the rhetoric, National Studies advocates' claims of scientific objectivity and political detachment could not help but place them closer to the tradition of Zhang Binglin than to that of Chen Duxiu. Like Kang Youwei and his New Text vision, Chen's radical activism had little use for the past or for the products of the old culture, whether literate or popular. Gu Jiegang, who developed the scientific approach in his journal *Critiques of Ancient History,* had first awakened to the importance of historical research as a prep school student, listening to Zhang Binglin before the latter was arrested in 1914. With his careful attention to details of text and context, Zhang demonstrated how Kang Youwei manipulated them to serve political ends. At that moment, Kang was pressing for state sponsorship of a new Confucian religion, and Yuan Shikai was giving the idea some play. Zhang became Gu's first model of empirical objectivity, a model that Gu and other New Culture academics struggled to live up to.[40]

Among the former rebels of the Changzhou Middle School, Qu Qiubai followed Chen Duxiu, coming to advocate an all-new proletarian literature to replace the vernacular of the new literary magazines. Liu Bannung, one of the five representatives of the protesting class, followed Hu Shi, becoming a collector of folksongs and advocate of the development of a new cultural spirit through folk revival.[41] Yet another of the rebels' five representatives, Zhang Xuan, helped launch the journal *National Heritage,* which attacked the new culture and advocated reviving the old.[42] Qian Mu himself read *New Youth* and other new culture journals in the Wuxi countryside, where he taught schoolboys Chinese. From that distance, and with his experience first in the world of the literati at the Guoyu school and then in the new-style school at Changzhou, he took the New Culture movement with a grain of salt. "I had already decided to immerse myself in the old books," he wrote in his *Memories of Teachers and Friends,* "so I was not caught up in the new wave. As I look back on it from the present, that was a great stroke of luck."[43]

The year Gu Jiegang heard Zhang Binglin denounce Kang Youwei, Qian Mu discovered the ancient division between New Text and Old Text studies in a college history textbook. He was teaching then at his old school in Dangkou, which had become a public primary school and now bore the name of its founder, Hua Hongmo, who had died in 1911. The more Qian studied, the more he regretted not having had the chance to attend college. But his education continued apace. While teaching in a village school in 1912, he had been introduced by the school's patron to translations of Herbert Spencer and John Stuart Mill's *Logic.* As Chen Duxiu launched his *New Youth* crusade against the old culture in Shanghai, Qian began applying Zeng Guofan's dictum that, when reading history, one should always read meticulously from beginning to end, to the 120-chapter *History of the Later Han.* As he gradually developed the habit of scrutinizing texts, their language became familiar to him, as did the writings of the great eighteenth-century scholars of Han Learning. By 1918 he had started publishing classics readers for primary schools, while discussing religion, politics, and even communism with young colleagues in Wuxi's rural schools. But not until 1918, when he set out to study the ancient non-Confucian philosophers, did he discover that what he was doing had a place in the larger cultural debates.

As a commission for his *Analects Grammar,* Qian received coupons for one hundred yuan worth of books from the Commercial Press booklist. Beginning to read an eighteenth-century edition of an ancient philosophical text, the *Mo Tzu,* he realized there must be errors in the text. After three or four days of studying it, he had compiled a long list of mistakes. How could the noted scholar who compiled the text have overlooked these errors, he wondered? And hadn't someone since then written about it? He found a likely looking title on the Commercial Press list and wrote off to a book dealer in Wuxi to see if they knew of it. They sent it to him: the classic 1893 philological study of the *Mo Tzu* by Sun Yirang, a man Zhang Binglin had met when Qian Mu was two years old, and a forefather of the science Gu Jiegang was learning in Beijing. Qian was shocked to find himself a "kindergartener among sages," and he set about learning the things Zhang Binglin had learned in his youth.[44]

But the life of a country schoolteacher differed from that of the city scholar. The foot soldier's choices in the two environments were similar in kind but different in substance. Qian Bogui, who had taught Qian Mu the political facts of life, helped start a primary school in his native village of Hongshengli before the revolution. Afterward he joined the victors, first as vice-chairman of the county assembly and then as a local judicial official. His brother joined the military and, after the the republicans seized power in Wuxi, pursued a military career.[45] Qian's closest teaching colleague in the rural schools marched off to join the new revolution in 1919, and others joined the Communists. But for those in the country who, like Qian Mu, chose to stand on politically neutral ground, the field was not one of scholarship, but of teaching.

In spring 1919 Hu Shi invited John Dewey to deliver a series of lectures in China on his philosophy of education. Dewey's approach was experimental, to attempt to find what has practical meaning in the life of the child and to use it, rather than to rely on the authority of teacher or text. The New Culture reformers viewed this as the way to eliminate from the curriculum what they saw as the useless parts of the old literati's culture. The lectures happened to coincide with the revival of student activism that began with the May Fourth incident. The differing appeal of the lectures and the student movement may serve to distinguish one generation of foot soldiers from the next.[46] For six years prior to Dewey's visit, Qian Mu had been teaching Chinese in the large marketing towns of Dangkou and Meicun, where his salary and privileges were slowly improving his lot. In autumn 1919, when the county announced its intention to convert a private school in the village of Houzhai to a public primary school, Qian jumped at the chance to head it up.

> There were two reasons why I decided to move to a primary school. One was that Dr. Dewey was in China lecturing on the philosophy of education. I had read his lectures in the journals and was very interested. I felt that although his philosophy was not at all the same as the old Chinese idea of education I knew from my native place, the two did have a lot in common. So I thought that if I went to a primary school and conducted an experiment, working directly with the children from the day they started, I could find out for myself what were the similarities and differences between new and old, Chinese and foreign ideas about education, and what were the strengths and weaknesses in each. The second reason was that everyone had been clamoring for a vernacular literature and the primary schools had already started using only textbooks that were written in the vernacular. The previous year I had published my *Analects Grammar* specifically to teach the fundamentals of classical prose composition. I was eager to examine the strengths and weaknesses of teaching primary students in the vernacular.

Qian chose two colleagues to accompany him to Houzhai on the condition that they would defer to his experimental design and confer daily on its application.

> I told them that it was my ideal to integrate the curriculum and the regulations into the lives of the students. I wanted to make their everyday lives part of the curriculum, but also to make the curriculum part of their everyday lives, so that the two were completely integrated and it would be impossible to distinguish one from the other. If the students were only to bring a part of their everyday lives into the curriculum and leave another part out in a world they call personal, that would be bad. My colleagues both agreed and asked how I planned to proceed. I said, "If we want to make the curriculum a living curriculum, then we'll have to change our idea of what we call classes. Physical education and music, for example, are clearly living things, but if we teach them in classes, then the students will treat them like classes. We should abolish those two classes and make music and exercise things that everyone does together, the three of us included, everyday." My colleagues were enthusiastic.

"If we want to make discipline a living thing," I said, "now that's a more complicated matter. To begin with, I want to abolish corporal punishment. I don't want the students to treat school regulations like laws; that would lead to the misconception that discipline is only a kind of bondage imposed from without. Isn't it, in fact, a primary goal of education to make discipline a part of everyday life?" My colleagues were not so enthusiastic on that point. They said I was being entirely too idealistic and ignoring the lessons of experience. Today's primary school students are six or seven years old. The oldest are never more than thirteen or fourteen. They are naive children who are quick to follow the crowd and the situation can easily get out of hand. Sometimes you have to use physical punishment.

"One is being idealistic about children the minute one lets them loose," I said. "If one is only idealistic and ignores practical experience, that's just empty-headed. On the other hand, if one only trusts in experience and doesn't pursue one's ideals, then one trusts in habit, and this is also quite meaningless. As for moral instruction, I am willing to take all the responsibility in order to experiment with my ideals, so long as you are helpful. You two can report your experience to me case by case to help me realize my ideal. If there are problems, we'll discuss them and consider a different course if that seems best. How about it?" They didn't object.

On the first day, I announced that when class was over everyone should go out to the exercise ground and no one was to stay in the classroom. But when I looked up, there was a child sitting stiffly in his chair. When I asked him why he didn't go out and play, he just sat there and didn't answer. I asked him his name, and still he didn't answer. So I went out and asked the class monitor about it. He told me that the boy's name was Yang Xilin, and that the previous director had told him he could not leave the classroom, except to relieve himself, because he had broken the rules.

"Now listen to the new director's orders," I said. "The previous director has left, and that order is no longer in effect. You take him outside with you." So the two of them went outside. Before long a group of students came to my office with Yang Xilin in tow and told me he had caught a frog in the ditch by the exercise ground and ripped it in two. One of them produced the frog's corpse. I said, "Yang Xilin doesn't understand some things as well as the rest of you do because he has had to stay in the classroom for so long. Now you take him and let him play with you. After a while he will learn from you. Wherever you are or whenever he needs it, you help him out, and don't make mountains out of molehills. If he does something wrong, then all of you come together and tell me about it. If it happens again after that, I will punish the rest of you, not Yang Xilin." Then they all went out, very quietly.

Then a pair of brothers by the name of Zou arrived. They were from another village, but their family was related to mine by marriage. A family member brought them, and after he had left, I told them to go out and play with the others. Before long a group of boys ushered the younger brother into my office. The older brother followed. The group accused the younger boy of hitting someone. I said, "He's really quite small. You are all older than he is, what is there to be afraid of? If he hits anybody again, you just hit him back. I won't punish you." The crowd went happily on its way, but the older brother stayed behind, crying.

"I can't just let my brother get beat up!" he said. I told him, "Don't you worry. Nobody will hit your brother if he doesn't hit them first. You just watch after him and tell him not to hit anyone again." There were no more incidents after that. After my colleagues saw how I handled those two cases, they were quite enthusiastic and never again spoke of using corporal punishment.[47]

Qian Mu's techniques resembled those of the great statesmen of the past. First, establish that there is a consensus about what is right and wrong, and assume that, given a fair chance, most people will do what is right. Then discourage wrongdoing by threatening the offender, or potential offender, with ostracism from the consensual group. Finally, prevent a division by allowing the offender to save face and threatening the group with alternative measures if they don't accept him. It was the same technique that Tu Xiaokuan had used to defuse the student protest at Changzhou Middle School, isolating Qian Mu, who had mistakenly assumed that the consensus was with him and against Tu. On one occasion, Qian even borrowed a strategy from the *History of the Han,* using a young thief's accomplice as an informant and then shocking the thief by reciting to him all the details of his behavior. When the culprit realized that he was not only found out but also alone, he was ready to reform.[48]

But only to be a statesman was not enough: the primary task was education. A Yang Xilin needed not just to be tolerated; he also needed to find himself.

I had two ways of testing the students' progress. First, I would write something on the board in Chinese characters, ask the students to read it over a few times, erase it, and then ask them to write it down from memory. Second, I would read the piece aloud, ask the students to listen to it three times, and then ask them to write it down. After we had done this a number of times, I learned that Yang Xilin rarely made mistakes in the aural exercise, and so I surmised that his ear was especially well-tuned. One day I detained him after class. I played the zither and asked him to sing along. His voice was elegant and harmonized perfectly with the strings. I asked him to follow me again, but this time I stopped short, and the voice continued without the strings. His manner was graceful and calm, and I applauded him. I asked, "Could you sing a solo for us tomorrow at chorus?" He nodded. "Could you go on singing when I stop playing, the way you did just now?" I asked. He nodded. The next day at chorus I asked for a volunteer to sing a solo, and Xilin raised his hand. He sang on when the zither stopped, and his classmates were so startled that they couldn't stop clapping.[49]

Qian's approach to the living classroom clearly worked for Yang Xilin, who went on to excel in music and acting and was accepted as a boy with talent. Hadn't Zeng Guofan written that human talent thrives only where custom permits, and that custom depends on individual efforts to maintain it? But the larger question in 1919 was whether a whole new generation would be taught to reject as dead what Qian Mu believed still lived in Chinese culture. Should that happen, he feared, the new China might have plenty of technological talent, but its soul would have been sold to the West. This is what Qian's experiment was designed to prevent.

In spring 1920 the "national language" (*guoyu*)—Mandarin Chinese, which was based on the northern dialects with Beijing as the standard—became the language of instruction throughout China's schools. The school in Houzhai, where a variant of the Wu dialect was spoken, hired an instructor to teach Mandarin to the whole student body. Qian's course in the national literature (*guowen*) was downgraded to a course in writing (*zuowen*). Still, he followed his living classroom strategy:

First I told the students that when it comes out of the mouth, it's called speech, and when it comes off the pen, it's called writing. Writing is just like speaking. However you would say it, write it. If there is something you want to say but, when you go to write it, you don't know the character it's written with, just ask. One day after lunch I had them write about lunch. When they handed their papers in, I selected a good one and wrote it on the board. It said, "Today's lunch was pork in brown sauce. The taste was great; too bad it was so salty." I told them that in speech there always had to be a little turning point, as in the last line of this piece.

Then another day, I selected a story from a collection of Lin Shu, the great contemporary classical prose stylist, told it to them in the vernacular, and had them write it down. I have forgotten the story, but the point was that there were five brothers. The first one dressed in his full uniform and went off to battle. Then the second dressed and went to battle. Then the third, and the fourth and the fifth. The students wrote it down as I told it. Then I told them that writing is like speaking, but sometimes speech can go on like this, where writing is more effective if it's simplified. Then I wrote Lin Shu's original story on the board, and they could understand the meaning immediately, even though it was written in the classical language. I said, "If you write this way, you can say in a phrase what you have just now taken five sentences to write. That's too verbose."

Another day I had the students take their slates and pencils and writing paper to a graveyard on the edge of the village, where there was a grove of perhaps a hundred pine trees. I had them each choose a tree to sit under, to observe what they saw around them, and then to try to write it down. We sat in a circle and I asked each student to explain what he had written. There was a rousing discussion about what various people had outlined quickly, completely forgotten, chosen to emphasize, or put in one or another order. Then I told them, "There is something none of you has noticed. Do you hear the sound of the wind over your heads? I want you all to listen carefully and tell me how that sound is different from the sound you usually hear." The students all listened for a moment. Then I said, "Because the wind passes through the pines, and the pine needles are thin and separated by small gaps, the sound is different from the sound in other places. It's called pine winds. Try rewriting your descriptions and see if you can write what that sound is like." They all thought hard about it and wrote something out, and then we discussed it again, and I pointed out where their strengths and weaknesses were. After spending half a day there, evening finally approached, and we returned with our heads in the air. In this way, the students came to think the writing class was fun, and they were always asking if they were going to have writing today.[50]

Qian Mu's experiments proved to his own satisfaction that the learning of the literati could adapt to the modern world and inspire the imagination of a new generation of foot soldiers. Perhaps it was uniquely suited to the needs of a people whose struggle against imperialism was complicated by its struggle against autocracy and the extreme concentration of coercive power. Qian's studies in Chinese history and classical literature, enhanced by the construction, under his direction, of the first rural public library in the county at the Houzhai School, were leading him toward a new interpretation of China's past. It was the literati, not as a class of gentry scholar-landlords but as the interpreters and transmitters of culture, who had prevented China's autocracy from achieving total authority over the Chinese people. The modernizing state, with its new military technologies and its claims on taxation and educational powers, threatened to destroy the literati's culture of resistance. But if he had proved that this culture could be transmitted in the modern world, Qian had also discovered that the New Culture, in its efforts to establish its own authority, was rapidly developing a stranglehold on those institutions that would allow this to happen. Journal editors balked at publishing cultural articles by an obscure country schoolteacher, and Dewey's lectures had already been claimed and given an orthodox interpretation by educational administrators. The New Culture would lead the Chinese resistance, and the problem of autocracy was blamed on the old. But perhaps the greatest blow of all for Qian was that the inspiration he provided the students was not sending them to the front. Most of them were sons of village shopkeepers, and after graduating they returned to family businesses. Their eyes opened, their sensibilities enhanced, they took their talents to the teashop, the wine shop, the butcher, and the candy store. Only the sons of the gentry went on to advanced studies.[51] The ways of wasting talent were more than one.

In 1922 Qian Mu moved to the Number One Upper Primary School in Wuxi City and then to a private school in Amoy. The next year, he was back in Wuxi, at the teacher's training school, where he remained until autumn 1927. From that vantage point, he watched the Guomindang-Communist party alliance grow into the wave of the future, as the new generation of primary school students began to mature. He watched Qian Zhongshu, the brilliant son of a kinsman and a teaching colleague, grow and thrive on the combination of Chinese and Western studies that was to make him the outstanding literary figure of the 1940s. Qian Mu began publishing vernacular textbooks on the lives and works of Chinese philosophers of the classical age. And he watched as the Guomindang's northern expedition approached Wuxi, as his former colleague at the Houzhai School was shot for making speeches supporting it, as the Guomindang turned on the Communists, and as sons of old teachers and friends joined the underground.

By the time Qian Mu moved up to the Suzhou Middle School in autumn 1927, he had identified himself with the political ideals of Sun Yatsen's Three Principles of the People. Sun published a full-blown manifesto with that title in 1924, elaborating on the slogan of the Revolutionary Alliance of 1905: *minzu, minquan, minsheng*—"for the people, their rights, and their livelihood," or as it is often translated, "nationalism, democracy, socialism." As political philosophy, the essay was designed to subsume Communist aspirations within those of the national revolution as Sun's Guomindang interpreted them. For Qian Mu, it was the manifesto's link between a much needed public spirit and the spirit of a Chinese people that warmed his heart. It was the first political program to acknowledge the possibility of a uniquely Chinese form of public spiritedness, a possibility that could lead China to democracy and social justice without discarding its culture.

So enthralled was Qian Mu with the prospect that he began to pull his lecture notes together for a book, which finally appeared in 1931, called *A Survey of National Studies*. The thesis was that Chinese intellectual thought had undergone many changes over the previous three thousand years. In each case, it had adapted to the challenge of a new age, just as the New Culture advocates said it must. But in contrast to Hu Shi's argument that Buddhist ideas, introduced from India after the Han Dynasty, diverted Chinese culture from its evolutionary path, and that values introduced from the West were closer to those of China's own ancient heritage, Qian Mu believed that something essential to Chinese culture was elaborated with each successive change. Only if one assumed that the course of evolution for all peoples is the same could one conclude that a diversion has occurred. It followed that Sun Yatsen's political philosophy, which allowed for a uniquely Chinese path toward democracy and socialism, was better suited to the Chinese people than anything imported from the West.[52]

That the emergent dictatorial Guomindang of Chiang Kaishek could make use of Qian's thesis to oppose liberals and Communists alike did not seem to deter him. Qian's obeisance was to Sun's political thought, not to the party. He refused to join the Guomindang, even though he later gave lectures and edited publications at the party's invitation.[53] In 1927 the important thing was to keep the schools open—Qian Mu taught without pay and counseled his students to stay with him rather than march on Nanjing to protest the lack of salaries—and to keep making sense of Chinese history. By the time Gu Jiegang met him in Suzhou in 1929, the New Culture movement was in disarray.

If *A Survey of National Studies* displays the teacherly side of Qian Mu's mind in those years, *Chronological Studies of the Pre-Qin Philosophers* reveals the scholarly side. It was the latter that Gu Jiegang discovered in Suzhou and that prompted him to invite to Beiping this opponent of the movement Gu had helped to launch. When the shooting started and funds for the universities dried up in 1926 during the northern expedition, Gu Jiegang and many others went south. On his return in 1929, he stopped in Suzhou and met Qian Mu. Qian showed him the scholarly manuscript and Gu told him he should be at a university. Qian's study of ancient thought, which Gu had recognized as an important contribution to scholarship, eventually became an authoritative reference for intellectual historians, and Gu's recognition led to Qian's appointment at Yanjing University in Beiping.

In addition, Qian's "Chronological Record of Liu Xiang and Xin, Father and Son" appeared in Gu's monograph series, *Critiques of Ancient History,* in 1930. The article marked Qian's debut among the professionals and established, once and for all, that the Han Dynasty usurpers could not have forged the ancient texts in the Confucian canon. It followed that no measure of New Text vision could justify excluding these texts from the sources of historical and philological research.[54] His reputation as a scholar thus established, Qian moved from Yanjing to Beijing University, where he became one of the most popular professors.

By 1930 the ideological battles that had developed with the emergence of the Guomindang and the Chinese Communist party had torn through the ranks of the New Culture movement. On the literary front, Hu Shi had raised the distinction between a folk tradition and a tradition of literati, arguing that the great novels of the past reflected the former and could serve as models for a vernacular literature. Liu Bannung and others turned to folksongs and folktales. But writers of fiction found the notion of traditional models absurd. On a visit home in 1921, Lu Xun, the era's greatest writer, found a wall between himself and the folk culture of his native place. Qu Qiubai called Hu Shi's vernacular "a mule," insisting that it reproduced neither the language of the old culture nor the language of the street. And Liang Qichao faulted the movement for romanticizing the folk, who had neither written the old novels nor read them. Like Qian Mu's childhood drill instructor, Liang believed the novels bred complacency and popularized the values that had destroyed the old culture.[55] In the midst of this confusion, the two political parties took sides.

For the politicization of the argument, the identification of "two cultures" was convenient. As folklorists, inspired by Gu Jiegang's call for a new history of popular culture, went to the countryside to find the culture of the people, Mao Zedong and other rebels in the revolutionaries' ranks went there to organize them. Gu Jiegang had identified the literati as parasites and assigned their culture to the museum. Peasant organizers, however, found that culture very much alive, in the form of deference to the rural gentry and avoidance of politics. The organizers saw their task as the destruction of literati culture and the class whose interests it served. The Guomindang, seeking once more to unify the people under a new authority, saw the problem differently. The literati culture was literate and could easily be transformed to meet modern needs. It was the folk culture, with its superstitions and clannishness, that stood in the way of progress. Thus their task was to destroy that, and to reform the people through education. Once again, the choice for the foot soldiers was to embrace the new authority, join the new wave, or stand on the principle of political neutrality.

Hu Shi, who had done much to encourage the idea of two cultures, tried to lead the New Culture intellectuals down the liberal middle. His faith in American pragmatism aligned him against the radicals in principle, but his ideal of gradual adaptive change and educational reform did not allow him to condone Stalinist tactics. The Guomindang's appeal to Sun Yatsen's Three Principles of the People in their attempt to resurrect "Confucian" authority Hu saw as a political nightmare. Still claiming political detachment, just like Qian Mu, Hu attacked the Three Principles of the People on intellectual grounds. Not only did this ideology link politics and education, reproducing what Gu Jiegang had been trying to show was the basic pattern of political manipulation of ideas in Chinese history since Confucius, but it was also explicitly elitist, antiprogressive, and antiforeign. But there was no political vehicle for liberals in China, and Hu found himself sharing the middle ground of political detachment with scholars like Zhang Binglin, Liang Shuming, and Qian Mu, all of whom had opposed the New Culture from the outset, and those who believed in pure science to the exclusion of moral principles, like Fu Sinian.[56]

When Qian Mu appeared on the Beiping intellectual scene, the focus of debate had already shifted from the understanding of history to the making of it. Fu Sinian, who had spent several years studying in Germany since the "renaissance" began, was now the director of the Institute of History and Philology at the newly opened Academia Sinica. Fu believed that it was time to "order the facts" of Chinese history, and he was overseeing the production of a massive history that would simply tell the truth, as empirically verified by historians, eschewing interpretation. Fu's position was one of extreme positivism, reflecting the debates on science and the philosophy of life in Beijing in 1923. Since then the positivists had held sway in the universities, and historians had paid the students of Chinese spirit and morality little heed. But by 1928 Marxist historiography had made sufficient inroads to force a new debate, this time among the scholars of Chinese social history. If history was indeed to be a science, then it must apply theories. Without them, Fu Sinian's array of facts would be meaningless. Moreover, history should be useful. The task of the science of history was to determine the course of change for the present, and scientific history was the application, testing, and modification of the theories of Karl Marx.

Suddenly, historical narrative was important again. As the choice between constitutional monarchy and republic had fired the controversy between Zhang Binglin and Liang Qichao, the choice between Guomindang reform and Communist revolution fired the social history controversy of 1928–1933. On the one side, it was argued that a capitalist economy had emerged in China in the fourth century B.C., before the imperial state, but the state had chosen to depend on landowners, adopting a feudal ideology, which prevented the state from developing the economy's systems of production and exchange. Now that the old ideology was discredited, the task was to preserve national unity and develop production, eroding the political power of the landowning class in the process. On the other side, there was a division between Trotskyites and Stalinists. The former argued that capitalism had indeed emerged in China, but it could only develop to the detriment of the nation because the growth sector was controlled by imperialists. They saw the task as opposing the imperialists and the big bourgeoisie. The Stalinsts argued that capitalism had not yet emerged—the relations of production and exchange were, in fact, feudal. The task in this case was to oppose the gentry and the state.[57] But the historians, no matter what their positions, saw their purpose as the production of new narratives that would demonstrate the pattern of the Chinese past.

Qian Mu was by then a veteran of eighteen years' teaching in the primary and secondary schools of Wuxi and elsewhere. He had observed successive waves of political revolution and had watched his students march off to join them or go home to tend the family store. He had entered the debates brought on by the New Culture movement from a distance, and he had seen its hopes rise madly and then fall. His *Chronological Record* filled a gap in the new history that Gu Jiegang had begun to explore in 1926. By the time Qian reached Beiping, however, the new history's empiricism had been superseded by the dialectical materialists. Qian Mu was still in his thirties. Perhaps in his eyes the world had not changed all that much. As he looked around him in Beiping, he saw a number of talented younger scholars, the poet and classicist Wen Yiduo among them, who had not been caught up in the New Culture debates. Perhaps they would have helped deliver China from this moment of cultural chaos, Qian reflected, if it hadn't been for the Japanese.[58]

Before the war with Japan, Qian Mu resolutely set out to reclaim Chinese history for the Chinese. First he revived a course that Liang Qichao, who had died the previous year, had planned to teach, on the intellectual history of the last three hundred years. Soon he had published, in two volumes, a definitive narrative on the subject. Its purpose was to call attention to the scholarship that Kang Youwei had dismissed, incorporating an exposé of Kang himself as an example of one who distorted the truth for political ends.[59] Then he engaged in a series of curricular battles to ensure that the university would offer expert coverage of the entire span of Chinese history. Disgusted with the government's support for Fu Sinian's project, he secured permission to teach the complete history of China in a single year-long course. The purpose was to show that history was interpretive, not just an ordering of facts. The only course of its kind, it attracted auditors from the other universities. The message, of course, was that Chinese history had a pattern of its own. The task was to learn it and to keep the faith.[60]

In all this one detects a stubbornness reminiscent of Zhang Binglin. It was Zhang who had inspired the first little foot soldier to extol revolution for the sake of freeing the people from their ancient habit of subservience. But it was the youthful Zou Rong, not Zhang himself, who had argued that revolution is "ordinary" and that "all of our current ideas were sifted down to us through the process of past revolutions." Revolution was not ordinary for Zhang, but necessary. Given the strength of the imperialist powers, the only choice for the Chinese people was to evolve into a unified and independent nation or into separate subjugated peoples. Revolution could make China independent, but it could not unify. Unity depended on cultural consensus. Continuing revolution, be it Liang Qichao's political one, Hu Shi's cultural one, or the Marxists' social one, could only serve to divide.

The scholars who groped for the key to a Chinese cultural identity in Beiping in the 1930s also had visitors from afar:

> One year Zhang Binglin came to Beiping to give a lecture, which I went to hear. He was flanked by five or six former students of his, who were by then professors at various institutions. One interpreted for him while another wrote words on the blackboard to the rear. Zhang's voice was faint, and he spoke in the Wu dialect, as he could not manage the national language. If his assistants failed to understand something he quoted from a classic—the name of a person, a place or a book—they consulted among themselves or asked someone else on the platform before translating or writing it down. And the audience remained silent and respectful throughout.

Zhang's two assistants were Qian Xuantong—the man who had moved from Zhang's tutelage to the New Text vision and had argued for disposing of the classical language—and Liu Bannung, Qian Mu's middle school classmate whose idea of the New Culture was rooted in folk traditions.

> It seems that even though the New Culture was ascendent in Beijing, these prominent professors were the very picture of the old

etiquette. It was clear that cultural change could not be accomplished with a flick of the wrist.

Later, in Suzhou, a student in Zhang's national studies seminar contacted me and I took advantage of the occasion to visit. It was the first and only time I met Zhang Binglin face to face. The two of us were alone in his room. I asked him, "I read recently in the newspaper that the government had invited you to be director of the National History Office in Nanjing; is that true?"

"That's quite impossible," he answered. "I am not in agreement with this government. The newspapers are wrong."

"If the government did invite you," I asked, "and if you accepted, what would be your idea of a new national history?"

"The people of this nation have already discarded their history," he said. "There is no longer any need for a new one."

"Well, let's set reality aside for a moment," I went on. "Supposing there were to be a new national history anyhow, how do you think it should differ from the traditional dynastic histories?" Zhang thought for awhile, then he said, "The basic chronicles and biographies might remain roughly the same. But the treatises would need to be totally redone. Take foreign relations, for example. The subject is too broad to be contained in the old treatise format. I would say that living in Shanghai has made me aware of the fact that the influence of the laws governing foreign affairs has been very great. If this were added to the histories as a topic, it would fill many volumes. The same is true of the economy and criminal law. There is an even greater need for specialized knowledge with respect to those subjects. These are the things that would need to be greatly revised. But there is little point in talking about that in these times."

We talked from three in the afternoon until early evening. Then, as he had also invited Zhang Yipeng and several other eminent Suzhou scholars for dinner, we ate and I retired. He virtually never discussed this issue with anyone else.[61]

Perhaps Zhang's notion was that the human element in the chronicles of dynasties and the biographies of historical figures displayed the influence of Chinese culture, while the institutions that men created and that, in turn, constrained them displayed the influence of social and economic structure. Whatever the notion, it was not timely. But, for Qian Mu at least, it was not simply a notion whose time had passed. Times got worse. In 1937 Qian Mu joined in the exodus of univer-

sity faculty and students who took refuge in the far southwestern province of Yunnan. As the Japanese occupied the major cities of the north
and east and as Communists and Nationalists spoke of a new united
front, the need for a national history seemed even greater than before.
At the suggestion of a colleague who had audited his comprehensive
history course in Beiping, Qian decided to write a two-volume narrative history of Chinese civilization.[62] As if to reinforce the notion that
the current situation was only a passing moment in a history that
moved in a rhythm all its own, he moved to a remote mountain villa
where he could concentrate exclusively on this work. The villa belonged to the Buddhist Precipice Spring Lower Temple. Qian's decision to stay there for a year and write occurred during an overnight
visit there with two friends.

Next morning, after they had left, the abbot came to discuss
my meals. He said that they served only vegetarian fare and was
afraid it wouldn't be sufficient for me. I said it was no problem and
that he could just send a portion up to me. I had not anticipated
that what he would send me would be so crude as to be inedible. I
tried to toughen myself up for a couple of days, but even though I
grew quite hungry, I still found it indigestible. So I had another
chat with the abbot.

"All the food in the temple is like that," he said. "Maybe you had
better switch to a meat diet."

"But it would be too much trouble to install a stove downstairs,"
I said.

"A meat diet can just as easily be prepared in the temple's
kitchen," he said. So I asked if he could look for a woman I could
hire, and he said, "There's Old Lady Zhang; we can ask her." I met
Old Lady Zhang and saw that she was clean and well mannered,
and so I was quite pleased. When I asked her about preparing
meals, she showed considerable self-confidence with regard to
cooking. When I asked her how much she would need to charge
per month to cook for me, she answered, "Six Chinese yuan is equal
to sixty New Yunnan yuan, and that would suffice for two meals a
day, one meat dish, one vegetable dish and one soup at each meal."
So we agreed to that. Later, I learned that the abbot had already
arranged for her to come to the temple to cook for me.

Not only was Old Lady Zhang a good cook, she also went to the
fields of the peasants around the temple to buy the ingredients
before each meal, so they were extremely fresh. One day she had

prepared chicken for me and for some reason I had to rush out right after lunch. As I passed the kitchen, there was the abbot sitting by the door with a chicken leg in his hand, resolutely chomping away at it. I could not restrain myself from asking if monks were now eating chicken legs.

"If a monk doesn't eat chicken legs, then what should he eat?" he answered. Then I saw a bowl of chicken soup by the stove and realized that it had all been arranged in advance that I should share my meat diet with the abbot. Later I learned that he had a family in a village nearby, that he came and went at odd times, and that everyone knew about it. One can easily imagine what else this monk was up to.

Once the cooking business was settled, I had a routine. Every morning after breakfast I went for a little walk to the spur of a hill from which I could view the peaks to the south of Yiliang. I would wait for the mist to rise and then return. After supper I walked at the foot of the mountain. There was a path leading east that was flanked by forested hills. Deeply shaded and totally secluded, the path was narrow and straight, with never any travelers to be seen. I loved that place immensely. I would not return until the blue sky was nearly black. When the days grew short, I went before supper. Except for these morning and evening walks, I spent the whole day in my study, writing the history. At night, I would read a few chapters of the *Draft History of the Qing Dynasty*, and then I would sleep. The sound of the spring below my study echoed more loudly in the night's silence, and my dreams were of boating on the country streams of my old home.

I had also contracted to write a weekly column for distribution among the newspapers in Kunming. Each Thursday I walked the four kilometers to the train station after an early breakfast and traveled to Kunming, returning on Sunday.

About four kilometers east of the temple was a hot spring, which I visited every Sunday after returning from Kunming. I took with me a volume of poems by Tao Yuanming, the fourth-century recluse poet, humming the poems as I went. There was a large pool with apartments lining one side of it. Stone steps led up from the pool to the apartments, a short wall separating each approach from the next, so that the bathers in the apartments couldn't see one another. After bathing in the pool, one could sit naked on the steps and sunbathe. With a pot of tea and a volume of poetry, I would chant poems over and over, not leaving until the spirit was exhausted. If I couldn't make it on Sunday afternoon, I would go on

Monday morning and stay until noon, then I would go another four kilometers into Yiliang City for lunch. Yiliang was famous for its duck. There was a restaurant that prepared it Peking style, wrapped in sesame rolls, for only six Yunnan yuan (sixty Chinese fen). I couldn't finish a whole duck by myself, but ate as much as I could put down.

Each week I called on the principal of the county middle school, who let me borrow books from the school library. They had the twenty-five dynastic histories and the ten encyclopedias, which were all the books I needed. Each week I would exchange one for another. In the school garden was an array of basins, some more than a hundred years old and similar to what I had seen in Suzhou. I would take a leisurely stroll there and then walk the four kilometers back to the temple. This became a weekly routine. . . .

There was also a Precipice Spring Upper Temple. The path there from the Lower Temple, where I was staying, was a stone stairway densely lined with trees that concealed the sky, so that only a few misty rays of sunlight penetrated at high noon. Another marvel of the place was the squirrels one could watch leaping from branch to branch along the route as one passed. The Upper Temple had become a Taoist retreat and was dominated by a rock and water garden. Next to the retreat was a pavilion where travelers could take light refreshment. There was a short wall around the perimeter of the pavilion so that one could sit with one's back against it and enjoy the view. As there weren't many travelers, I liked to sit there for half a day at a time, working on my draft.

A Taoist monk, whose fancy name was Jingan, meaning quiescent hut, lived at the retreat with his servant. He was an extremely pure and elegant man. Whenever I arrived, he would have the servant brew up the finest grade of tea. When I mentioned that the great Confucian scholar Wang Guowei in Beiping used the same fancy name, he said that he knew it well and that he liked reading Wang's poems. He chanted a couple of them for me. This was no vulgar man. He told me he was originally from Guangxi Province—he had come here with his family as a refugee from famine when he was seven years old. When the family went back, they left him at the temple and he had been there ever since.

Jingan was an opium smoker. He always chose the finest quality and cooked it himself. He pressed me again and again to try some. I had tried it before, when I was sixteen and so sick with typhoid that I almost didn't survive. As my condition deteriorated, an uncle of mine came every night to my sickbed with his opium, which he would light up and, once it was bubbling, make me smoke with him. He said it would keep my spirit going. I could remember what it was like even though twenty-eight years had passed, but I kept up my resistance as politely as possible. The monk also said that along with the spring grain crop there came a crop of soybeans, and that he went to a nearby market each year to buy up a quantity of them to store on his roof. Then when the price went up during the summer, the merchants would come and buy them. He made enough from this transaction to live on for a year. If I would like to invest a little, he could buy and sell for me, and I wouldn't have to worry myself about it. It would be no more work for him, and I would get some additional income from it. I politely refused that offer too.

Jingan also told me that it was common practice in the area to collect foster daughters. All one needed do was to select an intelligent girl of thirteen or fourteen in one of the peasant villages. For a very low price, she would wash, clean, cook, and take care of the household chores; then when she came of age, one could take her as a concubine or, for a small fee, arrange a marriage for her. If I wanted to move my family there, he told me, I could easily make a good life on that mountain, and he would gladly arrange everything for me. His servant was also a warm person, and I decided to move to the Upper Temple for the second half of the year. Jingan closed off the second floor just for me and occupied the first floor himself. Old Lady Zhang still cooked for me, although she continued living at the Lower Temple, making the trip up in the morning and returning in the evening.

There was a huge white orchid tree at the retreat. When it bloomed in late spring the fragrance of orchids filled the air. The monk would pick the orchids and sell them to a wholesaler at the railway station for marketing in Kunming. Old Lady Zhang also kept some in a vase on my writing table—the aroma was intoxicating. By the steps in front of the building, where the spring bubbled, were two pools that had been made by piling stones to trap the water. The pools were about two feet across and the water was so clear that it reflected the light like white porcelain. Old Lady Zhang soaked the lunch and dinner vegetables there for a while before preparing them, which made them taste even fresher than before.

Old Lady Zhang told me that if I should stay in the mountains she would never stop working for me. If I left, she wanted to find someplace in the mountains to build a hut and end her days as a nun. I was even happier at the Upper Temple than I had been at the Lower. I wrote all day long and was able to finish the draft of the *Outline History of the Nation* in just one year's time. And as I reflect on it, during that year it was as if I lived in the land of immortals.[63]

The history Qian Mu produced in this detached setting was a monument to national pride. Drawing on the author's thorough familiarity with the histories, the classics, the institutional compendia, and the literature of the past, it describes a pattern of native expansion and contraction, foreign invasion and assimilation, imperial coercion and amelioration, economic, social, and intellectual evolution over a period of three thousand years. The pattern, according to Qian, is China's, and it differs from the West's as a poem differs from a drama. The one develops in a meter from rhyme to rhyme, always by the same rules; the other develops in stages, from act to act, always with a different plot. The one expands to fill a space when it is ordered and disintegrates when it is not. The other progresses from conflict to conflict toward some inevitable tragic conclusion. The historians who tried to understand the course of Chinese history by applying Western science were right to look for facts. In this regard they surpassed the New Text revisionists. But they failed to comprehend that their theories presumed the universality of the dramatic form.

Thus did Qian Mu formally break ranks with the foot soldiers. Revolution, he argued, could never achieve in China what it had achieved in the West. In the West, he argued, religion had substituted for secular legitimation of the state in the Middle Ages. Religious revolution had been necessary if a modern secular state was to emerge. Scientific revolution had been necessary for the same reason. In every case in the West revolution was a means by which the people's culture overcame a state that had been strong and had suppressed that culture. But China's culture had always developed best when the state was strong, since the pattern by which it was strengthened made it one with the people's culture. For modern science to develop in China, the society must be pulled together, not divided, and the state must be founded on that unity.[64]

Qian Mu saw his history published in Shanghai in 1940 and spent a year hiding from the Japanese in Suzhou. After that he accepted Gu Jiegang's invitation to teach in Sichuan. After the war, he remained in the southwest to avoid the political pressures of the major cities. On a return visit to the villa where he wrote the history, he observed the dramatic effects of change:

> After the war, when I returned to Kunming, I couldn't stop thinking about the Precipice Spring Upper Temple, so I went there on a visit with a friend. I learned that it had become a billet for soldiers and had been completely transformed. I was told that Old Lady Zhang had moved to Kunming, and I got the address of the person she worked for, but when I looked for her in Kunming I had no success. The monk Jingan had also fallen on hard times. I was told that he depended on selling orchids for a living, but when I got to the temple he had already left and I never saw him again. The vicissitudes of life are cruel indeed. Recently, when I met my nephew Weichang in Hong Kong, he told me that he and his wife had just been to Kunming and had made a special trip to Yiliang to visit the two temples, but both had been torn down by the local people. There was nothing left but an occasional stone marker, identifying various sites. When I heard this, I could not control my sorrow.[65]

In 1948 Qian Mu joined the staff of Jiangnan University in the hills overlooking Lake Taihu in his native Wuxi. The university had just been built by the Wuxi industrialist Rong Desheng, who often retired there from Shanghai on weekends to discuss with Qian his dreams of constructing a highway to the lakeside tourist spots. In the spring of 1949, when friends urged Qian to stay as the People's Liberation Army advanced, he decided to wait and see how things would settle down for critical scholars like himself. He absented himself from the transition in Wuxi by taking a temporary job at the Overseas Chinese University campus recently opened in Canton. Invited by Yan Xishan, the new premier of the disintegrating Guomindang regime in Canton, to help rally intellectuals against the Communists, Qian advised instead that intellectuals should turn their efforts to education, because the Guomindang had lost the people and the Communists had won the war. The objective should be national unity and independence, not division and alignment of the two sides with the United States and the Soviet Union. But Yan's objective was to enlist the cooperation of small parties in an anti-Communist front, perhaps to influence American opinion. Those parties became pawns in the ideological struggle, and Qian Mu's plea fell on deaf ears.[66]

By August 1949 the propaganda had become so deafening that the very act of pleading was heard as an echo of counter-revolution by the other side. The U.S. State Department issued its "white paper" blaming the Guomindang for losing the people and the Communists for making the war. An enraged Mao Zedong responded with a series of commentaries setting history straight. It was no accident, he argued, that the Guomindang under Chiang Kaishek had lost the people, for it was only the last in a series of imperialist agents in China. And China's intellectuals—all but a handful—had come to recognize this fact. Representing the handful who had not turned against the "running dogs" of imperialism in Mao's commentary were three: Hu Shi, who as the Republic's former ambassador to the United States and Beijing University chancellor, was urging anti-Communist action; Fu Sinian, who had moved his institute to Taiwan and accepted the post of chancellor of National Taiwan University; and Qian Mu.[67]

His advice unheeded, the gentle scholar made his way to Hong Kong, where bookless and penniless but not friendless he started up New Asia College in 1950. He retired from the presidency of the college in 1965, after seeing it grow into a major liberal arts college with the help of several foundations and the governments of Hong Kong and the Republic of China in Taiwan. It was later absorbed into the Chinese University of Hong Kong. In 1968, at the age of seventy-three, Qian Mu moved to a house near the campus of Soochow University outside Taipei. By 1986 he had published more than fifty books on Chinese history, philosophy, and culture and was respectfully referred to as "teacher of the nation" (*guo shi*). He lives with his wife in a house the government built for them, which he named Plain Book Building after the place in Seven Mansions where his mother nursed him back to health just in time for the 1911 revolution.

III.

The Land of Streams

NINETEEN ELEVEN was not a good year for the peasants of Wuxi. The storm came in July, as the transplanted rice was still sinking its roots into the rich alluvial soil. For seven days and nights heavy rains pounded the crop, raising ponds and lowering dikes, until polder ran into polder and the whole was buried in a sea of mud. The stone dike between Clear Lake and Goose Lake held. Recently restored by Hua Hongmo, it stood like a monument to his ancestors, who had first reclaimed the land south of Dangkou with their waterworks around 1400. The muddy waters flowed past the old Qian homesteads in Hongshengli and Seven Mansions. It stayed within the banks of Whistle-and-Swagger Creek until it reached the junction at Xuesilang Bridge by the Lie Di Temple. There it rejoined the torrent flowing via the ancient Taibo Canal through the low-lying lake region, past the great "floating tomb" of the Hua ancestor, under the fifteenth-century stone bridge by the cluster of shrines and temples that marked the beginning of Dangkou, and around the bend below the stone dike into Goose Lake. But the crop could not sustain the flood. For the peasants who worked it, the idyllic land of streams (*shui xiang*) had become a cruel nightmare.

Sixteen-year-old Qian Mu lay on his bed in Seven Mansions, close to death from typhoid. His mother must have known of the unrest around them as she wiped away the sweat of his fever. A group of

69

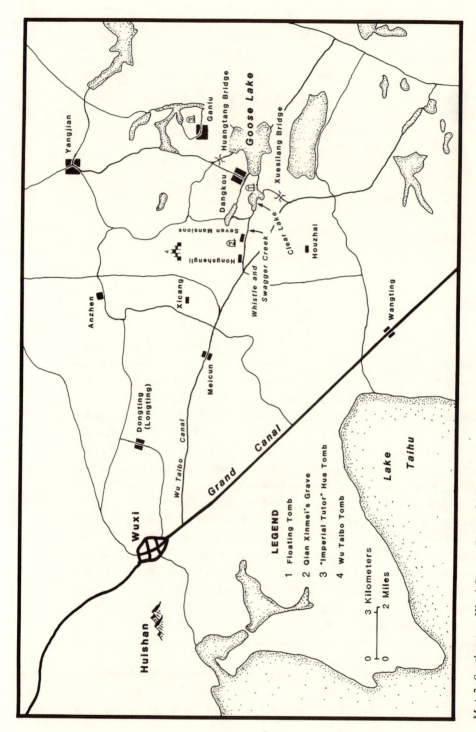

Map 3. *Southeastern Wuxi County. Drawn by Roy Doyon.*

peasants descended on Dangkou, demanding rice. Having lost their crops, they could look forward only to an autumn of haggling with rent collectors, pawnshop managers, and rice-shop owners. Hungry and burdened with new debts, they made the rounds of Dangkou's granaries. In response, the townsfolk locked their gates, waiting for temperatures to cool and level heads to intervene before beginning the painful negotiations over how to share the poverty without upsetting the cart. But the mob did not disperse. As if according to plan, its collective frustration came to focus on the gate of a certain landlord and rice dealer named Xu, whose reputation for driving a hard bargain was broad and whose granary was full. The peasants stormed the gate and emptied the buildings behind it, leaving Dangkou in a state of shock.

Before the young student rebel had recovered, order returned. As always, it wore an official hat and left a feeling of uneasiness—for some, a feeling of terror. There were no police in Dangkou, despite its population of more than five thousand. The magistrate's office was thirty kilometers away, about four hours by boat, in Wuxi city. But the size and wealth of Dangkou and its sister town of Ganlu rivaled that of many lesser county seats. The gentry families whose social and economic lives were centered there could count on the police in the event of disorder. A number of peasants thus went to jail that summer. One by one they were released, until only the one identified as the ringleader remained. His confession in hand, the police escorted him back to Dangkou, where he was beheaded before the usual crowd of curious onlookers.[1]

Hua Hongmo, beyond dispute the wealthiest and most influential man in Dangkou, also died that summer. The Qing Dynasty and the monarchy itself died in the fall, the day Qian Mu reckoned his recovery from typhoid was complete. There is no way of knowing how Hua might have felt about the rice riot, the execution, or the revolution. But for the young teachers and students in the school he had built and run, revolution was in the forefront. Qian Mu learned of the October 10 Wuhan uprising on the train to Nanjing the morning after. He had cut off his queue the previous year, after the abortive revolt at Changzhou Middle School, and once in Nanjing he prepared to join the revolutionary army on its way north. His old political tutor, Qian Bogui, led the Dangkou teachers and students to the police outpost in Wangting on the Grand Canal, where they stripped the submagistrate of his robes and ran his family out of town. Flags waving, they returned to Dangkou to herald the Republican era.[2]

For the peasants, the signals were mixed. The storm, the rice riot, the reaction, the seizure of police power from the Qing—the events unfolded like a familiar story. This was the end of a dynasty. Time for heroic action, for the righting of wrongs, for the taking of spoils. But who would lead, and where to, and who would follow? Were Hua Hongmo's school and the lineage shrine and the charitable estate granary, which lined the Huangting Canal with their arches and steles and marks of imperial honor, to be seized? The revolutionaries seem to have seized them already. What about the great houses and granaries at Seven Mansions, where rent collectors' boats docked beside those of yamen runners? The home of Qian Fenggao, who served the Qing as a magistrate, was there. But hadn't young Qian Shengyi, Qian Mu's brother, just opened a new school there last year and invited the local peasants to send their sons for free? What about that opium-sodden rent-collecting town of Xicang where the Cais lived?[3]

What would Lie Di, the local god and folk hero, have done in a situation like this? It was his image the peasants carried from village to village with all that fanfare every year. He was a martial hero one could pray to when one needed a little help from the other world. He had some clout. And he had fought his battles in this world over a change of dynasties back in the sixth century. But his message was mixed, too. He was so powerful because he was a loyalist, murdered for not joining a revolt. On the other hand, what mattered was that he died for what was right. In fact, he was loyal to the Sui Dynasty, which had already overthrown the Chen, which he had also served. Loyalty was to be repaid with trust. How did the message apply to the peasants who had stormed Xu's granary? They paid what rent they could muster, but Xu demanded more. Where's the trust? Where's the charity? Isn't that why gentry villages like Seven Mansions and charitable estates like Hua Hongmo's fed the revelers who followed Lie Di's image to their gates every year? Are we all in this together, or not? Now the dynasty's fallen, whose side are we (they) on?[4]

Qian Mu and his brother soon found themselves drilling their uncles and cousins in the use of firearms and standing guard at Seven Mansions Bridge. It took about a year for things to settle down. The new government in Wuxi City built a library and a public park. The school system developed. A county history and geography text for use in the new schools described the great potential for political, economic, and educational development, based on the local heritage, and decried the backwardness of the local folk religion.[5] One overly zealous reformer in Ganlu had the huge sacred image of Lie Di in the local temple destroyed. The new republican magistrate hastily had it reconstructed at the request of Ganlu's merchants: it seems the town's economy depended on the temple fair.[6] Hua Hongmo's grandson expanded the school in Dangkou along with the Hua estate, opened an experimental farm, and joined Wuxi City's new republican gentry elite.[7] Qian Bogui returned to Hongshengli, near Seven Mansions, where he added to the family estate by starting the steamboat company that monopolized the canal traffic.[8] Wuxi City began to industrialize during the First World War, and Seven Mansions continued its long, slow decline into poverty and irrelevance.

If the 1911 revolution changed nothing for the local peasants, neither did it mark a breakthrough for the local middle class. The opponents of Manchus and monarchy in the countryside were heirs to a hoary tradition of principled local leadership and moral opposition to the capricious use of imperial privilege and power. Their victory in 1911 was more a revival than a breakthrough. Neither aristocrats nor merchants, they stood with one foot on the backs of the peasants and the other in the schools, a stance that was entirely familiar. From this position they hoped to lead China out of the snare of imperialism and onto a new course. Because of it, however, they sank with the rice crop and with everyone else back into the mire.

Land and labor were the crux of the problem. Summer rice and winter wheat grew on all but a tiny fragment of the land around Seven Mansions. Mulberry shrubs for the developing silk industry were a new crop with an uncertain future, and whatever the previous extent of the local cottage textile industry, it had declined with the growth of Shanghai's industry and the appearance of machine-spun yarn. Peasants in this part of the land of streams lived off the grain they could produce and whatever they could sell their labor for on a small buyer's market. They sold half their grain to the rice merchants of Hongshengli, Ganlu, and Dangkou, who shipped it to Suzhou and Shanghai. The other half they delivered to the "inside" men—managers—at a number of landlords' estates or gave up to the most persistent of the "outside" men—rent collectors—who came to the village in their boats. Some managed to keep the other half by owning their own "subsoil" rights, but 80 percent of these rights were owned by someone other than the tiller. And for every tiny plot of ground there was a contract that specified who owned what.[9]

A typical plot of rice land covered 200–400 square meters, and a typical household tilled a dozen plots. It was common for such a household to pay rent to four or five subsoil owners; those who were better off owned the subsoil of half the plots they tilled. For hundreds of years the peasants of Wuxi had lived with this system, buying and selling surface rights, borrowing, mortgaging, lending, subletting, hiring in and hiring out. Fortunes waxed and waned. In the best of circumstances a single household might own a hectare or more of subsoil and pay their neighbors, or barter the use of their ox, for extra labor. If things went well, they might hire a tutor for their sons. In the worst of circumstances a family might have sold its surface rights, bit by bit, in order to pay subsoil rents. First the rights would be mortgaged, a small fee going to a neighbor in return for a loan. Then the neighbor would buy the surface rights and leave the tiller with a small percentage of the produce. Then, after a bad harvest, the tiller would give up the plot and send his sons to work for someone else for a small wage. If things went really badly, the sons could not marry, and the family would have to look for charity or for a wealthy indenturing household, or move out.

Inevitably, under such a system peasants scrambled for land to cultivate. And, inevitably, others scrambled for rents. With only 20 percent of the subsoil rights in the hands of peasant farmers, most peasants scrambled only for surface rights. But the teahouses and opium dens buzzed with the subsoil trade. Each year the larger landlords would meet to fix the rent schedule, some having already discussed the matter with relatives in other towns in Wuxi and neighboring counties. All would have heard the reports of their inside and outside men as to the projected size of the crop and other economic considerations. A consensus would form. For example, early payment would be accepted until such and such a date at the standard discount rate of 60 percent. After that date the discount would be reduced by 5 percent each ten-day period until the 100 percent figure was reached. The New Hua Charitable Estate agent would note the dates and add a further reduction of 5 to 10 percent across the board for the tenants on its 4000 *mu* as was the estate's custom (1 mu = 670 square meters, or 1/6 acre). Some of the others, including the charitable estate of Qian Mu's lineage, would follow suit. The tenants would be informed of the landlords' decision and would make their calculations as to whom to pay first and how much. When the pay period was over, the inside men would balance their books and landlords would decide whom to press, what to sell, and what to keep.[10]

The major buyers in the local subsoil market were traders and officials whose incomes were currently rising, and lineage charitable estates. The former might reinvest the income. The latter were obliged to use it for welfare services, and once they bought rights, the rights could not be resold.[11] Of about 47,000 mu owned by landlords in the early republic, 15,000 belonged to fifteen charitable estates and could not be sold. About 10,000 belonged to four major private estates. Perhaps another 8,000 belonged to thirty more.[12] The rest, some 14,000 mu, belonged to three or four hundred lesser landlords who were struggling to make ends meet.

Some pressed hard when rents fell short. Although the larger estates were not always averse to using pressure, the advantage of size came in being able to extend credit and to absorb the costs of operation. A larger estate could pay two or three outside men to negotiate with large numbers of tenants. Lesser landlords, who had a smaller margin to begin with, had to get more for less. Some even paid larger estates commissions to do the negotiating for them, a sign of resignation at best.[13] Some sold out to others with a stomach for extracting flesh from peasant bones. Perhaps as much as 10 percent of the total annual crop went into the estates of some three dozen gentry families. But most of the surplus that could be extracted from the peasants went to sustain the increasingly impoverished families of scholars and tradesmen, through either charity or scattered rents.

A handful of wealthy, influential families in Dangkou and the smaller towns tried to keep the lid on poverty. They were scholars, officials, rice merchants, shop owners, producers of wine and soy sauce—some with impressive gentry pedigrees and some without—and their means were sufficient to sustain a year's loss. They collected deeds to subsoil rights, hiring managers, clerks, and messengers to keep track of them. In bad years they lowered their rents and extended credit to the peasants who held the surface rights. Sometimes they overlooked the delinquent rent of an honest peasant. And greater acts of charity were also expected of them. In normal years their rents came easily, and if the gross income from rents was only 80 percent of the amount expected at the discounted rate, the estate still prospered.

For lesser landlords, 1911 was as hard as it was for the peasants. A typical small landlord held 30–40 mu. In a year with two good harvests he might count on grossing 1,300 to 1,800 kilograms of grain from such an estate.[14] A scattered estate of this size required a good manager. A good inside man would cost 270 kilograms per year plus bonus. Storage and delivery of the grain to market required additional labor, and transport cost money as well. In addition, a landlord who did not till the soil required a tutor for his sons. And marriage among nonpeasants was an expensive proposition. Yet an average peasant household with two working adults, an elderly dependent and one child needed 900 kilograms of grain just to feed itself on a near-starvation diet.[15] Should our typical landlord's household grow and the net income from rents fall below 50 percent of the amount expected at the standard rate, the family would not have enough to eat, let alone enjoy the benefits of gentry status.

And landlords' families did grow. The size of a peasant household was restricted by the amount of land it tilled. Daughters might join the network of "Dangkou girls" in Shanghai, working as maids there and returning to help with seasonal chores.[16] Eventually they left to join other households as wives and mothers. But sons took wives and added children. If there were more sons than the household or the village could bear, they moved out or didn't marry. Often they became "guest households" in someone else's village, tilling land where a holder of surface rights lacked labor. In any case if a young male peasant would increase the household's size he had to increase its resources or start up another household with resources of its own. But not so the landlord's son.

If a family tilled no soil in rural Wuxi, its sons studied. As students, their future was in teaching or trading. Some practiced medicine or carved seals; in rare cases they became officials. They might join the sons of well-to-do farmers up from the peasantry there. But that they should join the peasantry itself was not in accordance with plan. No matter how much land such a family owned, a son did not have to increase the amount before increasing the household's size. Other sources of income were forthcoming. Therefore, he might marry early and expect a little help from the family of his bride. Starting early, the landlord who lived comfortably was likely to have at least one son. He might even take a secondary wife to make it happen. If he had no son, he would adopt one. If he died without a son, his brothers or cousins might lend him one as an heir. The heir, in turn starting early, was likely to have at least one son. He was much more likely to see more than one grandson before he died than was a peasant. Inevitably, landlord households tended to grow larger than peasant ones.

Yet the need to increase the family's landholdings did not press the landlord as it did the peasant—not until the household divided, or the successful teacher or trader died, or the civil service exam system was abolished (as it was in 1905), or there was a surfeit of daughters, or the family was afflicted with physical or mental illness or opium addiction. Then, suddenly, the need was acute. Widows, orphans, illiterates, and opium addicts were poor providers, and the larger the household, the larger its share of them.

Opium was especially a problem in rural landlord families. There were more than forty nonrehabilitable addicts—adult males, presumably—among the landlords of Xicang in 1949, and the problem was not of recent origin.[17] Sometime before his death in 1889 Hua Yilun of Dangkou wrote an elegy for a gentryman who had forbidden opium dens in his home town right up to his death.[18] This man's town was the last in Wuxi to get its own opium den, Hua believed. By Republican times there were five illegal opium dens in Dangkou alone.[19] The drug, which may have killed Qian Mu's father in 1907, played no small part in the economic and spiritual decline of the scholar-gentry class.

Yet for every landlord household there were twenty or thirty peasant ones. A rough estimate would locate eight to ten thousand households in the villages around Dangkou, Ganlu and Hongshengli in the early republic. Perhaps forty-two thousand people lived off 58,000 mu of paddy.[20] Some, like Lu Ajin's grandfather, were recent arrivals. Lu had moved to the village near Seven Mansions to work the land of another peasant. As was the custom for guest households, during the first three years he paid only the subsoil rents, keeping the rest for himself. After that he paid an additional 50 percent to the peasant who owned the surface rights. By working hard and wasting little, he saved enough to purchase surface rights to 40 mu before he died, and to raise four sons to share it.[21]

Others, like the two Hua households of Hua Family Village just north of Seven Mansions, had been there for generations. The first was well off. Owning 6 mu outright and surface rights on 14 more, it could afford a rice mill, an ox, and hired hands to help with the work. The second owned only 1.5 mu of surface rights and was working another 32.5 mu on contract. The land it had contracted to cultivate, perhaps in the previous generation, was more than it could till with its own labor. But rather than give up the land, the family hired seasonal help. The Huas also did sewing for other peasants and sent their son to Qian Shengyi's primary school for four years.[22]

In such a competitive world, where land was scarce and peasants mobile, some were bound to lose out. While the Lus were taking control of the land they tilled to the west of Seven Mansions and the Huas were holding onto their cultivation rights to the north, another household to the south of the landlord village was sliding into debt. Shao Genrong's grandfather had been tilling 6.5 mu, paying subsoil rents to two Hongshengli landlords. Qian Jiansan, the owner of 4 mu that the Shaos worked, had no doubt noticed that industrious guest households like the Lus were more consistent in their rent payments, even though they had to pay both surface and subsoil rents. He surely knew as well that the Sea of Caring Charitable Estate, the one that supported widows and orphans among his kinsmen and paid for Qian Shengyi's new primary school, remitted 50 percent of the rent for tenants in dire straits. But the Shaos had enough able-bodied family members to work their land, and Qian was within his rights to demand payment in full. In accordance with custom, he had allowed the delinquency to pass the first year. Now it had been two years in a row. The outside man had pressed the Shaos without results. Then the yamen runner had come with his boat, taken the old man on board, and demanded payment plus expenses, again in accordance with custom. But the Shaos could not pay. Qian confiscated the 4 mu and demanded a son's labor to pay off the debt.[23]

Not many were as hard pressed as the Shaos. The yamen runners were not called into service all that often, and confiscation was rare.[24] But the threat was always there and the Shaos' story served as a reminder. Without land to till, the peasant was no longer a peasant, the son no longer a son. For centuries the peasants of Wuxi had lived with the terrible prospect of becoming something less than a free person. For centuries they held tenaciously to their land. And so had the Shaos.

What was the debt-ridden peasant to do? Shao Genrong's grandfather dug in his heels and tried to stop the slide. With only 2.5 mu of surface rights remaining to him, he had little hope of finding wives for both of his sons. Feeding them was problem enough. But through friends he learned of an heirless couple in Dangkou who were looking to adopt a son. There a boy would have the chance to receive an education and find a wife. He would not be a Shao, and his duty would be to his adoptive parents—but he would survive and so would the Shaos. So the peasant gave away his younger son. The elder succeeded his father as head of household and as a "small person" (*xiaoren*), or servant, to Qian Jiansan, as custom demanded.

A small person, like a child, was a dependent. Some were totally dependent; in Qian Jiansan's household there were four. Others, like Shao Genrong's father, had households of their own. Unlike a serf or slave, Shao could not be forced to work, and he could work for other landlords for a wage. But the household was, in effect, operating at a deficit without assets. Its only resource was its labor, to which the Qians had a prior claim. Under these conditions, the Shaos could rarely afford to pay off the creditors who made the rounds on New Year's Eve. When they failed to pay, the creditors would add another 20 percent to the bill and extend it another few months. As the debts mounted, the Shaos worked harder, but they never managed to remove the stigma imposed by the Qians.[25]

Since the formal prohibition, in 1727, of enslavement of tenants by landlords with official status, a peasant could not become the landlord's property anywhere in China. But in rural Wuxi, the currents of obligation and dependency ran deep. Small persons who joined their master's households worked not for wages but for life. The master fed and clothed them. He might educate them and find them mates, or he might not. The choice was his. A woman could be given away as bride or concubine—her dependency was complete. Her children, in turn, were also her master's dependents, and as dependents, they had no property of their own.

The same currents of obligation and dependency had moved countless numbers of other peasants into semidependent positions vis-à-vis other households. Cooks, musicians, itinerant priests, and gravekeepers still owed services to the descendants of lords their ancestors had served because they could not hold onto their land. In return for these services, the landlords' descendants provided security. Once the obligation was incurred, it could not be transferred easily to another. The Qians of Seven Mansions provided this kind of security for the Dings of Ding Family Village. By the end of the Qing over a hundred Qian households were obliged to call on the Dings whenever they needed music, and the Dings were obliged to provide it.

Music was more than entertainment in rural Wuxi. It was the voices of gods and ancestors, a spiritual ordering of the wind. It marked the seasons of the year and the stages of life with its staccato rhythms. It restored the basic harmonies of nature and society with its familiar, repetitive tones. Music spread the news of a death or a marriage. It announced the arrival of Lie Di's procession on his birthday. It heralded the opening of the temple fair. Music filled the pauses in the lives of peasants, students and traders alike, reaching their ears through the sounds of ancient instruments.

The Dings taught their sons to play music in the Kunqu style, which originated with the musical drama of the Wu dialect area in the sixteenth century. They played *pipa, sheng,* and *xiao*—instruments similar to the mandolin, bagpipe, and flute—as well as gongs and drums. The poorer Qians called on them for weddings and funerals, the richer for important birthdays as well. The standard funeral required four musicians for one day. A wedding required eight for two or three days. Pay varied with the musician's rank; the headman received the clothes he wore for mourning and all the musicians were fed. Beyond this, the Dings earned whatever the Qians decided to pay them. Customarily, those who could afford to pay more did so.

Just exactly what kept the Dings making music is not easy to tell. But it is clear they were too many to live as peasants on their own land. At least one household lost the surface rights to its 3.5 mu some time after 1911 and went on cultivating it for a higher rent. The landlord was a Qian. On the other hand, their rights as musical headmen guaranteed them a source of income, and they could afford to have sons.

In fact, like the peasant farmers, the Dings could not afford not to have sons. Whether or not their ancestors had once been servants in a large landowning household, they themselves were not. Like the Shaos, they were only semidependent. Unlike the Shaos, however, they had inherited customary rights that were entailed in their ancestors' relationship with the Qians. The musician householder passed these rights on to his heir. Like the peasant's surface rights or cultivation rights, they were the musician's security in his old age. Like land rights, they could be transmitted or sold. When the Qians of Seven Mansions needed music, they had no choice but to call on the Dings. Other musicians recognized Seven Mansions as Ding territory, and the Dings respected the territories of others in return. Should the Dings receive two calls at once, the Qians had priority. The others could be contracted out. Just which musician should play where was the Ding headman's decision. If he lacked sufficient numbers on a given day, he could hire more from other headmen. A headman might have rights to as many as two hundred households, and never would another musician encroach on them.[26]

Even better protected were the rights of *daoren*, the itinerant priests who presided over weddings and funerals. Only the poorest of families—like the Shaos, who buried their father in a casket hewn from a door of their own house—sent their dead to the other world without the help of a daoren. The wealthy might need as many as six to keep away the hungry ghosts and malevolent spirits who tended to pick on people of means. If one worried about getting one's parents through the difficulties of the underworld to a place of comfort and influence beyond, then one also preferred to deal with daoren who were familiar and not to rock the boat. The same held for blessing the marriage of one's children, which one hoped would produce grandsons who were not possessed. Some of the well-off worried hard enough to invite a Buddhist monk to the wedding in addition to the daoren. All worried enough to pay off beggars—living hungry ghosts that they were—before the funeral. So ritualized was all this that even the beggars had territories, perhaps left over from a time when they had prepared the dead for burial. The daoren, like the musicians, inherited their territories. Unlike the musicians, they paid the head priest of a Taoist temple to keep interlopers out.[27]

If life is a calculated struggle for economic ascendence or even survival, the musicians and the daoren were sliding off the scale. The measure of economic success was land and they had little. But if life is a passage to the other world, they were agents of the forces that govern it. Without them the passage would be rough. In either case, their lives intersected with those of peasants, scholars, and traders in a pattern that conflicted with the economic one. Castelike, they married their own kind, as peasants with land rights married peasants with land rights. Their own territorial systems were the heritage of an earlier time, when powerful families divided the land and the tillers served them. But the musicians and daoren did not fade away, for nothing had appeared to replace them. They were performers of ritual, the glue of a culture that gave life a meaning land rights could not give it;

they were the makers of an aesthetic context in which people observed the rhythms of the seasons and of their lives. The centers of this other kind of life were not the granaries but the temples.

It was the Taoist priest (*daoshi*) at Taibomiao Temple in Meicun who protected the daoren around Seven Mansions. Built in 1499, the temple was itself a product of the age of great gentry patrons. It enshrined the spirit of Wu Taibo, legendary bearer of civilization to the south from the Yellow River basin in the eleventh century B.C. The local people believed that Taibo was buried on the southwest slope of the hill called Hongshan, a few kilometers north of Seven Mansions. Ancient records placed the tomb not far from a place called Meili (Plum Grove), where he had lived and where the people had built a shrine in his memory after he died. Since the beginning of the Confucian revival in the eleventh century A.D., Taibo had joined the ranks of the Confucian sages, for not only had he brought civilization to the south, he had also intentionally left the north to his younger brother, the father of Wen Wang, whose virtues as a leader he had recognized. It was Wen Wang's virtues, in turn, that brought the state of Zhou to power. And it was the rites and songs of the state of Zhou that Confucianists looked to as the font of Chinese culture, a model for civilized man. The revivalists in Wuxi had built Wu Taibo a temple in the eleventh century, but it had not survived. In 1499 the gentry of the area persuaded the magistrate to sponsor official ceremonies in spring and fall commemorating the sage. They would donate the funds and the labor for a temple where the rites could be performed, and it should be at Meicun (Plum Village) by the canal Taibo was believed to have dug. As Confucianists had no priests, they attached a Taoist retreat and invested a Taoist priest to watch over the temple.[28] Four hundred years later the ceremonies were drawing celebrants by the thousands, and the priest collected 15 percent of the daoren's fee at every marriage and every funeral to which they were summoned.

The Taibomiao temple, for all its appeal to fanfare and glory, was only one in a vast collage of religious establishments covering the rural landscape. Taoist and Buddhist temples, monks' retreats, temples to local gods and national folk heroes, ancestral shrines and gravesites all found places in the busy ritual lives of the people. Some administered to particular personal needs. The Buddhist monks, who lived in scattered retreats, prayed for the souls of those who had built them and for poorer folk who shared their devotion but not their means. It was

8. *Wu Taibo's canal, near Dangkou.*

9. *The dike at Goose Lake near Dangkou, built by Hua Leqin in the early 1400s, restored in stone by Hua Hongmo in the early 1900s.*

10. *Rare surviving merchant quarters at the scholar-gentry settlement of Xicang.*

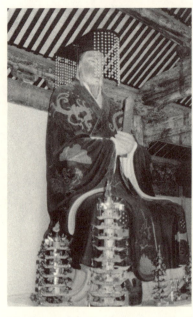

11. *Entrance to the shrine of Filial Son Hua, fourth-century spiritual ancestor of all the Hua of Wuxi, at Huishan.*

12. *Image of the Confucian sage Wu Taibo, recently restored in the temple at Meicun, with Taoist-style offerings made by local women.*

14. *Stone horse at the tombsite of Hua Cha, the sixteenth-century Hanlin academician remembered in local legends as Imperial Tutor Hua.*

13. *Entrance to the tomb of Wu Taibo at Hongshan, Hongsheng Township.*

15. *The shrine of Hua Zhengu, fourteenth-century progenitor of the Hua of Dangkou,
built in the 1630s by the Ming loyalist scholar Hua Yuncheng.*

16. *Eighteenth-century buildings of the Old Hua Charitable Estate, Dangkou.*

17. The kitchen in a typical scholar-gentry settlement house near Dangkou.

most often the women who tended the candles and incense sticks at miniature shrines on household altars. And it was women who knew the Buddhist prayers. Perhaps the overwhelming dominance of male symbols in the rituals of family and folk religion was responsible. Or perhaps it was the family system itself, which demanded that daughters move to husbands' households, serve husbands' parents and raise sons to succeed them. In any case, the popular Buddhism of the sixteenth and seventeenth centuries had spread with the blossoming culture of the townsfolk who were less dependent on land and lineage than either the peasants or the great gentry landlords had been. And its symbols of a paradise without hierarchy, a Pure Land where gender and status did not matter, lived in the shrines and on the golden squares of paper one could burn before them. Its Goddess of Mercy—Guanyin—stood beside the martial figure of Guan Di in the Guandimiao temples where villagers prayed for sons.

Praying for sons and for success in this life required no more help than praying to Guanyin or the Pure Land Buddha for success in the other. The smaller Guandimiao temples usually supported a caretaker with the income from two or three mu of land. Guan Di and the other folk gods had no priests. A warrior whose story was known through dramas and through *The Romance of the Three Kingdoms,* Guan Di had no doctrine. Many other gods shared the space in his temples and people might disagree about the powers of each. What mattered was that one visit the sacred place they occupied when one was troubled and leave a message in hopes of gaining some solace. Perhaps the act of faith would have some small effect in the places where fate was determined. Anticipating trouble and knowing the fickleness of fate, the villagers tried to control it by imposing cosmic order on their off-springs' lives. Noting the hour of each birth, they recorded the eight signs—two each for the year, the month, the day, and the hour—and delivered them to the temple for safekeeping. There they could re-trieve them for matching with those of prospective mates when the time for betrothal arrived.[29]

More help was required where ghosts were involved. They were the products of past troubles—a widow who, forced by her in-laws to re-marry against her will, took her own life; an infant girl drowned by desperate parents; a prodigal son who died by violence; a fisherman slain by pirates. The souls of the improperly buried and unmourned of generations past haunted the land of streams and possessed the souls of the unwary.

It took the powers of a trained exorcist, like the priest in the Taoist temple in Dangkou, to deal with possession. The shelves of the old Sea of Learning Academy, which the temple had taken over from its Confucian owners, were lined with jars full of exorcised spirits being held under the priest's spell.[30] The priest's services were expensive. No wonder the townsfolk had donated so much land for free burial and spent so much time and money to do the job properly when refugees from the Taiping war, with their dead and dying, flooded Dangkou in the 1860s.[31] No wonder the well-to-do continued to call on the daoren to keep the spirits at a distance when they buried and married off their own. The rituals were a fixed part of the larger spiritual picture of which this cycle of life on earth was only a part.

The daoren and the musicians were there at Lie Di's festival day, too, for the same reasons. They knew the rituals that kept the spirits at a distance. But unlike the celebrations at Seven Mansions, Lie Di's festivals were public affairs. The temple at Xuesilang Bridge opened its gates twice each year, once in the fall for a day of games and drama and once in the spring for two days of feasting and parading.[32] Lie Di also had his territory, and all the villages within it had duties they owed him. Daoren and musicians were paid—slightly better than the men who carried the palanquin with Lie Di's image—but the peasants worked out of obligation.[33] The better off the household, the greater its contribution and, most likely, the more respectable its place in line. For two days in the spring the procession of dancing lions and stilt walkers, flowing silk gowns and painted faces moved from station to station about the god's territory, pausing for a few hours at each. There the peasants would refresh themselves as guests of the local householders. If one had no relatives there, someone else surely had. One could count on something to eat and drink on those days. And the stations were well chosen. Of course Seven Mansions was one, for that was where the landlords lived. Lie Di did not look kindly on landlords who failed to feast the peasants at planting and harvest time.[34]

In the classic *Book of Songs,* it is written:

With twin pitchers they hold the village feast,
Killing for it a young lamb.
Up they go into their lord's hall.

Raise the drinking-cup of buffalo-horn:
Hurray for our lord; may he live for ever and ever![35]

The days when peasants sang of the lord's glory as they shared the harvest were gone long before Lie Di walked the earth. But scholars knew peace and stability still depended on the peasants' acceptance of their patrons' terms. The songs of the people, in local dialect, sometimes expressed bitterness:

Spring is sparse: make the congee a little thin.
Summer's long: do some gleaning late at night.
Autumn's tough: nab half an ear before it's ripe.
Winter's hard: all that's left is a cold stove.
All year long I grow grain for food;
Why does growing grain leave my belly empty so?[36]

Lie Di saw to it that the peasant's plaint was ritually heard and that the landlord ritually responded. The haves and the have-nots sealed their contract as Lie Di watched: no one would starve to death and no one would riot, so long as the spirits could be kept at a distance.

Lie Di himself had a much better claim to this territory than did its temporal rulers. His largest temple, in Ganlu, had been built some decades before the Qing conquest of 1645, and smaller ones may have preceded it. His title, meaning Patriot God, had been granted him in 944 by a Southern Tang emperor who fought the king of Wu-Yue for control of the area.[37] And he sometimes disguised himself. At Huang-tang Bridge, halfway between Ganlu and Dangkou, he was known as the local earth god (*tudi*). Some in Seven Mansions called him the rampart god (*chenghuang*). And in Dangkou he had taken over the shrine built for Hua Cha, the place's most powerful native son in the Ming period.[38] His temples were supported by the villages that surrounded them. His festivals were their collective affair.

When gods walk the earth, mortals tremble. But when their paths are cleared by priests and musicians, their behavior prescribed by ritual, mortals gawk. Trembling also becomes a ritual affair. In Wuxi it was a hubbub. Gods had walked the earth for centuries here, on prescribed days and in prescribed ways. For centuries the crowds had gathered to gawk and to play, until Lie Di's peasant communities could not contain them. Thousands gathered for Taibo's birthday after New Year's Day and thousands traveled to Taibo's grave at spring festival time. And the nighttime festival for hungry ghosts at the Chenghuang temple in Dangkou in August drew better than Lie Di's. But the champion festival in the area was the early autumn temple fair in Ganlu.

Ganlu had been the center of a small peasant cosmos at least since the 870s, when the Tang emperor established a Buddhist temple there. The name, meaning sweet dew, was given to sacred places, blessed with the sweet substance by the gods, and to the sacred words of Amitabha, the Buddha of the Pure Land. Legend has it that a market was built on the site in Han times—two thousand years ago—because the sacred substance had been found there and that the temple took its name from the market. Eventually it became a military outpost—first for the Tang, then for the state of Wu, then for the Southern Tang—the last line of defense against the kingdom of Wu-Yue, which controlled Suzhou.[39] Dynasties rose and fell, but the sacred place at the center of the community endured. By Qing times Lie Di had imposed himself upon it.

According to legend, the man who became the god had owned a villa by the lake where Ganlu was situated.[40] Another legend told that his mother was buried near Huangtang Bridge and that he had built his villa there to be close to her grave.[41] He first appeared as a god when, from a chariot in the clouds, he fired the arrow that killed his own murderer; he had appeared periodically at times of trouble ever since. Occasionally he was sighted on the lake at night, his purple face glowing as his boat sailed to and fro. It was only fitting that his temple should join the Buddhist and the Taoist ones in the center of Ganlu by the Incense Burning Canal. And it was only fitting that his image there be twice the size of the ones at Huangtang and Xuesilang. For here was a place blessed by the gods and frequented by worshipers for more than a thousand years.

A hundred boats from three counties jammed the canal when Lie Di came forth each September. Thousands of celebrants visited the temples and the shops that specialized in religious goods. Here one could buy the Buddhist shrines and ceramic images for home altars and incense of all kinds. The golden paper squares imprinted with red images, the silver paper money one burned to bribe officials in the underworld, images of the kitchen god to be sent on his way before New Year's, his mouth sealed with sweet congee—all could be found. Here one could have one's palm read or consult the *I Ching*. Here one could visit the exorcist or ask the monks to say a prayer. And above all, one could delight in the display, have tea with a friend, gaze on the ancient ginkgo trees whose spirits sanctified the Buddhist temple's compound, and return with a sense of fulfillment.

Lie Di was not the only one who had imposed himself on the small peasant cosmos. A few kilometers to the south of Ganlu, by the side of Clear Lake, was a most remarkable tomb. Travelers who saw it from their boats said it seemed to float on the water, and the local legend explained why. It was the tomb of Hua Leqin, ancestor of the Huas of Ganlu and Dangkou. He was a rich man whose father had been a refugee in the area during the upheavals between the Yuan and the Ming in the 1360s. Accused of some crime by a poorer neighbor, he had been forced to spend some time in the magistrate's jail. Hua had protested his innocence and charged his accuser with fraud. In such cases it was the law that both accusers should be detained until the truth was established. But if one of the contestants should die before that happened, the other would be absolved and set free.

Knowing of Hua's wealth, the jailer had visited him, offering to kill his accuser for a fee. Hua refused, and assuming the jailer would then make a deal with his enemy, he resigned himself to the likelihood that he would die in jail, saying, "who would have guessed the bones of this incarnation should be laid to rest in this place." That night a spirit in the form of an old man appeared to him in a dream, saying his bones would not be laid to rest here but rather at a place yet unknown to Hua called Thatchgrass Embankment. In the end fate rewarded Hua for his uprightness. His accuser admitted the falsehood of his accusation and Hua was set free.

One winter, some years later, Hua Leqin happened to be traveling through Clear Lake by boat when he decided to drop anchor for the evening meal. After dinner a servant dropped Hua's favorite jade cup in the water while rinsing it. Heartbroken, Hua tried to recover it, but the water was too cold for the servants to bear. Determined to try again when it was warmer, he had the long punt pole stuck into the mud to mark the spot. When he returned the next spring he found that the punt pole had sprouted leaves. Sensing the intervention of something otherworldly, he asked someone the name of the place. It was Thatchgrass Embankment. Then, said he, I shall be buried on this spot. And so his filial sons filled it with earth to make the tomb that seemed to float on Clear Lake.[42]

For five hundred years the descendants of this early Ming refugee had settled around Goose Lake and Clear Lake. Some had prospered, and as had been the custom since the time of Wu Taibo, so far as anyone knows, the prosperous divided their riches equally among their sons. They built dikes and bridges, dug ditches and canals. And as they prospered a new town grew up by the place where the streams flowed into Goose Lake. The town was known simply as Dangkou—Lake Entrance—as if there were no other reason for it to exist. By the end of the Qing it was home for some forty rice merchants—as many as in Ganlu—and several thousand people, most of them Huas.[43]

If fate had determined that the Huas should come to dominate the earthly aspects of this little cosmos, it was not without the help of good character. The legend of Hua Leqin, which was transmitted orally and virtually unchanged between the sixteenth and twentieth centuries, exemplifies the way virtues such as honesty, perseverance, and filiality meshed with the cosmic order. Fate was not blind in this world. One could convert its lessons into practice. In fact, if one enjoyed the privileges of wealth and education, one was obliged to convert them into practice. The gods, as well as the ancestors, were watching.

The crowd that gathered at the floating tomb each year at spring festival time included not only the Huas. The spring festival was for sweeping ancestral graves, but it was also a time for an outing. The Tangs of Lesser Tang Embankment, some thirty households in all, would visit their own ancestral graves at the village's edge first and then join the crowd at Clear Lake. So would the Huas of Fifth Branch Village, and anyone else in the vicinity who wasn't trekking to Taibo's grave on Hongshan. Some seven hectares of pine and cedar, the tomb was a veritable country park. There were those who claimed that their right to celebrate there was inherited from ancestors who had been servants of the legendary Ming Imperial Tutor, Hua Cha.[44] But most simply took the right for granted. Fate and human virtue had worked together to give Dangkou to the Hua clan. It was only fitting that the Huas should give Dangkou a spring festival park.

Not all the ancestors who had imposed themselves on the peasants' world were refugee settlers. Even the Huas themselves had other, later ancestors to emulate. Most imposing of all was the Imperial Tutor, whose tomb dominated the landscape a kilometer to the east of Ganlu. Stone horses stood by the spirit path that led from canal to gravesite, reminding the visitors of the path to the Ming founder's tomb outside Nanjing.[45] Chances are that many of the visitors had seen that grave too, for Nanjing was the site of the provincial civil service exams and

Hua Cha's descendants included many scholars. The legend of Imperial Tutor Hua was told more widely than that of the Hua founder. So powerful was he, it is said, that the emperor he had tutored suspected him of a plot to usurp the dragon throne. The story of how he escaped the emperor's wrath is part of the origin myth of eastern Wuxi County's busiest market town, and one of the best loved folktales of the region.

According to legend, when Hua Cha retired from his official career in the capital in the mid-sixteenth century he built a villa as large as an imperial prince's estate in the small town of Longting. In front of the villa he built a pavilion and opened a market, widening the canal to receive traders and guests. In the process he had consulted an expert in geomancy—the science of wind and water, which applies to the auspicious placement of graves and buildings—who gave him some bad advice. The siting was suspiciously like that for the Son of Heaven's palace. What's more, the villa and its market had put Longting on the map, and the local people wrote the name with characters meaning "Dragon Pavilion." Palace eunuchs, in league with jealous court officials, asked the emperor to put two and two together and soon a contingent of the dreaded Embroidered Guard was on its way to investigate.

Hua's friends in the capital caught word of the trouble, the story goes, and sent a warning by express messenger. What was to be done? The clever former tutor quickly commissioned the market's bean curd shop to put up ten thousand cakes of dried bean curd using a luxus recipe and to stamp the product with a new label: Dongting, or "Eastern Pavilion." Overnight the Longting Bean Curd Shop became the Dongting Bean Curd Shop, and the next day Hua had the product distributed throughout the area as a gift to the people. When the emperor's spies arrived, they were easily persuaded that the Dragon Pavilion story had been the concoction of jealous court officials, for everyone they asked displayed the bean curd cakes with the town's name impressed upon them. The guard returned to the capital with some dried bean curd for evidence. From then on the town was known as Dongting, the name chosen by its patron. And its most famous native product was Dongting Dried Bean Curd, a delicacy still popular today.[46]

In reality, Hua Cha was not Imperial Tutor at all, but a scholar in the Hanlin Academy where imperial papers were edited, chief examiner in the civil service exam, and special envoy to Korea. The remnants of his villa in Dongting are nonetheless imposing, and the record shows that he personally financed the repair or rebuilding of nearly every major temple and bridge in the Dangkou-Ganlu region. The Lie Di temple in Dangkou was first a shrine to Hua Cha himself, and the jars full of exorcised spirits in the Sea of Learning Academy claimed space he had intended for educational pursuits. As undisputed leader of the local landed elite, he built a fortress against pirates, set aside a thousand mu of land for charity, spearheaded the reform of the tax system, and built a shrine in Dangkou to the provincial and county officials who had carried it out. He was the very model of what Qian Mu called a shiren.[47] In the folk culture he was remembered as the man who fooled the emperor and shared his bounty with the people.

Men of such stature ceased appearing in recent centuries but the legends lived on and the graves survived. The same currents of obligation and dependency that ran beneath the struggle for land rights kept the symbols of gentry patronage alive. The same need for ritual reassurance of one's place in the cosmos that kept the trees growing in the central temple grounds and kept the processions moving through their stations on the periphery sanctified the burial places of great patrons of the past. If the magistrates, prefects, and governors who served the empire were sometimes called "father and mother" of the people, they were nonetheless distant figures on this landscape. But the symbolic link between parent and gentry patron was close at hand.

When the Shaos buried their father in his makeshift coffin, sacrificing a door from their broken home, they sent him to the other world with a degree of filial respect matching that of Hua Leqin's sons when they built the floating tomb. When Lu Ajin's family swept the grave of his immigrant grandfather, their offering matched that of Hua Leqin's descendants when they swept theirs. And as the Shaos and the Lus divided the fruits of their respective families' labors after their patriarchs' deaths, so had the Huas divided theirs, along with the ritual duties owed the deceased. The complex system of rights and duties that linked the living and the dead took on its peculiar shape for each family in the arrangement of ancestral tablets in the household shrine. From there it extended to the larger family and, for many, to the lineage shrine. As the landscape was cluttered with graves, fancy and simple, so was the world of the dead crowded with ancestral spirits, great and small. The rights and duties that ordered that world were reflected in the world of the living.

Wang Atu's grandfather moved his family from the ancestral village in neighboring Jiangyin County to East Creek near Ganlu in 1905 because there was not enough work to be found at home. He had a wife, three sons, and two daughters to feed. Soon they would be an aging couple with three sons, three daughters-in-law, and grandchildren on the way. The sons were healthy. If they had more land to work, even poor land, they had the time and the muscle to apply to it. But the land was already too crowded. There were three hundred households in the Wangs' village and people were leaving all the time to look for work. Relatives had just returned from East Creek saying there was an empty room in the old farmhouse they had moved into the year before. The rent for one room would not break the Wangs, and they could borrow enough from the relatives to get through one harvest of mulberry leaves. They could contract with the county, which owned the subsoil rights to most unirrigated land thereabouts, for thirty mu, rent free and tax free for the first three years.

The Wangs planted mulberry trees on the highest of what was generally high ground. It was the heyday of silk industry development, and credit was available for those who would take the chance.[48] They turned the lower ground into paddy fields, building ridges and digging ditches to distribute the water that was yet to be found. First they brought the water in buckets and then by treadle pump, and when the three years had passed they were able to pay the rent. Eventually the Wangs bought the surface rights on their thirty mu, and when Atu's grandfather died his sons split the rights three ways. Along with twenty or thirty other households from the ancestral village, they had become the Wangs of East Creek.

For three sons to work together with their father to build an estate under conditions of such scarcity required some certainty that the outcome would be fair. For relatives and neighbors to provide credit for such an enterprise required some trust. Ancestors were the guarantors of fairness and trust. The arrangement of their tablets showed precisely how their rights had been divided and the exact degree of ritual obligation that was owed to each in return. The rights and obligations were shared by everyone whose ancestors' tablets were at the shrine. The Wang brothers shared the chores in their father's household in accordance with their rank in age. Under his watchful eye they performed their duties. When he died, they assumed their ritual duties, again in accordance with their rank in age. Still under his watchful eye, they divided the property, 13–11–9.[49]

As for trust among relatives, more distant ancestors were there to watch. The Wangs were only peasant farmers who understood little about compiling genealogies. Moreover, they moved from their ancestral village in 1905, leaving behind the genealogies that told the story of their lineage ties to others who migrated to East Creek. By the time a new generation might have thought about clarifying matters, the land of streams was engulfed in war and revolution. But the migrants themselves still lived in a world where lineage meant security, even after lineage members moved.

The guest households of East Creek could not have failed to notice that the Huas of Ganlu followed the same rules. The largest branch owned a charitable estate in an ancestral village west of Dangkou, from which it distributed welfare to descendants of Hua Leqin's older brother.[50] As with the other charitable estates, the principle involved was the obligation of descendants to share the wealth. Payments went to widows and orphans first, then to students, and then for coffins for the poor. Hua branch shrines and charitable estates dominated the town of Dangkou, and legend made the Huas themselves out to be immigrants. The Qians of Seven Mansions, with their seven branches and three charitable estates, also claimed descent from a guest household like the Wangs.

Ancestors, like folk heroes, tended to be long on virtues and short on faults, and the Qians' were no exception. As a general rule, character improves after death—and the less one knows about one's ancestors, the more efficacious they are as moral witnesses. About all anyone knows about the man called Xinmei, whose grave lay a kilometer northeast of Seven Mansions, is that he was said to be a guest cultivator who made good and that all the Qians of Seven Mansions, and no one else, claimed descent from him.[51] The genealogical records of the Qian descent group, compiled and printed by the shrine in Hongshengli, identified Xinmei as the twenty-second generation descendant of the first king of Wu-Yue. The claim to royal blood mattered little—everyone named Qian in the whole Wu dialect region was descended from the Wu-Yue kings. It mattered more that Xinmei was the seventh in a ritual sequence of nine male cousins whose tablets were arrayed as *fang* (houses, or branches) in the shrine of their paternal grandfather. No one knows when Xinmei was born or when he died, but he must have settled in the area in the latter half of the sixteenth century, after the tax reforms, giving his family's homestead the name Seventh Branch.[52]

Perhaps it mattered also that Xinmei's grandfather was one of thirty-four great-grandsons of another early Ming refugee in the area, that he himself had had five sons, and that Xinmei was the sixth son of number three. Like the Huas, the Qians had been wealthy gentry patrons once. [53] But even if they had controlled ten thousand mu, Xinmei's share, by the time the land had been divided among so many, would have shrunk to the size of one of the Wang brothers' in East Creek. Like many other sons of the landed gentry, Qian Xinmei resettled. If the legend is correct, he started by cultivating someone else's land.

Whatever Qian Xinmei's economic circumstances after he resettled, the family did not grow larger. One son and one grandson were buried by his side and the genealogy shows no collateral lines. But great-grandsons he had five, and in the next generation there were fifteen males. One of the great-grandsons earned a large, new gravesite, complete with a grave watcher paid for by rents from land donated by descendants in two lines. From then on, birth and death dates were meticulously recorded, along with spouses' fathers' names. The Qians of Seven Mansions were becoming a lineage by the middle of the eighteenth century.[54]

As the Qians became a lineage, Seven Mansions also became a village of landlords and scholars. No one knows where the money came from. Perhaps Qian Xinmei or his progeny invested in the new textile market at Dongting, or perhaps sons who moved away sent home earnings from commerce in Suzhou. Whatever the source, the money was there by the early Qing. Not only did the Qians grow in number, a sure sign of increased wealth, but they began to marry Hua women in large numbers, an apparent sign of status. Xinmei's gentry ancestors had arranged one-third of their marriages with Hua women, and although neither Xinmei's grandfather or father, Xinmei himself, nor his son married Huas, six of fourteen grandsons who married did marry Huas. The pattern held thereafter.[55] By the 1720s the Qians were purchasing Imperial Academy scholarships for their sons, and by the 1760s they had in-laws with provincial degrees. At its height before the Taiping rebellion in the next century, Seven Mansions was a classic scholar-gentry village with a small core of imperial licentiates, prefectural and county stipendiaries, Imperial Academy scholars, and a number of citations for relief work. In 1841 one household with seven males in the fourth generation was cited by the emperor for achieving the impossible ideal of five generations under one roof.[56] No one in Seven Mansions tilled the land.[57]

Like other scholar-gentry lineages, the Qians of Seven Mansions had their rich and their poor. Like Wang Atu's grandfather in East Creek, their ancestors watched as they divided the wealth. But scholar-gentry ancestors demanded fairness on a grander scale than peasant ancestors did. Perhaps it was because the gods demanded it of them. Perhaps it was because they had seen what could happen when gentry sons were left out in the cold. If partible inheritance was their way of solving the Wangs' problem—how to assure brothers a fair share—the charitable estate was their solution to Qian Xinmei's problem of diminishing returns.

Qian Xinmei himself must have benefited by the reforms that Hua Cha and the prefectural officials devised in part to treat the problem of diminishing returns in the 1560s. By then the large estates of the previous century had devolved into paper holdings with tax obligations, the tax for each cluster of villages being shared by the landowning householders. Landlords who inherited diminished estates locally were dunned for increasingly larger shares of the tax duties as others sold their rights to speculators or moved away, taking the rights with them. Absentee owners collected rents and evaded taxes, while local landlords won exemptions by taking civil service degrees. Hua Cha and his relatives collectively donated 2,400 mu to the tax district, the rents from which were to go to pay the entire tax bill. The inequitable tax burden having been lifted, the landlords submitted their holdings to a new survey. Duties were attached to the land at equitable rates and the flight of subsoil rights was halted.[58] Qian Xinmei and his descendants could collect them without the protection of powerful degree holders or the agents in the city who specialized in buying and selling tax-privileged real estate.

For men like Hua Cha, keeping the land in the hands of local landlords was more than just a contest for wealth: it was essential to the ritual ordering of that small cosmos of which their ancestors were such a large part. The property, having been divided, should not be lost to speculators. The small share of rights carried with it a small share of obligations, both to ancestors and to descendants. By law the subsoil was the source of tax revenues which kept the Son of Heaven in his place. By custom it was the source of a special kind of status, symbolized by the great floating tomb and others like it. Where the earth was barren, the ancestors had made it fertile. When Heaven failed to produce a crop the ancestors had provided relief. When the Son of Heaven failed to protect against bandits, the ancestors had raised a defense. And what the magistrate—distant and short-term servant of the emperor that he was—could not know about the soil, the seed, and the spirits of this particular cosmos, the ancestors had taught the people. One did not live on in the countryside and take such a heritage lightly. As if to demonstrate the link between land rights and public obligation, the Huas who donated the tax relief land stipulated that rental income remaining after taxes were paid be used for charity for other Hua descendants, the victims of diminishing returns.

If the lives of musicians and daoren, small persons and grave watchers intersected with the lives of peasants, scholars, and traders in a pattern that conflicted with the economic one, so did the charitable estate (*yizhuang*) serve as witness to an age when great gentry patrons walked the earth. The obligation (*yi*) for which it stood was that of a ritual descent group (*zong*) to its members (*zu*), the model being the kin group of the ancient Zhou overlords. The lord who feasted his peasants in the *Book of Songs* was also the ranking descendant of an ancient kin group. The land and the produce were held as an ancestral trust. In that long-gone era, patronage, not property, had determined the rights and duties of lords and peasants. Descent, not property, had determined the rights and duties of lineage members. In a world where property rights had split and devolved, wealthy landowners had taken over the obligations of the kin group. Or so they explained it.

The charity givers knew they were fighting the effects of the exchange of private property. But where the rules demanded egalitarian devolution, why should the rich get richer and the poor get poorer? The ancestors watched and the charity givers invoked their blessing. Scholars watched, too, and some even noticed a fundamental moral contradiction. The perceptive sixteenth-century statecraft writer Tang Shunzhi pointed it out in his commemoration of charity land in another Hua estate:

The ancients established descent groups (*zong*) for every set of agnates (*zu*). The members who had a surplus gave it to the zong and those who had not enough took from it. They treated one another as parts of a single body.... With the decline of the zong, private property came to determine status among agnates.... Charity land exists only because there are men of means, whereas under the rules of the zong (*zongfa*) everything, no matter how valuable, was shared. With charity land, it is only the benevolent man, acting as a single part of the body, who provides for the commonwealth, whereas under the rules of the zong nothing, no matter how small, was hoarded.[59]

In short, currents of obligation and dependency ran together with currents of egalitarianism to produce an institution peculiar to late imperial times. The charitable estate reinforced the moral heritage of the scholar-gentry, and it slowed the defection of their sons and daughters into the ranks of the merchant class.

The Song statesman Fan Zhongyan had invented the charitable estate in the eleventh century. A key figure in the Confucian revival, Fan had borrowed the idea of charity land from a Buddhist temple and adapted it to the lineage. The Fan estate had disappeared and reappeared over the centuries, providing relief for widows and orphans of the Fan lineage in Suzhou. It was the model for many others which began to spring up throughout the region in the fifteenth century. Few survived. Hua Cha's grandfather had tried to create an estate with some permanency by attaching it to an ancient shrine on the sacred mountain Huishan, west of Wuxi. But the land, like the charity land of other private estates, soon went the way of all ancestral land—through partible inheritance and back into the real estate market.

Not until the Qing emperor Qianlong gave the institution Heaven's blessing in 1739, with a law prescribing punishments for those who alienated lineage property, did the charitable estate truly mature.[60] Any estate that registered its deeds directly with the Board of Revenue in the capital, removing them from the rolls of the villages in which the land was located and arranging to pay the tax in a lump sum, would be protected from that time on. Not that Heaven was eager to change the custom of partible inheritance. Quite to the contrary: it was happy to have the world's property divided into small plots. In fact, the emperor explicitly forbade the creation of inalienable estates of any other sort. But ancestral shrines and charitable estates were institutions dedicated to the maintenance of ritual order on earth. Heaven had its reasons for keeping the sons of the scholar-gentry close to home, and charity was a good way of keeping them dependent. That it made the tax easier to collect was simply a good side effect.

With Heaven's blessing, the last intruders into the small peasant cosmos took their place. The Old Hua Charitable Estate in Dangkou, founded in 1745, started with 1,300 mu and grew to 3,500. In Hongshengli a branch of the Qian lineage started an estate with 200 mu in 1763 that grew to 900 by the 1810s. As the estates grew they took hold of the earthly aspects of the small cosmos in ways the ancestral tombs and shrines had not. Their power was collective and their finances secure. When the rice merchants' association met in Dangkou to negotiate seasonal prices they had to know the estates' intentions. When landlords met to fix rent schedules the estates' managers had to be heard. They were major contributors to temple fairs and the primary dispensers of food and clothing to the poor as the merchants started their year-end settling of accounts. The estates lowered rents and extended rent schedules, retaining the good will of their tenants. Their managers, chosen collectively by lineage leaders for their proven ability to manage, were a powerful force in the community. And their scholarships gained them the support of students whose influence would reach beyond that community. As the estates grew, they rescued the spirit of scholar-gentry patronage from the doldrums of diminishing returns and placed it in the minds of teachers and managers. This was the spirit that possessed Qian Shaolin when he saved his scholarship from the Hongshengli estate and used it as seed money for one in Seven Mansions.

Qian Shaolin had reason to worry in 1841. Not about himself: he had only accepted the scholarship because the Hongshengli estate rules said that every student descended from the common early Ming ancestor should receive one. The family was well enough off, and Shaolin had gone on to pass the prefectural exam and win the rank of senior licentiate in Nanjing. In 1841 his first great-great-grandson was born and his household received an imperial citation for achieving five generations under one roof. But there was the rub. His sixth and seventh great-grandsons were also born that year. If he could have seen the future he would have counted seventeen males in that generation and thirty-four in the next. Among the latter was Qian Mu's father, a bright boy whose family was not well off. Shaolin knew his ancestors from the genealogical record he had compiled some years earlier. They helped him see the future and urged him to start the Sea of Caring Charitable Estate.[61] Qian Mu and his mother were living off it in 1911, and his brother was running its school for peasant boys.

Yet the spirit possessed more than country scholars and influenced more than peasant boys. The charitable estate had become the core of a local political culture in which men of talent sought to influence the course of events. As Qian Shaolin was planting the seed of an estate in Seven Mansions in the 1840s, Hua Hongmo's father and three uncles were doing the same in Dangkou.[62] But these Huas were not scholars. They were local merchants, manufacturers, and purveyors of the wine and soy sauce for which Dangkou was known.[63] A brother of their great-grandfather had been manager of the Old Hua estate in the previous century and an uncle had helped compile the genealogical record of their branch some years earlier. But unlike Hua Yilun and his uncles, who were descended from the founder of the Old Hua estate, they held no degrees and wielded no influence. When their father died in 1840 they decided not to divide the property but to manage it jointly and add to it until there was enough for a charitable estate. With that their influence would grow.

It was also the year of Hua Hongmo's birth. He was one of only four male offspring of four brothers. This fact complicated their move into the scholar-gentry world. The sons had to study, but they also had to learn the business. Because they had the means, they could hire managers and apprentices to help. But they would have to succeed in three realms—commerce, scholarship, and gentry management—with whatever talents they possessed.

Had the spirit of scholar-gentry patronage not possessed them, Hua Hongmo and his father and uncles would have applied their talents differently. The years they spent building their estate were years of crisis for the old regime. By 1840 the outflow of silver and inflow of opium had already affected the local economy and the swelling of the population did not help. There were 130 widows and orphans from Hongmo's branch receiving charity from the Old Hua estate, which could no longer provide them all with the stipulated 15.5 liters of rice per month. The land tax was payable in silver and as the price of silver rose landowners were harder pressed to pay it. The Old Hua leaders were involved in a countywide struggle of local gentry managers to wrest control of tax policing from corrupt clerks and tax farmers (men who paid taxes for others, cheating both the taxpayers and the state), while small landlords like Qian Shaolin put their land into lineage estates where it was beyond the clerks' and speculators' reach. This was the struggle that the New Hua founders vowed to enter in 1840. And the struggle had just been complicated by British gunboats.

For the Qing regime the Opium War was a conflict with foreigners over trading rights on the empire's periphery. But when British gunboats sailed virtually unopposed up the Yangzi to Nanjing in the summer of 1842, the depth of the crisis was clear. The emperor's special commissioner, Lin Zexu, had precipitated the crisis in the spring of 1839 by confiscating the traders' opium and dumping it into Canton's harbor. The British gunboats had prevailed, and Lin was dismissed. The first negotiated settlement had failed. Now the British brought their demands further north. The Treaty of Nanjing, signed in 1842, opened the sleepy coastal town of Shanghai to the foreigners and gave them extraterritorial rights.

The scholar-gentry world buzzed with news of the regime's failure. The new crisis represented a more advanced stage of the disease that was killing the Qing. Unable to control the malignant growth of interlopers between Heaven's appointed officials and the hustle-bustle of the people's economic life, the regime grew weaker as the people grew thin. As governor of Jiangsu in the 1830s Lin Zexu had tried to eliminate the tax farmers and control the revenue clerks. He and other students of statecraft had recognized the outflow of silver due to the opium trade as another symptom of the same disease. The scholar-gentry movement to gain control of tax policing in Wuxi continued the struggle for a local cure. By 1846, the Wuxi reformers had succeeded, winning local tax districts the right to select their own constables and outlawing the use of tax farmers.[64] But as the Old Hua leaders and others celebrated their success in Dangkou, the scholar-gentry of the southern provinces found themselves face to face with armed rebels.

The Taiping rebels rose up in Guangxi in 1850, and the threat to both the Qing Dynasty and the landed gentry was immediately apparent. Hua Yilun, a provincial degree holder and great-great-grandson of the founder of the Old Hua estate, went off to serve as chief military adviser to the Guangxi governor, another Wuxi native who had been a major spokesman for reform back home. As Qing defenses crumbled before the Taiping onslaught in the south, resistance fell to gentry-led militia units, coordinated by the tent government of Zeng Guofan. Hua Yilun returned to Dangkou to head up the militia for eastern Wuxi county. By 1856 Nanjing was in rebel hands. In 1860, when Wuxi and Suzhou fell, Dangkou was headquarters for the last line of defense. Before the Taipings arrived, the Hua lineage leaders called a meeting, attended by seventy-two men representing all the Hua branches. The three surviving sons of the wine and soy sauce merchant, all of them now serving as officers in Hua Yilun's militia, presented their plan for a New Hua estate. As if to affirm that this crisis would pass and that the survivors could count on the lineage leaders to help them recover from it, the Hua brothers donated the 375 mu they had accumulated to the Old Hua estate for safekeeping and promised to take over relief for their own branch within five years. The branch heads endorsed the plan, which was formally drawn up in quintuplicate, with seals affixed and deeds attached. The meeting adjourned and the war commenced. Hua Hongmo was twenty years old.

For four years the land of streams ran with the blood of soldiers and militiamen, rebels and refugees. Dangkou and Ganlu, the towns farthest removed from the centers of imperial administration, held out the longest against the Taipings. Settlements with granaries, like Seven Mansions, became militia headquarters, while tumuli of forgotten ancestors more ancient or more peripheral than the Huas' became Taiping bunkers. The public cemetery at Dangkou grew amoebalike around the coffins of refugees from Suzhou and Wuxi. When local defenses finally collapsed, Hua Yilun and the others retreated to the foreign concessions of Shanghai. Some, like Yilun's son Hengfang, joined Li Hongzhang's tent government as advisers—Hengfang was a ballistics expert, trained in Western mathematics at the new Shanghai armory school. Others, like Hua Hongmo, pressed on with their studies for the civil service exams. When Zeng Guofan's armies finally captured Nanjing in a bloodbath in 1864, the experts went to new professional careers and the others returned with their deeds and their imperial honors to the family ruins in the land of streams.[65]

Hua Hongmo passed the prefectural and provincial exams in 1873 but never served the Qing. Within two years he had formally established the New Hua Charitable Estate. By the time of his father's death in 1882 he had begun compiling new genealogies for several of the branches and built a lineage temple for his own.[66] Over the next three decades he saw the estate grow to nearly four thousand mu. Leaving the wine and soy sauce business to his cousins, he opened a rice warehousing concern in Wuxi City and began to invest in urban real estate. His warehouses, among the first in a new wave that soon made Wuxi the site of the largest grain commodity market in eastern China, became the property of the charitable estate, channeling into the Huas' Dangkou projects revenues earned from storing the grain of inland merchants en route to Shanghai.[67]

The New Hua estate extended its charity first to in-laws, and then to widows and orphans in other Dangkou families. Where the old estate had supported a lineage school, the new one opened an academy, inviting scholars from neighboring counties to discuss the issues being raised by the new "foreign" studies and by Kang Youwei and the reformers. As the reformers made their way to Beijing in 1898, the estate published the essays of its invited scholars. And when educational reform took hold in 1904, the academy became the school. Along with the new private girls' school opened by the Old Hua branch, this was the local scholar-gentry's center of intellectual and political ferment.[68] A spiritual renewal had run its course with Hua Hongmo and a handful of others as its agents, just as the social and political fabric of the little cosmos unraveled, preparing the ground for the flood of 1911.

No wonder, then, that Qian Mu's experiments with learning, undertaken as they were within the confines of that little cosmos, reconfirmed the ancient values of his civilization. The world of bureaucratic empire and rural exploitation that was unraveling had been not the source of these values but the diseased body against which the spirit struggled for survival. And what was that spirit? It was the spirit of Lie Di, the ancestors, and the scholars, the spirit of the ancients that possessed the teachers and makers of whatever is good and beautiful. The good and the beautiful reveal themselves in familiar forms. Remove the forms, and where will inspiration come from? The currents of obligation and dependency run deep, but so do the currents of egalitarianism. Block them and only exploitation remains. Who will be inspired to rebuild the little cosmos after the revolution?

Qian Mu was not yet asking that question when he rose from his sickbed in 1911. But by the time he taught young Yang Xilin to sing in his "living classroom" in Houzhai it was very much on his mind. That was in 1919, after eight years of teaching the sons of scholars, traders, and peasants, the year the New Culture movement took to the streets. Almost sixty years had passed since the "restoration" movement that had inspired the scholar-gentry to take hold of their world, stop the Taipings, and resist the foreigners by reviving the spirit of the past. For most intellectuals history seemed to have displaced the values that Zeng Guofan and the other restorationists had fought for. "Chinese learning for substance, Western learning for practice" had been the restorationists' slogan. The master formulator of their program, Feng Guifen, had projected a world in which experts trained in science and technology would develop China's defenses while institutions inspired by kinship ideology and managed by enlightened scholar-gentry would order its society and economy.[69] Feng's experts showed an uncanny resemblance to Hua Hengfang, his managers to Hua Hongmo. But for all its sentimental appeal and theoretical elegance, the idea had failed. China was undefended, its society and economy in chaos. The May Fourth generation needed a revolution. There was no inspiration for that in China's past.

But what if history was inseparable from value? And what if the values that inspired the makers of history were derived from the familiar forms of their culture? Then the makers of revolution were simply products of a chaotic era, destroyers of corrupt and decadent forms of exploitation and builders of new, more efficient ones. Their success or failure could only be measured by the degree of annihilation of the old and efficiency of the new. If they would destroy the basic values of the culture in the process, then what was it they hoped to defend? If they would destroy the forms that had inspired their ancestors to love order but keep both the emperor and the spirits at a distance, then how did they hope to inspire their descendants to resist imperialism and foreign gods?

If Zou Jingheng, a native of Houzhai and a budding young student of economics, did not reflect on such questions just yet he was typical of the May Fourth generation.[70] His inspiration came from his teachers and fellow students in Tianjin, and when he returned to Houzhai in the winter of 1921 full of hope for the future, he found the place embarrassing. Jingheng admired Qian Mu for his missionary-like zeal, helping to build and stock the little library the Zous were starting up. But he could have predicted Qian's disappointment. Of course the students would settle down to run the family store. The land of streams was hopelessly mired in parochial familialism. This is what the New

Culture advocates were at last identifying as the ultimate source of China's backwardness—its patriarchal family system, an adjunct of feudal society reinforced by Confucian ideas. Without the empire and the exam system that drew scholars into its service, the country boy who could read and write was only a slave to his family. To teach him to love his culture would hardly help set him free. But when Zou Jingheng tried his own enlightened ideas on the person in his own family who was most clearly a victim of patriarchal oppression, the spiritual problem was presented to him with a slap.

Ten years had passed since Jingheng's older brother's untimely death. The young woman he had left a childless widow after only sixty-four days of marriage was still with the Zous. Although illiterate, Hua Ruizhen was a product of the same scholar-gentry world as Qian Mu's teachers. Born a Hua in Dangkou, her father had been a teacher and her brother a promising young calligrapher who studied with Hongmo's grandson. Her place in the complex network of kinship relations that tied Houzhai to Dangkou was another small part of the ancestors' heritage. Like any other woman she was excluded from the bloodlines that connected males to the other world. Like many she was a link in the uterine chain that connected them in this one. For her maternal grandmother's sister was paternal grandmother to her husband of sixty-four days.

The center of a woman's world in Houzhai was not the study but the kitchen. Lord Zao, the kitchen god, watched as she performed her ritual duties for the family, and four times each year the family assembled before him in ritual expression of the order she enforced. On the twenty-fourth day of the last month he traveled to the other world to report on what he'd seen, his lips sealed with the sticky sweet congee she had made for him. When the children misbehaved she lined them up before him, directing their apologies to him. It was in the kitchen that Zou Jingheng advised his aunt Ruizhen that it was now "considered backward to remain a chaste widow; she should give more attention to her own happiness."

Ruizhen's response burned in his ear and in his memory. Sixty years later, after learning of her death, he respectfully recorded it:

> No sooner had the words escaped my lips than she changed color and burst into tears. She set down her work and scolded me: "Your brother's body is hardly in the grave and already you have

forgotten how I took care of him when he was dying. You must find me loathsome! I was born in a scholarly household. I learned how to be a daughter and a wife there. I'm not the kind of person who serves one country at dawn and another at dusk. We may have been married only sixty-four days, but we knew each other and we loved each other. It is my wish to be loyal to him until I die, but you come with your concern for my personal happiness. Why aren't you concerned about your brother? If everyone was only concerned for himself, there wouldn't be any loyalties in this world. If I wanted to remarry why should I wait for you to tell me! I belong to the Zou family in this life and I'll be a ghost in this house when I die. I know you mean well, but I'm not interested." Completely cowed, I apologized and felt intensely the absence of any place to hide.[71]

Zou Jingheng was neither the first nor the last young man to be shamed by a virtuous woman in the land of streams. Ming loyalists of the 1640s often compared themselves to chaste widows as they took their suicidal stands. And every mother's son lived through the struggle by which his wife established her rights vis-à-vis her mother-in-law. Where close intermarriage among particular patrilines was common, as in the case of the Qians, the Zous and the Huas, the weight of ancestors on both sides might be brought to bear on the struggle. When the Huas married their daughter into a cousin's household, therefore, they had reason to expect she would be respected for her service. If there were any doubts, she was prepared to remind them of their obligations as scholar-gentry sons.

Like daoren and musicians, women's interactions with peasants, traders, and scholars conflicted with the economic mold. Hua Ruizhen was dependent on the Zous because she was excluded by custom from her father's inheritance and obliged by custom to join her husband's parents' household. Neither law nor custom would have prevented her from succeeding her husband as household head if he had lived long enough to become one, but whatever property rights she might have controlled in that position belonged to a male bloodline. Her sons would have been her security. Lacking sons, she found security in her brothers-in-law, the eldest of whom was Zou Jingheng. If she were to remarry she might have sons of her own, but her original husband's share of the Zou property would be divided by his brothers. Ruizhen would thus progress from her second dependency to her third, one step further removed from her ancestors' eyes. At Jingheng's naive suggestion, she raised his brother and the host of ancient loyalists from the dead and shamed him before Lord Zao the kitchen god with the ultimate symbol of dependency, a woman's tears.

Confucius called the bond between husband and wife one of the five basic relationships. An ethical world order depended on it, along with the other four. The bond between lord and servant was strengthened by loyalty and trust, the bond between father and son was strengthened by forgiveness and respect, the bond between brothers by deference for age, and the bond between friends by shared feelings and knowledge. The conjugal bond was the only one to be strengthened by a virtue that was explicitly feminine—submission. And, as the *Book of Changes* would have it, through submission the principle of Heaven—the principle of goodness for Neo-Confucian China—was able to complete itself in human form.[72]

Submission went hand in hand with dependency, and nowhere was the nature of it made clearer than in the ways property devolved. Property, real and movable, belonged to the household. No matter how many generations of conjugal pairs or how many brothers there were, the household had only one kitchen and the kitchen had only one god. Should the household divide, as usually it did after the household head died, the property devolved onto the sons' new households. Only if there were no sons could the property be passed on to a daughter's household, and then only by giving the daughter in marriage to an adopted heir.[73] A man became household head when his father died. A woman became household head only if her husband died without an heir or before his heir became a man, and then only if her husband was already head of the household.

In rare cases, real property could devolve onto a daughter's household as part of her dowry. The early Ming ancestors of the Qians of Hongshengli and Seven Mansions established their households with landed dowries. Civil war had left the Qians landless in the 1370s. But with their pedigree, their education, and their experience in elite circles, their sons were a good match for the daughters of lesser landowners in remote places. Just what sort of obligations the Qians incurred is not known, but as their progeny were among the greatest gentry patrons of the next century, the dowry givers would seem to have made a wise investment. Two hundred years later, a landed household named Jin by Whistle-and-Swagger Creek followed the same strategy and set up the first Qians of Hongshengli with dowry land.[74]

But dowry land was rare. More common was the dowry of movable goods and money. The size of it reflected the status of the wife givers and in this little cosmos it could become twice the size of the betrothal gift that came from the groom's household. For a poor household the betrothal gift could amount to compensation for a dowry it could ill afford. In the worst cases, it was simply compensation for the cost of raising a daughter. But for most it was a signal from the groom's family of how much dowry they thought the new couple should receive. It guaranteed that marriage would be restricted to families of similar status and that the bride would enter her new household with whatever support this fact provided. Mostly it provided face.

If life for men was a struggle for property rights that are transmitted from one generation to the next, life for women was different. A woman took from her mother not property rights but a sense of shame. It was her mother who scolded her in front of the kitchen god and taught her the value of face. She brought face with her into the alien environment of her husband's household, and she appealed to face when she scolded her own children in turn. As the men in her life reminded her that submission was the virtue through which she could better this world, she reminded them in turn that wealth and the power of literacy were nothing without a sense of shame.

The ritual of marriage, with its elaborate exchange of gifts and visits, eased the passage from daughterly respect to wifely submission. The new wife made her first ritual offerings to her husband's ancestors and her brothers ritually gave her leave to do so. The exchange of betrothal gifts and dowry followed careful prescriptions leaving no doubts about the obligations incurred. As the daoren and musicians kept the spirits happy, the two families displayed their faces and the ancestors watched. The bride's family made certain the ancestors knew they had gained nothing in the exchange, which would be tantamount to selling a daughter. The groom's accepted responsibility for the woman's welfare and that of her children. And finally, in the ultimate ritual of submission, the bride accepted instruction in her duties to her husband and his kin.[75]

Hua Ruizhen had learned how to be a daughter and a wife in a scholarly family. Her scholarly ancestors had preserved the instructions written down by Hua Leqin's father five hundred years earlier, as the refugee family struggled to build a farm from scratch at the swampy end of Goose Lake. They include these words on the instruction of the new bride:

> It is the wife who determines the success or failure of a family. It is a matter of urgency that a woman is taught when she first arrives. The first priority is instruction in the morality of the family—how to follow submissively and apply oneself respectfully, to serve the elders and the husband. Practical instruction—the business of food and clothing—comes second. Placing relations with the husband first gives them a special importance. In sum one should say that in our family since the time of the earliest ancestors husband and wife have been bound together by mutual trust and there has been neither jealousy nor bad conduct. Now, when you have just arrived, is the best time for you to learn the right things. In serving parents be filial. In serving your husband, be submissive. Toward the other son's wives exercise restraint. Toward the lineage be harmonious. Treat inferiors with kindness. Carry yourself with dignity and caution. Speak little and never speak wildly. Neither hear nor speak ill of others. Be neither lazy nor greedy. As for the business of food and clothing, you should replace the labor of the older generation with your own. For the sake of the younger generation, you should tend the hemp and the silkworms and produce cloth. It is up to you to preserve our family line and to maintain our family economy. This is how to become a worthy wife in our family. Be one who puts into practice what you learn, not one whose promises are false. One who can do all this brings happiness to her husband and happiness to the whole family. One who cannot does the opposite. That is why it is said that it is the wife who determines the success or failure of the family. These words are worth heeding.[76]

The woman who heeded this lesson accepted her submissive role. But once she accepted it, she had the right to expect her instructors to keep to their Confucian roles as well. Her weapon was shame.

The Taoist sage Lao Tzu taught the power of submissiveness even as Confucius taught the value of the five relationships. "Know the male / but keep to the role of the female / and be a ravine to the empire," he said.

> In the world there is nothing more submissive and weak than water. Yet for attacking that which is hard and strong nothing can surpass it. This is because there is nothing that can take its place.

That the weak overcomes the strong,
And the submissive overcomes the hard,
Everyone in the world knows yet no one can put
    this knowledge into practice.[77]

The Taoist-inspired martial arts taught one how to restrain oneself
and use the strength of one's opponent to defeat him. And Confucian
statesmen had learned how to withhold their services or otherwise
shame a superior in order to see that the right thing was done. For a
woman, these were the only tactics available. The attentive son might
learn from her as well.

No family was without strong women ancestors. Many of them
must have broken with their prescribed role in order to manage a
household for a weak husband or dominate an only son. As with other
key ancestors, their characters must have "improved" after death.
Their success must have been made possible by their devotion to husbands and sons: the stronger the woman, the stronger the devotion.
Perhaps the chaste widows listed in the local gazetteers and honored
with memorial arches in the countryside were more powerful than
their submissive images imply.

The story of the woman named Yang, who married a widower
named Qian in Hongshengli in 1730, is a case in point. Her father, a
scholar in Wuxi City, died when she was fifteen. Perhaps her mother
was incapable of arranging a good marriage at that point, or perhaps
Yang insisted on staying home to help manage the household. For
whatever reason, she worked at her loom until her younger brothers
had finished their studies, which otherwise they might not have been
able to afford. At twenty-three, she was older than most brides when
her mother and brothers found a match for her. She was given to a
forty-four-year-old widower with three sons and two daughters, all
under the age of fifteen, and an aging father. Three years later she
bore a son of her own, and by 1735 she was the only adult in the family.

As a twenty-eight-year-old widow, Yang faced the problem of arranging marriages for her stepsons and stepdaughters while protecting
herself and her own son. She arranged the marriages and presided
over the family's fortunes until her own son came of age. Then, setting
aside a portion for her own support, calling it "boarding" land, she
divided the rest evenly among the heirs. By then the second stepson
had died, leaving a childless widow who was, like Yang, a second wife.
And the third stepson was a remarried widower as well.

It was Yang who made the Qians see the future. By the time she was sixty-five there were fifteen grandsons and thirteen granddaughters in the family. The other widow, named Zhou, had offered 160 mu of her husband's inheritance to the sons of her husband's two younger brothers to support them in their studies. But the oldest brother had already assigned his second son as an heir to this property and the younger brothers refused to receive it. Yang then reminded them all that their father had instructed her before his death that he hoped his sons would establish a charitable estate with the inheritance. Wasn't the purpose of such an estate to provide support for widows like her and Zhou and students like her younger grandsons? As if to shame them for their own slowness with regard to the matter, she took 40 mu of her own boarding land and donated it to the yet nonexistent Hongshengli charitable estate, inviting Zhou to add her 160 mu to that. It was Yang's own son, the youngest of the brothers, who saw to the paperwork. The women thus found a way to break the rules and Hongshengli got its first charitable estate.[78]

Yang and Zhou were not the only chaste widows to influence the distribution of wealth in this way. At least 800 mu of the estates in Seven Mansions were donated by widows and their heirs. One large grant came from a seventeen-year-old boy who shared a household with his mother and the wife and two concubines of his uncle, for whom he was also the adoptive heir.[79] The result, in Hongshengli and Seven Mansions, was that more relief was provided for widows and orphans of the various Qian lineages and more scholarships were given to the Qian boys. The ancestors watched, and they were happy.

Qian Mu scarcely knew his father and he has never seen the genealogical records in which the history of the Qians is told. In his "Reminiscences on My Parents at the Age of Eighty," he attributes what he did know to his mother, whose stories were always instructive. It was she who recounted the legend of the women's protest when the gentry managers of the village allowed the prodigal son of a widow to die in jail. It was she who told of his father's fight with corrupt gentry managers over control of the charitable estate when the managers diverted funds for their own private use. She told him of his father's diligence as a young scholar, of the respect he earned as a leader in lineage and community affairs, and of other things that happened before the time when he lay ill on his opium couch mumbling incoherent lessons to his disheartened son. Nothing troubled her more than having to live on

charity, the ultimate proof of her dependency. But she refused merchants' offers of jobs for her sons, because she was determined they
finish their studies, as their father had wished. Her very presence
confirmed the power of Confucian values, with their emphasis on human bonding through family roles, and her stories showed how an
ethical world order depended on such bonds.

The world of Seven Mansions weighed heavily on Qian Mu when
he rose from his sickbed in autumn 1911. His deep respect for China's
ordinary people, with their sense of place and the duties attached to it,
and for China's country scholars, with their sense of equity and their
dedication to achieving it, remained with him throughout his life. In
1911 the revolution had begun, but the spirit of the old culture was
very much alive. Perhaps for Qian Mu, the two were inseparable.
China was sick. Revolution was the cure. But it would succeed only if
administered with compassion. For his own part, he combined his hope
for a new China with compassion and the dignity of a scholar.

IV.

"Reminiscences on My Parents at the Age of Eighty"

QIAN MU (CH'IEN MU)

TRANSLATOR'S INTRODUCTION

Qian Mu's career as teacher and scholar began in 1911, when he was sixteen. The year marked the fall of the monarchy and the beginning of China's earnest search for a new political form. Nearly thirty years later Qian wrote his comprehensive *Guoshi dagang* (*Outline history of the nation*), a highly learned plea for unity based on historical consciousness, an argument for the relevance of a history that most intellectuals had rejected.[1] If China is to survive as a nation—united, strong, and independent—it must recognize its own heritage, Qian argued. Western civilization, which includes Russia, has produced parliamentary democracy and Leninist party dictatorship, and each of these has been instrumental in the development of strong Western states. But these forms cannot be grafted onto China. The instruments for modern political development in China must be native products, the result of a native process. So far, China has failed to produce its own modern political forms and is therefore in the process of being divided up by foreign powers and foreign ideologies—all of them instruments of Chinese dependence. Should those with the potential for leadership fail to rediscover the processes that in the past unified China and made her strong and independent, then China is doomed to dependency and weakness in a world whose political forms are determined by foreign powers.

Through the more than forty years since Qian Mu first laid down these arguments, the issues have not changed for him. Like nationalist and historicist thinkers in other traditions, Qian Mu roots his country's uniqueness in the people's experience of their culture.[2] History shapes culture, and for Qian Mu the motive force in Chinese history is spiritual.

In 1940 the spirit of Confucian humanism helped Qian Mu to make sense of the imperial past. In 1983 the spirit of the rites, li, helped him explain the cultural integration of the Chinese people, as told in the first chapter of this book. But if Qian's argument that the uniqueness of China's past should determine the course of its modern development is to have any force, the spirit of the rites must be shown to have remained alive in Chinese culture even though the traditional material basis of the rites has declined. Otherwise, how can the culture be said to live on? Or, at least, how can China's history be said to have relevance beyond the arrival of the West?

In 1975 Qian Mu for the first time applied his historical vision concretely to a small portion of the world he wants to keep alive. "Reminiscences on My Parents at the Age of Eighty" is not history, at least not in the sense that the *Outline History of the Nation* is, but it is nonetheless part of the same narrative.[3] It describes the spirit of the rites in a setting where the rites themselves did not prevail. Since we are now familiar with that setting, perhaps we can understand why Qian Mu takes the spirit of Chinese culture for granted: the world of his youth was steeped in its traditions. But the historical role of this spirit can be derived only from Qian's interpretation of Chinese history.

Qian Mu did not intend his "Reminiscences" as history. But they are, in fact, an expression of the idea that he first encountered in the writings of Zeng Guofan, that custom begins "with the echo of one mind in the mind of another."[4] That idea is as close as one can come to an explanation of what Qian means by the spirit of the culture, the motive force of history. In the "Reminiscences" we can see this force limited by historical circumstances but very much alive. Because the account is personal but concerns the lives of people long since dead, it is both subjective and objective, a better vehicle than history for describing a spirit that lives as an echo in the mind.

"Reminiscences on My Parents at the Age of Eighty"

1   Foreword

I was orphaned at the age of twelve. When Father died, I was still a naive boy. When Mother passed away, thirty-six years later, I was forty-eight. But then I was off in Chengdu by myself, unable to return and tend to the burial. Because of the national crisis I was afraid even to circulate a death notice. So there was no proper mourning ceremony and all I could do was to lock myself in my room and wail at the darkness. At the hundredth anniversary of both my parents' birth I was seventy-one. I had retired from my position at New Asia College by then. I suffered from an eye ailment for which I underwent surgery. Soon thereafter I was occupied again, lecturing at Kuala Lumpur. I had hoped to write this essay then, and I managed to prepare a rough outline of it, but in the end it came to naught. This year I am eighty, and next year will be the one-hundred-and-tenth anniversary of their birth. And so, while traveling in the mountains between Hualien and Taipei on the occasion of my eightieth birthday, I have seized the opportunity to write.

My poor mother and father—how they suffered to give me life! As I look back on their earthly lives my sorrow is great. To think that my own living flesh, bones, skin, and hair were all transmitted to me by them. And now, suddenly, I am old and gray, my spirit declining, my goals unachieved. In shame I look back on the gift of parental care and instruction. How can I redeem myself for even a small fraction of my errors? Events of the past, piled one upon the other, remain to this day lodged in the crevices of my brain. I shall extract a few and write them down. Perhaps someday the descendants of my parents' four sons, back on the mainland, will happen to read about them and so learn of the virtue of their ancestors.

2   Seven Mansions

I was born in Yanxiang Township, Wuxi County, Jiangsu, in a village on Whistle-and-Swagger Creek called Seven Mansions, to a family in Five Generations Together Hall. The village originated with my eighteenth-generation ancestor, whose family was wealthy and powerful. Altogether they controlled tens of thousands of mu of rich paddy land along the creek. But my ancestor had lost his parents and, having no children of his own, he lived alone with his wife. At the age of thirty he fell ill. The best physicians from near and far could find no cure and his condition grew steadily worse. One day, in the midst of his decline, his wife said to him, "There is something I have wanted to say for some time but have not for fear you would reject my advice and reprimand me." He replied, "I am already so ill, I can scarcely imagine any advice that I would not heed. If for some reason I cannot accept it, there is no blaming you for it. What is it?"

"I think medicine will not cure your illness," she said. "If you keep taking medicine, it will only lead to new complications. Only the long road of quiet self-nurturing will work. But there is no way the two of us can go off to the mountains to live in a monastery. So, I have taken it upon myself to prepare a place for you in the cottage in the west garden. If you would stay alone in the cottage, I could manage the family affairs and you would not have to worry about them. I have had a small door cut in the gate through which food can be delivered. You could just come get it when the bell rings. It would be hard at first, but after a week or so you would get used to it. If you had to, you could open the gate and get out. I would prescribe three years of this. I have spoken to two physicians about it and they both said it is worth trying."

My ancestor consented to his wife's plan. After three years he emerged, his health restored. Then his wife said to him, "While you were in seclusion I made a promise to the Buddha to abstain from eating meat. I have vowed to remain a lay disciple and live out my life in solitude. But because you should have an heir, I have found two young women of good character who are a good match for you. For the past two years I have been instructing them. If you take them into your house you should not have to worry."

And so my ancestor was persuaded by his wife to take the women in. In the end he had seven sons and at the edge of Whistle-and-Swagger Creek he built seven mansions for them. Such were the origins of Qifangqiao (literally, Seven-branches Bridge) Village. The story is recorded in the family record book. I have not seen it myself, but I tell it as it was told to me in my youth.

The seven houses stretched in a line from east to west along Whistle-and-Swagger Creek, each one a mansion of considerable proportions. Each mansion was a separate compound, surrounded by walls. Outside these seven compounds there were neither peasant houses nor shops. Some thousand paces to the east was a bridge, hence the name Seven-branches Bridge. Just north of the bridge was a small village—I've forgotten the name—where the hereditary servants of Seven Mansions lived. It was they who, generation after generation, preserved the ritual incantations of our ancestors and performed them at weddings and funerals. Whenever a Qian household had need for them, the entire body of servants would gather there.

Some five hundred paces to the west was another bridge, named for Ding Family Village, which lay to the north of it. Here lived the hereditary musicians of Seven Mansions, heirs of a tradition dating from Ming times (1368–1645). In accordance with this tradition, the musicians performed southern-style opera—sixteenth-century Kunqu—to the accompaniment of gong and drum. They, too, gathered on ceremonial occasions to perform their art. At weddings, depending on the scale, one or two platforms would appear for a day, sometimes two or three days, before the great hall in one of the compounds. The musicians would sing opera and beat the gongs and drums. As children, my brother and I feasted on the sound, and as adults we remained fond of it.

3   Five Generations Together Hall

The population of the seven branches did not grow evenly. In the beginning there were some ten thousand mu of paddy for each branch, but as the population grew, those who divided the property more often had less per share. Only those families whose numbers were few were able to preserve their wealth for long. Therefore, after the inheritance passed through a few generations the differences in wealth among the seven houses became greater and greater. The descendants of the senior house were the most numerous, and with the birth of my father's oldest cousin, the ideal of "five generations in one hall" was achieved. In my great-grandfather's generation there were two brothers, the elder having seven sons who comprised the senior branch, the younger having five who comprised the junior branch. These two branches then divided further into twelve separate sub-branches. My grandfather's generation, then, numbered twelve in all.

Now, each mansion had from front to rear seven rows of buildings, each row having seven sections, or spaces between pillars, with a great hall in the center and living quarters to the right and left. In addition, each row was abutted by side chambers, which also served as living quarters. Running the length of the mansion on each side was a passageway. The seven families of the senior branch came and went via the eastern passageway, and the five families of the junior branch came and went via the western passageway. The main gate remained closed except for special occasions.

Then each family in turn had its own offspring. My grandfather, Master Juru, had four girls and two boys for a total of six. I had four paternal aunts and one senior uncle, my father being the youngest of the lot. The other families in the mansion also proliferated rapidly, so that living space was limited and each family's share of the land was quite small. In my own childhood the rare family that had a hundred mu of paddy was considered well-to-do, as most had only a dozen or two. My father and uncle, neither of whom could claim a foot of soil, had sunk into poverty. Of the original seven branches there were three wealthy ones, consisting of single households, who still held several thousand mu each. The other three branches were just as poor as Five Generations Together Hall.

Everything sorted itself out according to this division between the rich and the poor. The three wealthy branches took turns serving as local gentry. They were the ones who had access to officials above and who managed locally the public business of tax payment and labor recruitment. Whenever some dispute arose, it was turned over to the gentry for settlement so that the cost of litigation could be avoided. In Seven Mansions, the gentrymen of the three wealthy branches gradually assumed responsibility for the affairs of the whole lineage. The other four branches did not get involved in decisions.

There was a legend about a widow of the western branch of Five Generations Together Hall. She was well off and had one son and one daughter, neither of whom had married. The son had little respect for rules and was often in trouble with the law. By that time, even though the large extended family still existed, the rites and regulations that had governed it had disappeared. None of the hall's elders knew what to do. The man who served as gentryman at the time was from the third branch and lived next door. After lecturing the son repeatedly to no avail, he had him sent to the county jail. The hall's elders went to the third branch and pleaded with the gentryman to have the boy released. But he refused, saying that if he were locked up for a while there might be some hope of reform.

Unfortunately, the son starved to death in jail, and the gentryman of the third branch also fell ill. Then, suddenly one night, the mother dreamed that her son had returned to lodge a complaint. He had reported his grievance to the authorities among the shades and had obtained justice. Now he requested that a large sum of spirit money be burned so that he could use it in the underworld to hasten his tormentor's death. When the mother awoke she told the dream to her daughter. The daughter had dreamed the same. Next morning the mother related it to several women to whom she was close and found others who had had the same dream. With that, she went to the market and purchased a large amount of spirit money. The women of Five Generations Together Hall gathered in the yard outside the main gate and consigned it to the flames. When the large pile of paper money had finished burning, the ailing gentryman of the third branch breathed his last. This story was still being told in my childhood. One can imagine how divisive the feelings among the branches were.

At the main gate of Five Generations Together Hall there hung a placard commemorating the hall. The great hall of the second court-yard was called the Hall of Profound Deliberation and was the largest great hall in all the seven mansions. It took its name from the strategy meetings that occurred there during the defense against the Taipings, when Huai Army troops were garrisoned in the village. The great hall of the third courtyard was called the Plain Book Hall. The rest were smaller and unnamed.

The living quarters to the west of the Plain Book Hall had been those of my fifth great-uncle of the western branch. I am not certain how, but someone had climbed to the roof and demolished them. Only the eastern half of the great hall itself and the plaque identifying it remained. The tiles and beams had all been sold. No one seemed able to prevent this destruction. The Hall of Profound Deliberation had originally had twenty-four hinged double doors among its pillars. They were made of fine cedar and inscribed with the complete text of *The Romance of the Western Chamber*. These doors, too, had been stolen and sold by one of the family. The hall's long meeting table and chairs had also been sold off. The disintegration and neglect of family regulations within the branch of Five Generations Together Hall had reached this extreme. The demolished living quarters by the Plain Book Hall we called "the ruin." There was no way to reconstruct them.

The education of the youngsters is even more painful to write about. Most of the older boys of my own generation and the men of my father's whom I knew in my childhood had read no more than the *Four Books*.* Those who could read the *Odes* and the *Tso Commentary* were as rare as phoenix feathers and unicorn horns.† Virtually none of the sons had a comprehensive knowledge of the classics. The three wealthy houses could have afforded fine tutors, but they were too pampered and self-indulgent to think about advancing themselves, so their learning was in no way superior to the other four houses. If a son succeeded in passing the examinations, it was as if he owed nothing to the rest of the lineage. A small number of the poorer members managed to leave home and find a place in business, working for someone or opening a shop to eke out a living. But the vast majority depended on rents from a few dozen mu of land, just floating along and engaging in nothing productive.

About half a kilometer west of Seven Mansions was a small market called Hongshengli, most of the inhabitants of which were also Qians. Every morning shortly after sunrise a contingent of thirty-odd persons of all ages would set out from Seven Mansions for the market to drink tea and eat noodles, not to return before noon. Some went back in the

---

*The core of Neo-Confucian teaching was based on four ancient texts: the *Analects of Confucius, Mencius*, the *Great Learning*, and the *Doctrine of the Mean*, collected and edited, with commentary, by Zhu Xi in the twelfth century.

†The *Four Books* were often grouped together with five classics to form the basic Confucian canon. The five were *Odes, Documents, Changes, Rites*, and *Spring and Autumn Annals*—all allegedly transmitted by Confucius to his followers. The *Tso Commentary* was an expansion of the *Spring and Autumn Annals*, a work of history.

afternoon and some just stayed all day, returning only in the evening. At home they raised canaries and crickets for fighting, amusing themselves with grand contests each spring and fall. Contestants sometimes traveled great distances to compete at Seven Mansions, or the local contestants would travel elsewhere to compete.

In addition to bird and cricket fights, there was a grand kite-flying festival every spring. No two kites were alike and they came in all sizes. One uncle of the fourth house, who had at least five or six hundred tubs of crickets, hired help to build a kite so large it took eight men to carry it to the fields. Strings of small baskets dangled from the kites so that the sound of whistling filled the air. At nightfall, lanterns hung from the kites, as many as twenty from the largest; the glow could be seen for miles around. Seven Mansions was renowned locally for this display and the lineage members, young and old, were delighted with themselves. By the time of my youth, the decline of the extended family was nearly complete.

4   My Grandfather, Master Juru

The only place in Seven Mansions from which the smell of books had not disappeared was Five Generations Together Hall. My great-grandfather, born in 1810, held the rank of imperial academy scholar, and my grandfather, born in 1832, was a county scholar. Of the former I knew nothing and will not presume to tell; the latter left behind a copy of the *Five Classics* in his own hand. My father had had a boxwood case made for it; the phrase "Bearing the copier's handprints," in his own calligraphy, was engraved on the case. The paper was the highest-quality Xuancheng.* The characters were large, resembling those in the *Imperial Four Treasuries* collection but more refined.† Each one was perfectly shaped—there was not a single reckless stroke in the entire work. And the density of the ink was consistent throughout, as if it had been a single day's work. The copy included only the texts, no commentary, but there were phonetic symbols in the margins. My brother informed me that our grandfather had excelled in phonetics and that these marginal notes were the results of his own original research. Unfortunately, I was unable to comprehend them.

xuanzhi is paper valued by calligraphers, produced in Xuancheng, Anhui.
†The *Imperial Four Treasuries*, or *Siku quanshu*, was the imperial compendium of the Qianlong emperor (r. 1736–95), copied by the emperor's finest calligraphers.

Grandfather was not a healthy man. He died at the age of thirty-seven, not long after completing this work. My brother pointed out to me that there were slight tear stains on the pages after the middle of the book, toward the end more and more. This was because Grandfather had an eye ailment by that time, and when he bent over the book his eyes ran and left these stains. My brother and I could not understand the texts, as there were no commentaries, but we examined those tear stains on the pages many times and I was left with an unforgettable impression.

There was also a large-character, woodblock print edition of the *Records of the Grand Historian* in the family that had been punctuated and underscored in five colors by my grandfather.* The margins and spaces between the lines were also filled with his critical notations. I have loved the *Records of the Grand Historian* from the time I first learned to read. It all started with this book. As I studied more, I learned that grandfather's punctuation and emphasis followed Gui Youguang and Fang Bao† and that his critical notes were similar to those in *A Bouquet from the Grand Historian*.‡ The notes were intellectually stimulating and they filled the pages of every chapter with comments from other works and Grandfather's own insights.

5   My Father's Boyhood Studies and Examinations

My father's name was Chengpei. He was born in 1866, the Year of the Tiger, in the Tongzhi period of the Qing Dynasty. When Grandfather died, Grandmother was forty-one and my father only three. He was a child prodigy and it was said that his eyes glowed with a certain lucidity, as if he could see through things. It was also said that he could see ghosts until the age of twelve. Grandmother directed his studies, which he took very seriously. There was no proper study in the house, but there were three dilapidated rooms behind the ruin beside the Plain Book Hall, where no one had lived since that side of the hall was demolished. Most likely they were vacated because the mystical symme-

---

*Shiji, by Sima Qian, the classic history of ancient China, was written in the first century B.C.

†Gui Youguang and Fang Bao were literary style-setters. The former propagated the *Shiji* in the sixteenth century, the latter in the eighteenth. An edition of the text was published with their comments.

‡*Shiji qinghualu*.

try (*feng-shui*) of the place had been destroyed. Father secluded himself there, braving the heat of summer and cold of winter, buried in his studies.

When mosquitoes raged on summer nights, Father thrust his legs into old wine jars and studied on. Every night he studied. Sometimes he worked on beyond midnight until someone had to call him home to bed; chances were, next morning he wouldn't remember who had called him. His first tutor was Old Mr. Wang of Yiqiao, some five kilometers south of Seven Mansions.

My brother and I could not find any examples of Father's early examination essays after he died. But we did find two composition books filled with rhyme-prose poetry. I used to enjoy chanting them; unfortunately, I've forgotten them all now. I remember two of the titles. One was a piece of rhyme-prose called "Mountains in Springtime, Laughing." I was fond of the mountain imagery, as one could just barely see from Seven Mansions a row of hills called Qinwang Shan. This piece was the beginning of my fondness for the parallel prose style of the post-Han period—I love to chant the works of the masters of that style—and for landscape painting.

Another rhyme-prose piece I remember was called "Yue Fei's Retreat." The rhyme scheme was determined by the eight-character line, "ten years' achievement wiped out in a day" (*shi nian zhi gong fei yu yi dan*). The last word in the last line of each of eight sections of the piece rhymed with the word whose place in that phrase corresponded to the number of the section. This ode to the Song patriot, Yue Fei, was the longest one in the book and I loved to chant it. My awareness of my national identity began here, as did my attention to the virtue of loyalty. But the versification itself was spiritually transforming. Later, as I came to know and love the accented, regulated prose style of the Song "ancient prose" masters, I was constantly reminded of my father's rhyme-prose piece.*

Father formally became a scholar at the age of sixteen, placing first in the county examination. The chief examiner called him in, together with the second-place candidate, and said to him, "Your prose is highly

---

*Yue Fei was the patriotic general who was executed for refusing to obey imperial orders to abandon the fight when the Song gave up north China to the Jurched Jin Dynasty in 1126. The Jurched were ancestors of the Manchus. Yue Fei became a folk hero and, in many places, a martial god. The stylists Qian refers to belong to a tradition that includes Sima Qian, Han Yu, Ouyang Xiu, and Gui Youguang.

expressive and perfect in form. You will excel as a writer, but finding someone who can appreciate your writing will not be easy." Then he said, "You are still young but your prose is well seasoned." Turning to the second-place scholar, he remarked, "Even though you are older, you rank below him on the list. But your prose is not yet seasoned. If you are fortunate, you may yet do better than he."

Father had always been physically weak. After becoming a candidate he took the provincial examination three times but fell ill in the examination cell each time, never completing it. After that he gave it up. One essay topic was on the passage from *Mencius,* "Qi is going to fortify Xue."* Father barely finished the essay before leaving, but it was meticulously written. It was an argument in the manner of the *Gongyang Commentary* (the progressive New Text school of criticism), focusing on the word *going to.*† The essay made him famous overnight and students began to seek him out. Altogether some forty people came to study with him. But when those who understood and mastered what he had to teach them tried the examinations and failed, he determined not to live by teaching.

6   The Sea of Caring Charitable Estate

There were three charitable estates owned by the Qian lineage of Seven Mansions. The oldest and largest had been founded by ancestors of the Five Generations Together Hall branch and was called the Sea of Caring estate. The estate hall and granary were located east of the village and this was the place where lineage meetings were held. As it happened, Five Generations Together Hall had become the poorest branch and had a large number of widows and orphans. There were insufficient funds to provide proper burial for poor widows or to educate the orphans. There was not even enough for marriage arrangements or for the support of people who wanted to leave the village in search of employment. The estate's resources were managed by the three wealthy houses and there was nothing Five Generations Together Hall could do about it.

Mencius, I.B:14 (D. C. Lau translation, p. 71). Mencius advises Duke Wen of Teng to do what he knows is best for the people, given the circumstances.

†*Gongyang* was a commentary on the *Spring and Autumn Annals,* which interpreted passages by analyzing Confucius's choice of words (the *Annals* are attributed to Confucius). As read by the New Text school, it was full of cryptic political messages.

Father had grown up as an orphan himself and he was especially sympathetic toward others of his own mansion. He knew that their ancestors had founded this estate to protect them against disaster and impoverishment. Now it was the estate that was improving while its owners declined. Father thought it should be opened up and put to its intended use of providing relief. He discussed this with the members of the wealthy houses who managed the estate, but to no avail. After several discussions they failed to reach an agreement and, as Father was dissatisfied with this hearing, he took his grievance to the county magistrate. The estate managers responded with a joint defense on behalf of the three wealthy houses.

Seven Mansions was thirty or forty kilometers from the county seat and the three wealthy houses all kept boats with glassed-in cabins for such trips. There was room to sit or lie down in them and they had all the comforts of home. Although the boats were moored on the creek at Seven Mansions, Father made the trip to Wuxi on foot. Had he been a healthy man, it might have taken half a day, but as it was, he set out at daybreak and arrived, exhausted, in the late afternoon.

When the magistrate read Father's complaint he was favorably disposed. But although Father's case was well grounded, it worried the magistrate that he was such a young and eager advocate. His opponents were not only more than twice his age, but they were articulate, well mannered, and familiar with official protocol as well. After careful deliberation, the magistrate sent them all home and urged them to reach an informal agreement.

Some months later, the two sides decided once again to seek a legal settlement. This time the wealthy elders invited Father to share their boat out of respect for his determination and sympathy for his poor health and impoverished circumstances. He accepted, riding in their boat and even sharing their accommodations in the city. But once they were in front of the magistrate, both sides held firm to their positions. After several such meetings, the magistrate grew to understand something of Father's character, and he summoned him to the yamen for a private talk. "I have read over your complaint several times," he said. "It is both compassionate and reasonable. And although you are raising points of contention you are not contentious, but sincere in your concern for fairness. What would you say to this? I could order them to turn over management of the estate to Five Generations Together Hall. How would that be?"

But Father protested, "The elders of my branch have no experience with that sort of enterprise. I'm afraid no one could do the job."

"Then why don't you do it?" the magistrate said.

"I am the youngest member of the youngest generation in the branch," father said. "I should not be given such a position."

"Then, what would you have done?" the magistrate asked.

"I would leave the estate's financial management in the hands of the other three houses," Father replied, "but I would try to put someone new in charge of distribution, to adjust the string on the bow, so that no one is cold and hungry."

"Who do you think should take charge of this?" asked the magistrate. When Father responded that uncle so-and-so of the second branch would be rather good, the magistrate said, "You are surely wrong. He is a peaceful and passive man. I don't think he would want the job."

"That is precisely why he would be good for it," Father said. The magistrate was delighted. "Of course, of course!" he said, jumping up. "I'll call in both sides tomorrow and we'll discuss it."

Next day the magistrate summoned Father and the other three to his office. "It is not right for members of a lineage to be involved in litigation among themselves for such a long time," he announced. "I have a plan that I hope will help you bring this case to a close. Tell me what you think of it." As no one objected, he turned to my father first and said, "I think it would be best to leave the estate under the supervision of the other three houses, as is their desire. What do you think?"

"That is what I have always preferred," Father said.

Then the magistrate turned to the other three. "I also think the estate should have a new manager who might help you to carry out some reforms. What do you all think?" All three nodded their agreement. Then the magistrate pointed to uncle so-and-so of the second branch and said, "You, sir, I hope you might be willing to take on this burden. What do you say?"

"Your honor shows such concern for the affairs of my humble lineage," he responded, "that even though I might be unable to do it myself, I shall continue to consult with the plaintiff's side when we return and see that your honor's sincere wishes are upheld."

"Very well," said the magistrate, and with that the case was decided. Once they had returned home, this same uncle so-and-so called

Father in and told him to draw up a detailed set of regulations for the charitable estate concerning welfare categories, relief payment periods, and the like. "We shall do just as you suggested," he said, "and hire someone to keep the welfare accounts of the estate." From then on, all the children of Five Generations Together Hall had enough to eat and the aged had something to depend on. Everyone enjoyed the protection their ancestors had provided for them, and no one came to grief. Nor was the property base endangered. Everyone in Five Generations Together Hall was pleased and the three wealthy houses accepted the regulations father drew up.

Soon after that, welfare recipients began coming to Father to complain about the miserable quality of the rice. Father had them bring him some samples, and with two small packets of this rice in his pockets, he went to the estate granary. The new clerk offered him tea and Father stayed for lunch. As they were eating, Father remarked, "You do all this work just for the weakest and poorest people in Five Generations Together Hall. But since this is the main part of your job, these weak and poor people are, in effect, your real masters!"

"That's right," the clerk admitted. Then Father displayed the contents of the packets he had brought with him and compared it with the rice they were eating. "This is what your real masters are eating," he said. "How is it that you eat so much better than they?" The clerk admitted his fault and the widows and orphans began to eat good rice.

After that, whenever anyone in Five Generations Together Hall had a family problem, great or small, they turned to Father. He could settle a dispute with a single word and sweep away grudges of long standing. Soon, the three wealthy houses began to call on him whenever there were lineage problems. Next they sent lineage members to him directly with their problems. And eventually he became the chief problem solver for the larger community of which Seven Mansions was a part. In effect, Father was both lineage head and local gentryman by the time he was thirty, and as public affairs pressed in on him, the life of the study slipped away. All of this occurred while my older brother was in the nursery. He heard it from Mother and passed it on to me.

I observed my father's efforts in one of these public affairs after we had moved to the town of Dangkou. I was ten years old. One evening after supper there was a knock on the door. It was a woman and her son, who was about my age, dressed all in white mourning clothes. When they saw my father they knelt down and knocked their heads on the floor, wailing, in spite of his efforts to get them to rise. By the time they were again on their feet, they were in tears. They told us they were Qians, like us, from a village many kilometers away in the neighboring prefecture of Suzhou. Their household was the richest in the village, but the woman's husband had died and this, the only son, had been adopted from outside the lineage. Another wealthy family of the lineage was trying to win their property by expelling the boy and forcing the mother to accept a designated heir. The designated heir was already grown, married, and father of a son. Although he was in no position to take her in, her property was to come under his control. The woman and her son were powerless to resist.

Someone had told them there was a man of the Qian clan in Wuxi who had extraordinary strength of character and was able to help people in trouble. Why shouldn't she try him? So she had packed up her goods in three cases and left the village under cover of darkness. Now they had arrived.

"I can't have these valuables here," Father told them. "I can only help you after you have taken them somewhere for safekeeping."

"But I brought them with me because there is no one near my village I can trust," she said. "And I don't even know anyone anyplace else. What can I do with them?"

"If you trust me, then take your things by boat to a certain gentry-man's house in Dangkou and beg him to keep these cases for you. If he is willing, then come back here." She did as he suggested and came back to spend the night.

I don't know the details of what followed, but I later heard that the woman kept her son and only a portion of the property went to the designated heir, and that this good deed owed entirely to my father's intervention. When Father died, both the mother and the son came to our house to pay their respects, dressed in mourning as if they were his own offspring. They made the long trip to our house several times before we moved back to Seven Mansions.

7   Receiving Father's Instruction

Father loved his children passionately. He said to his friends, "For me, getting a son is what getting a couple hundred mu of land is for others." I am told that I cried for three whole days after I was born and that Father paced the room with me, blending his voice with mine. He told people, "I guess this boy was intended for a nobleman's house and got born to us by mistake!"

Among my earliest memories is this: Whenever Father returned late from Hongshengli he brought back a treat—a small cake or sweet of some sort—and placed it on the table covered with a cap or a rice bowl. I would find it when I awoke and I was allowed to eat it first thing in the morning. But when I turned seven and started school there were no more treats in the morning.

"You have started school," Mother explained. "You are a young scholar now and should begin to learn about growing up. You are no different from your big brothers and sisters and should not expect treats any longer when you get up in the morning."

My next younger brother, whom Father loved dearly, died when he was still a baby. Father held his body and cried, "You must come back to us!" When my next little brother was born with a mole over his eyebrow, Father took it as a sign that his boy had indeed come back!

Father hired a tutor for my brother and for the son of the uncle who flew the big kites. His name was Hua and he came from Dangkou, the town just two or three kilometers east of Seven Mansions; he lived at my uncle's house. The tutor's son joined the others to make a class of three. The second year, Father signed me up too, and I bowed to the sage Confucius for the first time.

This tutor was extremely irritable. In the afternoon, after his nap, he would scowl at us and pace about the room nervously. But we were just foolish boys, and one day, when my brother and cousin were teasing me, I got a bit loud. The next day I was required suddenly to learn thirty characters rather than twenty. Fortunately, with some effort, I was able to remember them all the following day, but then the quota was increased again, to forty. The quota continued to increase in this manner until I was forced to remember seventy or eighty new characters in a day.

Under this pressure I once left the room to urinate and when I returned the teacher called me to his desk. "Why did you leave your seat?" he said, and he gave me ten hard strokes on the palm of my hand. After that I didn't dare to leave the room to urinate but I began to wet my pants rather badly. My mother would find me out when I got home and ask what had happened, but I wouldn't respond. When she learned the truth from my brother she said nothing more about it.

One day along about evening Father came to the classroom and stood behind me. I was chanting the introduction to Zhu Xi's *Commentary on the Great Learning* and had just come to the word *mo* in a passage that had not yet been explained to me.* Father pointed to the word and asked, "Do you know what this word means?"

"*Mo* is like *luo*," I said, "to fall into the water, as in *mo tou dian dao*, 'head under and topsy-turvy.'"

"How do you know that *mo* means to fall into the water?" he asked.

"I guessed it, because the character *mo* has the symbol for water in it," was my reply. Father patted my head and said to the teacher, "Maybe this boy learned to read in a previous incarnation!" Only then did the teacher begin to think I had any intelligence.

When Father told Mother this story, mother told him about how I had been wetting my pants. So at the end of the school year, Father released the teacher, closed the school, and moved the family to Dang-kou for the sake of our education. This time he found a reputable teacher, also named Hua, who lived by the market in the east side of a mansion called Kefu Hall. We rented a place in the west side of the hall to make it convenient for my brother and me. I was eight years old by then, and the teacher taught me two texts, an outline history and a geography in verse. I recall being especially fascinated by things like the length of the days and nights in Norway and Sweden. Unfortunately, by the time we finished those two books, the teacher became seriously ill and could not continue his classes. His students still went there, but all they did was play with the fish in the garden. Our education came to a halt.

After that, we moved again, this time to an old, multistory dwelling north of the marketplace. It faced north, and we were the sole residents. My brother and I no longer attended school. I spent the days sequestered behind a rock pile in the garden, sitting with my back to the wall, reading novels. As the sky darkened, I would crawl up onto

---

*The passage is "Ji Mengzi mo er qi chuan mang yan." Zhu Xi was the synthesizer of Neo-Confucian thought. His commentaries were the orthodox interpretation.

the roof to read. This was when I started learning how to see with my own eyes.

Mother's and Father's way of dealing with the children was not to use harsh words and stern looks when we did something wrong but rather to turn on the kindness, in the hope that we would discover the feeling of regret inside ourselves. A cousin of mine from Seven Mansions was staying with us in town during that time, and one day late in the afternoon he suggested that the two of us go home to the village. I was to tell "Auntie" of our plan. But when I told Mother, she assumed I was joking and paid me no mind. Only when we failed to appear at dinner did she realize we had gone. Father and his servant, Yang Sibao, came to fetch me in the middle of the night, lantern in hand. I woke up with a start, threw on my clothes and followed them home to Dangkou. Father said not one scolding word to me all the way home. Instead, we stopped in town for a bowl of dumplings. The rest of the family was waiting anxiously when we got home. "You had yourself a bowl of dumplings?!" they said. I had no trouble sleeping.

Every evening Father went to the opium den. That's where things got decided in town. Once father let Yang Sibao take me along. There were twenty-odd lounging platforms set up on three sides of a large room. One of the loungers spotted me and said, "I hear you can recite *The Romance of the Three Kingdoms* from memory. Is that right?" I nodded, and someone else said, "Will you try a bit for us?" I nodded again, and a third said, "I have a request!" It was the famous episode in chapter 43, "Zhuge Liang Disputes with the Scholars."*

So that evening I turned actor, reciting and playing the parts. When I finished, the loungers had nothing but good things to say to my father, who just nodded politely without a word.

The next evening Father let Yang Sibao take me again. But on the way, we came to a bridge and Father stopped to ask me a question.

"You know how to write the character *qiao*, meaning "bridge," don't you?"

"Yes I do," I answered.

"What is the signific in that character?" he asked.

"*Mu*, meaning 'wood,'" I answered.

"Now, what if you exchanged the signific 'wood' with the signific 'horse'?" he continued.

---

*The episode is recounted in chapter 2, above.

"Then it would become *jiao*," I said.

"Do you know what that word means?" he asked. It means "arrogant." I understood the word and told him so. Then he took hold of my arms and said softly, "Were you close to this *jiao* last night?"

Father's words struck me like a thunderclap. I lowered my head and had nothing to say. When we got to the opium den the loungers were all ready to hear another episode. One of them spoke up, "I have a request! How about the one in chapter 93, 'Zhuge Liang Shames Wang Lang to Death.'" But when they saw how ill at ease I was, they did not press me. After that, Father warned Yang Sibao not to invite me to go with them to the opium den. I was still only nine years old.

Every night Father went to the opium den, my mother and my sister retired, and my brother waited up to let Father in. Since my brother was in charge of me, he let me stay up late to keep him company. When we heard a knock on the door, he sent me scurrying off to bed before going down to open it. Father told my brother what to read while he was out, then he quizzed him on it when he returned. For a while Father had him reading the recent history of the Qing Dynasty and its civil servants, especially about Zeng Guofan's Xiang Army and the campaign against the Taiping rebels. I recall one night in particular when they came to the subject of Zeng Guoquan's recapture of Nanjing and the achievements of Li Chengdian and Xiao Fusi, who were the first to enter the city. Father explained that there were polite constraints in these passages.* Once my brother had finished his narration, Father said, "When you study, you must also understand the meaning of what is not said. For every word written, there may be three that are not written. For every sentence written, there may be three sentences not written. When you come upon such passages you must use your native intelligence or you won't know how to read them." Eavesdropping from my pillow, I was so excited I couldn't sleep, even though I didn't know what it was they were reading. After that I eavesdropped routinely. It was often after eleven before my brother came to bed. Father would dim the lamp and read on past midnight.

Father was very strict in his supervision of my brother's education, possibly because he knew he wasn't well himself. My brother competed

---

*The Qing reoccupation of Nanjing was a bloodbath. Qian's father was likely suggesting that the choice of words contained secret political meanings, as in the *Gongyang*.

in the last round of old-style examinations and didn't pass. Then a new primary school appeared in Dangkou, called the Guoyu School. It was the beginning of the new-style education in our area. Father sent both my brother and me there, where we were enrolled in the upper and lower schools respectively.

Since Father paid relatively little attention to my education and supervised me hardly at all, I was surprised one evening to overhear him saying to a couple of guests in the next room, "This boy also knows something about letters." He was referring to some essays I had written in school. They were imitations of essays of my brother's that I had seen at home, ten essays on Guan Yu, Zhang Fei, and other characters in *The Romance of the Three Kingdoms.* I had kept them a secret from my brother and to hear Father alluding to them was a shock. From then on, I was sometimes allowed to listen in as Father instructed my brother and to interrupt if there was something I knew and wanted to recite.

My father's health grew worse, until finally he could no longer visit the opium den. After that he just kept to himself, lying on his couch, smoking and eating, while mother and my sister sewed and spun and my brother studied. Occasionally Father would call me over to his opium couch and talk to me. He could talk for two hours without stopping. The others all teased me. "You're the ugliest of all the kids," they said, "but you hold his attention for the longest time. What is he chattering about?" I was embarrassed and couldn't tell them. Now that I think back on it, I cannot remember anything my father said to me during that time. But the essence of it was not so much head-on instruction as oblique insight. The meaning was so obscure to me, that I have not been able to make use of it. What a shame that this flood of nurturing advice from my father's troubled mind was wasted on me.

8 Father's Illness and Death

My fourth aunt and her husband, who lived in Shanghai, were acquainted with a certain Cantonese family in Hankou (Wuhan) called Zeng. My parents arranged for my sister to marry into this family. The formal introduction occurred in Shanghai, where the bridegroom and his father came as part of their business and where we sojourned for about a month in order to carry out interviews. It was upon returning to Dangkou from this sojourn that Father fell ill.

The doctors said he had consumption, and his breathing grew more and more phlegmatic. Sometimes he slept past eleven, and Mother sent me upstairs to rouse him and help him down to lunch. Father preferred light dishes to heavy ones. Under normal circumstances he would eat things like soup made with bream, silverfish with eggs, glutinous pork dumplings, smoke-dried fish, meatballs made of lean pork, boiled peeled shrimp, and the like. Mother was a superb cook, and when Father told her of some delicacy he had been served elsewhere, she would always be able to concoct it on the basis of what he told her, much to his pleasure. Now that he was ill, he scarcely ate a single dish served to him at lunchtime, and he ate only half a bowl of rice. In the evening he had a bowl of gruel. Mother prepared a variety of spiced and pickled dishes to go with this gruel. They were truly outstanding dishes, and although she taught her daughters-in-law how to make them after Father died, no one could make them the way Mother could. She knew that my brother and I liked these dishes, so she continued to make them for us when we came home for holidays. Eventually, my brother died, I moved away, and Mother grew old. Some forty years have passed since I last tasted those precious foods.

When Father's illness became grave we moved him downstairs, where he lingered, confined to his bed, for more than two months. In the night he would lie on his side facing the wall and words would often escape his mouth as he slept, words to the effect that it was still early and he could wait a little while. At first we didn't know what he meant. Then my fourth aunt from Shanghai came with her two sons, and other relatives came to stay with us, more each day.

Suddenly, on the twenty-third of the fourth moon, in the middle of the night, Father told the family, "Tomorrow morning I must go. It's time to leave instructions." He called my mother over first, then my brother, then me. He had only one thing to say to me: "You must study hard." Then mother led my two little brothers over, and Father said, "These two boys should follow their older brothers' instructions." Next came two younger cousins from the lineage. One belonged to Five Generations Together Hall and the other was the brother of the uncle who flew the big kites. Father had groomed these two to succeed him as leaders in lineage affairs. After that came our closest relatives, each for a separate word.

At the first sign of light, Father said, "There are many people in town who have been kind to me in my illness. I would like to take leave of them. If they come before ten in the morning I can wait for them. Tell the neighbors and have them spread the word." Once the sun was up, the neighbors were informed, the word spread, and they began to come. Father propped himself up against a tall pillow and met them as they came. He folded his hands as one does when taking one's leave and said, "I'll see you in the next life." There were store clerks, servants, even people he didn't know, who had heard the commotion and walked in off the street. Father took leave of them all with these same words. When ten o'clock came he said, "I'm going now" and closed his eyes. Outside, the mountain of fragrant flowers and paper bridges that people had sent was burned, and latecomers lingered by the flames.

Father was forty-one years old. The year was 1907, the thirty-second year of the Guangxu reign. My brother was eighteen; I was twelve; the little brothers were seven and three. Together with the sons of Father's brother, we assumed our ranks within the generation for purposes of mourning, my brother being first, I fourth, my younger brothers sixth and eighth.

9 Mother Joins the Family

My mother, née Cai, was born the same year as my father. Her family lived at the edge of a pond in a place called Cai Shi Tang, just north of Hongshengli. Her father and his brother were scholar-farmers. They raised fish and geese in the pond, which covered four or five mu, kept an ox, and hired three or four men to do the farmwork. One of the brothers was a teacher and the other practiced medicine.

When the go-between was negotiating with my mother's family, someone told them, "That house called Five Generations Together Hall is a perfect example of what's meant by the phrase, 'the saucepot is broken, but the rack it sits on remains.' The whole clan lives together on the edge of poverty but they keep up their pretentious style. I've heard that the prospective bridegroom is a student. If so, he's probably not at all practical. If you marry your daughter to him, you are asking for trouble."

But Mother's father thought differently. "A house that lives by the *Odes* and the *Rites* doesn't count its wealth in money," he said. "I'd like my daughter to go some place where they know the meaning of propriety" (that is, the rites). So he agreed to the marriage.

Father and Mother were married when both were sixteen, the year Father began to sit for the examinations. Father's parents were both alive then and they were immediately impressed. My grandfather shared responsibility for my great-grandparents with his six brothers. Each household cared for them in rotation for a period of five days. When it was Grandfather's turn, Mother became chief cook and had to provide meals that were both plenteous and nutritious. Her meals were so well received that my great-grandparents often invited their youngest son, whom they favored, and his family to come to the Hall of Profound Deliberation and share in the bounty.

My great-grandparents also admired the new bride for her attention to propriety, a quality that had become rare among lineage members. Males had forgotten about generational rank, and the names that would have indicated it were not even used. Instead, everyone had a nickname. For example, my fifth uncle in the western branch of the house had the character *ai,* meaning "love," in his name. But everyone called him Wogai, meaning "lid-lifter," as the two characters *wo* and *gai* had the sounds that the dictionaries used to indicate pronunciation of the initial and final phonemes in the word *ai.* My brother and I only learned his real name after we had grown up and made an investigation. Before that, we called him Uncle Wogai.

My father was known as Master Number Two and mother as Number Two's Bride. Everyone, including the lineage elders, called them that, even behind their backs. Father was busy; so when some lineage member came to him with a problem, it was often Mother who treated it. The disputants were usually older and of higher generational rank than mother, and she treated them with both sympathy and deference, so they could not leave feeling dissatisfied. Still, no matter how much she might bend the solution, she never contradicted Father's intent in the matter. So it was that the lineage members came to see Mother and Father as one.

When Father was tutoring examination candidates, a number of them occupied the rooms by the Plain Book Hall where Father had studied as a child. There were never fewer than six and sometimes there were more than ten of them, all grown men. Mother had to feed them, without the aid of a maidservant. She hired a couple of poor lineage members to help, but the brunt of the work was hers. The students learned to call her Worthy Mother Tutor, a title she was known by for decades thereafter.

Mother gave birth to four girls and five boys in twenty-six years of marriage. Only one of the girls survived, but of the boys she salvaged four. Mother and Father remained affectionate throughout their marriage. Even behind closed doors they treated each other with the respect some people reserve for public exposure. They never quarreled. Yet they were so busy we scarcely had time for family entertainment. I can remember only two family occasions. Once was during Dragon Boat Festival, the fifth day of the fifth moon, in Dangkou. People came all the way from Suzhou for a spectacular on Goose Lake. Father hired a boat for the family, and the townspeople put it at the head of a line of forty or fifty, right behind the dragon boat. On the dragon boat there were towers and pavilions four or five stories high, full of musicians. The lanterns lit up the sky and the sound of gongs and drums, strings and pipes filled the air. The flotilla slithered into town on the canal from Goose Lake while the townspeople poured out of their houses and lined the banks. The family sat up front in the boat's cabin to take in the sights. We didn't get home until midnight.

The other occasion was the winter fishing spectacular. Goose Lake was two-and-a-half kilometers across and five kilometers long. Normally fishing was forbidden, but one day each winter the lake was opened.* On this occasion, people sank nets, used cormorants, or dropped lines from rowboats, and the townspeople turned out in pleasure boats to watch. One year Father hired a boat for the family and we wobbled to and fro, taking it all in. People shouted to their acquaintances across the water, and young people sometimes leapt crazily to their friends' boats. Fishermen offered us their catches and we cooked and ate fish on board. We set out in the chill of dawn and returned in the glimmer of sunset, moved by the play of the clouds' shadows with their reflections in the water. The thrill of it has never been equalled. The next day, dozens of fish arrived from well-wishers around town. Most were pickled and saved for New Year's. In my experience, however, family occasions were either occasions for hard work or for rest. Only twice were they for entertainment.

---

*Fishing was licensed and commercialized, so that normally only fisher households worked the larger lakes (Shen Xiaodi, December 3, 1985).

10   Mother as a Widow

The community respected Father for his literary talent and trustworthiness, but he never spoke of his private needs to them. Although he was constantly exchanging favors with people, he observed the strictest proprieties and was never casual or extravagant, nor did he display his poverty to others. No one was aware of our economic situation. My cousin once had a conversation with a stranger on the street in which the stranger kept remarking on how self-effacing my father was. My cousin told him, "Everyone knows what kind of person my uncle is but no one knows about his economy!" When father heard about it he scolded my brother and my cousin. "Every family's economy is different. Young people should not ask about such things and you should never discuss them with strangers." So it was too with Mother. Never, in all her daily business with her relatives, did she mention the family economy.

Not until my father's wake did our kinsmen, who gathered at the house, realize what the family's circumstances were. They urged us to accept relief from the Sea of Caring Charitable Estate, as we were clearly eligible. But Mother refused. In tears she said, "My husband often told me that nothing left him as shaken as that case against the lineage uncles over the charitable estate. The only way he could redeem his guilt even the slightest bit was to disavow any selfish interest in that estate. His casket is not even in the ground yet! How could we face him in the other world if we took rice from the estate now?"

But the relatives argued, "He never had a selfish interest in anything. His kinsmen know that and even the man in the street knows it. It was the intention of a long line of ancestors that the charitable estate should provide relief for widows and orphans. The widows and orphans who have taken relief are too many to count. How could those of us who remember forgive ourselves if you, alone, did not take it?"

There was nothing else Mother could do. She called my brother and me over and stood us there and said, "Did you two hear that? At least you can resolve yourselves to become self-sufficient as soon as possible."

Mother was illiterate and had been married at the age of sixteen. My earliest memories are of things I picked up from the conversations between her and my older brother and sister. Later, as I reflected on them, I realized that Mother never instructed or reprimanded us, but only chatted about daily life. Yet the talk always eventually led to Grandmother or to Father, who were her authorities on everything involving the lineage or the community. Although she seemed only to speak of trifles, of idle gossip, in fact she was instructing us and there was always something at the heart of her words.

After Father died, his authority was even more evident in Mother's words. No matter how destitute and isolated the family was, we children never knew the bitterness of poverty or the loneliness of the orphan. Father's spirit was with us, all around us. Every day we heard about something Father had said or done, and this was our only joy.

The year Father passed away we moved to another part of Dangkou, right next to the Guoyu School. That New Year's Eve was a terrible one. My brother went to Seven Mansions to pick up the stipend from the charitable estate in the afternoon. My next younger brother was in bed with a fever, clutching the quilt, intermittently too hot and too cold. Mother and little brother were watching over him, and I sat alone at the threshold, waiting for my brother's return. Wisps of incense and the sound of firecrackers emanated from the neighbors' houses. There was a wealthy old couple from Huizhou (in Anhui) who lived in our compound, and when they noticed there were no lanterns in our windows and no fire in our stove, they wanted to have us over for the New Year's meal. Mother kept refusing and they kept inviting us, until she told them, "I don't mean to be unappreciative, but we have to wait until my eldest returns, because we have to burn incense to the ancestors together before we can prepare dinner." After that, the old couple never stopped praising Mother for her unexcelled attention to family affairs. My brother came hustling home in the evening mist, then he went out once more for ceremonial goods. We burned the incense and made our offerings to the ancestors, and only then did we put together a hasty meal, well into the night.

When Father was alive, we did not pay cash at the shops in town but settled our accounts on New Year's Eve. After Father died, Mother often sent me out to buy things. One day she sent me for some soy sauce and told me to pay cash for it. But no matter how much I insisted, the shopkeeper would not accept payment. "Your family can buy on account. What are you worried about?" It was the same everywhere; I had to keep the cash.

"But this means trouble," Mother said. "We could always get by when your father was alive, so long as we economized. But it's different now. What if we are unable to pay at New Year's?"

The shopkeepers' custom was to send bill collectors out on New Year's Eve, starting in the villages, then covering the town, neighborhood by neighborhood, family by family, saving the most dependable until last. They never reached our house until after midnight, and some didn't arrive until it was light. The custom was to keep a lantern lit to show that the night was not over. Mother had us watch to see that the gate wasn't locked so that no one could claim we were in arrears. We often sat up all night waiting, and some collectors never did show up. Mother's response to that was, "When you have money, you don't need to keep accounts in your head; but when you have none, how can your head hold anything else!" So it was until we moved back to Seven Mansions and my brother and I started teaching. Then we turned over our earnings to Mother each month, and at New Year's we gathered in her room, opened the drawer, took out the eight or ten yuan that remained, and said with happy faces, "There's a surplus again this year!"

After Father died my mother received numerous offers from relatives to provide introductions for my brother to trading companies in Suzhou and Wuxi, but she turned them down. "My husband put his heart into the boys' education," she said, "and the oldest hasn't finished yet. It was my husband's will to preserve a few seeds of learning for the Qian lineage. I must respect that. I can't let our son abort his education."

The following winter, the new Changzhou prefectural high school was established. My brother passed the entrance examination for the teacher's training class, and I passed the examination for middle school. The teacher's training class was to graduate after one year. It was a class of forty, most of whom were over thirty years old; some were grandfathers. My brother was just nineteen, but because he was intelligent and respectful, he was made class president. The superintendent wondered at his intentions.

"You are a young man and should be thinking about more advanced studies," he said. "Why throw your lot in with the teachers' training class?" My brother told him that he needed to support his mother and his brothers, so the school gave him a stipend and put him in charge of the physics and chemistry laboratory.

My brother graduated first in his class the following year. His superiors and even his classmates were ready to recommend him for available teaching jobs, but he preferred to return home, where he could look after Mother and do some good for the village. The lineage at Seven Mansions hailed his return and used income from the three charitable estates to build a school for all the children of the lineage. The school was named Youxin, meaning "renewal." My brother was principal and the school hired two additional teachers, one a former student of my father's and the other a classmate of my brother's. Both were over forty.

Now that my brother had a job, Mother gave up the relief payments from the Sea of Caring Charitable Estate. But since my brother earned only ten yuan a month, the family was in even more desperate straits. Fortunately, the principal of the Guoyu School got me a scholarship from a benevolent association in Wuxi City, and I was able to continue my studies.

When my brother finally married, the following year, the entire lineage at Seven Mansions celebrated the event. Not since Father's and Mother's wedding, thirty years earlier, had there been such a wedding ceremony at the Hall of Profound Deliberation. Mother sat in her room, choking on her tears, until the ceremony progressed from the paying of respect to Heaven and Earth to the paying of respect to parents. The crowd brought Mother from her room to the hall. She was wiping her tears as I watched from the side, overcome with melancholy. I reflected on the years since Father's death and the present moment seemed only a dream.

My brother's reputation continued to grow. In addition to being head of the primary school, he began to take on the affairs of the lineage. The spirit of felicity returned to Seven Mansions.

In 1911, the year of the Revolution, I transferred to Chongying Middle School in Nanjing. That summer I was stricken with typhoid, for which I received improper medication, and nearly died. A well-known physician by the name of Shen lived in Houzhai, some five kilometers away. He had a deep respect for my father and brother and had arranged for his daughter to marry me. The arrangement was made after Father's death, and he had invited my brother and me to his home. He told his sons, "Now we are relatives, and you shall have the additional guidance of two exemplary brothers."

Under normal circumstances it took most of the day and well into the night to walk to Houzhai for medical aid and back again. If one went by boat, one would not return until the next morning. When the doctor heard I was ill, he said, "I had better go to my son-in-law and not wait for him to come here!" He made the trip many times and saw to my recovery. Unfortunately, my intended bride died, but her brother, who went on to make a name for himself in Western medicine at Tongji University in Shanghai, always treated us as relatives.

My nurse during this illness was my mother, who was by my bedside from dawn to dusk and who shared my bed at night. Without a fan in the intense heat, she never allowed her eyelids to droop. When after two months, I was at last able to consume a thin gruel, Mother rose before dawn to prepare condiments. After three months I could take plain rice. During this illness, I received a second life. It was a gift from my mother who nurtured me. To keep this gift always within my memory, I have named my house in Waishuangqi, outside Taipei, Plain Book Building, after the hall we lived in at the time.*

After three months of illness, the very first day I went back on a normal diet, I demanded to return to school. My brother packed my bags, and the next day I took a boat from Hongshengli to Wangting Station, where I boarded the train for Nanjing. It was the twentieth of the eighth moon (October 11, 1911), but only after I was seated on the train did I learn from the newspaper of the revolutionary uprising in Wuhan the night before.

My classmates had scattered by the time I arrived at the school, but I decided to stay and join the revolutionary army when it reached Nanjing. I stayed at the school, foolishly, until events reached a crisis. Suddenly, the school was closed to everyone. Teachers, students, and staff were forced to leave. The last train out of Nanjing did not stop in Wuxi, so I had to ride to Shanghai. It was the ninth of the ninth moon, and revolutionary flags and slogans were in evidence everywhere. I had lost contact with my family and when I finally got home my mother hugged my head to her body. Close to tears, she said, "I had hardly celebrated your coming back to this life before I thought I would not see you until the next."

In Seven Mansions we organized a self-defense corps. My brother

---

Su Shu Lou: the derivation of the name is obscure. It is either from one of four categories in the Han Dynasty's imperial library, where historical records were stored, or from a Han syncretic Taoist text.

was captain and my uncles were all corpsmen. We procured some breech-loading rifles in Shanghai and I was named drill instructor. I taught my uncles the military drills I had learned in school and how to follow commands. We also hired an instructor in martial arts—boxing and sword-fighting. Every night we posted sentries all around the village. My brother and I and the elder uncles were the inspectors. We linked ourselves to neighboring village corps, all of which were under my brother's command. He was twenty-three then, and I was seventeen.

I did not return to school the following spring because the village situation was still unsettled. I was unwilling to be so far away, but neither was there any way to pay my tuition. So my brother got me a teaching job at a newly consolidated primary school in a certain Qin Family Village, just three or four kilometers from home. This was the beginning of my teaching career, which has continued for sixty-three years now. My brother sent our next youngest brother, who was just thirteen, with me. He said, "You may be a better teacher for him than I can be, and I would like him to get used to being away from home." The next year the third brother went on to Changzhou Middle School.

I was married in 1917, and shortly after that, Five Generations Together Hall suffered two fires. The first was in the front, where no one was living. The second was on the east side of the Plain Book Hall, where Mother was living with me and my wife. The two bedrooms and a study were reduced to ashes. The copy of the *Five Classics* in my grandfather's hand, his punctuations and annotations of the *Records of the Grand Historian,* and father's compositions were all lost to the same blaze. Five Generations Together Hall had become an unbearable wasteland, and since we now had no place to live, we moved once more to Dangkou. My sister brought us enough clothing to cover our bodies, but Mother suffered a stomach ailment, was able to take nothing but liquids for a whole month, and didn't recover for half a year.

Eventually, my youngest brother graduated from Changzhou Middle School, and the four of us had all become teachers. The two younger ones married on the same day, and after that we had a fraternal conference. My brother told us, "It is time to take the burden off Mother and divide the household. We're going to have separate stoves." Since the younger ones' wives were new and unfamiliar with Mother's moods, they could not be expected to serve her; so they were exempted.

"But now I have nothing to do," Mother said. "Let me help my grandson with his lessons." So she tended the lamp and listened to her grandson recite his lessons every night. Whenever I was home I joined them. We were three generations together at the table. It is a kind of recreation that the poor can enjoy.

My older brother's and my styles, or literary names, which indicated our rank in the mourning grade, were chosen by my father. With the revolution of 1911, we changed our given names to erase the heritage of the Qing Dynasty that was reflected in them. The younger brothers' names and styles were chosen by my older brother. And my older brother's son's name was chosen by me.

11   My Brother's Death and Mother's Last Years

My wife and her newborn infant both died in the summer of 1928. My brother was teaching at the new private middle school built by the Rong family in Rongxiang, west of Wuxi. He came home to help me make the funeral arrangements. The strain was too much for him. An old stomach ailment flared up and, before we knew what had happened, he too had passed away. Three tragic deaths in two months' time.

My brother was only forty-one and left a wife, two sons and two daughters. His eldest son, who was sixteen, followed me to Suzhou and entered high school there.* My brother thus joined his father and grandfather in failing to live to an advanced age, and for the third consecutive generation there were widows and orphans in our household. One can imagine my mother's grief at having to endure such a tragedy once again.

My brother loved music. He could play many instruments and was especially skilled at the Chinese mandolin and pipes. I played the flute, and when we were home for summer and winter holidays we often played together. My brother was also good at directing gong and drum ensembles. At spring festival time the sound of gongs and drums, under my brother's direction, filled the air above the Hall of Profound

*Qian Weichang originally intended to specialize in Chinese history and literature, following his uncle's excellent tutoring. He later graduated from Qinghua University and the University of Toronto and earned an international reputation in physics. In 1986 he was a national leader of China's scientific community (I interviewed him on May 29, 1986).

Deliberation. He was also a talented calligrapher, and traces of his ink found their way to the city and were spread around the countryside.

After my brother died, I kept a copy of the classic narrative history, *A Comprehensive Mirror for Good Government,* in ten volumes which he had punctuated by hand. When the war broke out, I had to leave some fifty thousand volumes in Beiping as I fled south. All fifty thousand were entrusted to a bookshop for a hundred piculs of rice. Later in Hong Kong, of the fifty thousand only these ten found their way back into my hands. That is something to marvel at.

My brother also loved to chant poetry, and Zeng Guofan's *Poems Copied from the Works of Eighteen Masters* was always at his fingertips. He was especially fond of Lu You's seven-syllable regulated verses, which served as a model for the poems he wrote.* After he died, I selected three hundred of his own poems, had them printed, and distributed them to his closest friends and best students. Unfortunately I no longer have a copy and I wonder if there are any left on the mainland.

A year after this tragedy I remarried in Suzhou and Mother came to live with me there. When we moved to Beiping, Mother went with us. Then, when the wind turned foul with news of the Manchurian Incident, I took her south again, promising to return for her when the wind subsided. But Mother refused to hear of it.

"Your father's and brother's fate was to die young," she said, "but you three are all on your own now. Your nephew has passed the entrance exams at Qinghua University; so the next generation has started to college. What more could I want? I just don't want to die of cold or starvation, and I am assured of that. I won't miss the comforts of Beiping. Besides, life must end and I am growing old. What if I should die up north? It would be a burden for you to bring me home for burial." It was clear that Mother had made up her mind, so I took her to live with my little brother in Dangkou.

When Mother turned seventy, I returned from Beiping to Dangkou during the summer to celebrate. She was in good health and her spirits were high. A stream of well-wishers poured into Dangkou from Seven Mansions and elsewhere. Farmers and merchants, servants and housemaids, Mother received them all cordially and tirelessly. I could see

---

*Lu You was another patriot who was removed from office in the Southern Song period. One traditional school of poetry writing began with him.

then that she was happy to be able to live without changing her way of life. In three months' time I never felt it appropriate to mention her age. It was all I could do to persuade her to undergo a physical examination in Wuxi and to spend the afternoon with me and the other brother's family at Turtle Head Islet on Lake Taihu.

12   Mother's Death

When the war broke out, I went south alone to Changsha and Kunming. During the summer of 1939 I returned alone to Suzhou. My wife also returned from Beiping with the children, and Mother joined us. During the war, my mother had been living with my three brothers' families in Dangkou, and this was her first chance to see my three sons and my daughter since the war began. Although she had known the oldest boy, the second had been an infant and the other two had not been born. Now she looked over the whole brood like a mother hen. I found an abandoned house with a garden and settled the family there. I changed my name, locking myself in the house, and kept Mother company for a year.

Mother, who was seventy-six then, could still prepare a fine meal all by herself. She would make something I had always liked and we would eat it together. She ate as much as I did, and that made me happy. But rather than talk about the past, she preferred spoiling the children in the garden, which she did everyday.

In the autumn of 1940, I returned alone to the interior, leaving Mother for the last time. She brought the children from the garden and accompanied me to the front gate, some several hundred paces. I watched her expression as she blurted out her feelings on that walk. It was totally absorbing. Later in the season she was bitten by mosquitoes in the garden and stricken with fever. The family had two good friends who were physicians. One was Doctor Shen, the graduate of Tongji University in Shanghai. The other, who was even better known than he was, was the daughter of my friend and colleague Xu Peiruo and a graduate of Union Medical School in Beiping. Both of them treated my mother with the greatest respect and were willing to interrupt anything to see her at a moment's notice. They both agreed that she should have quinine for the fever because of her age, but it unexpectedly aggravated the stomach ailment she had had for forty years. Her digestion failed, and on the fifth day of the new lunar year, 1941, she died. Everyone from the four brothers' families, except for myself in Chengdu and my eldest nephew in America, was by her side. And they saw to her burial. Mother was seventy-seven and I was forty-eight.

As I reflect on my life, I realize that I hardly knew my father. What little I did know of him, I learned from my mother and brother. And most of what I learned from my brother, he learned from her. As for me and my mother, we spent little time together and much apart. I was still in primary school when Father died, so I was with her mornings and evenings. But at thirteen I started middle school and could only be with her for school holidays. In 1912, I started teaching and still could see her only on holidays. She was with me for half a year in Suzhou in 1930, then a year and a half in Beiping. After that, I had her company for a year in the garden in Suzhou during the war. When we parted, she could not accompany me beyond the gate, nor could friends or relatives share the pain of parting with us. Although my life spans the entire life of the Chinese republic, I spent only three of my adult years in the company of my mother.

On the outside, Mother was kind. On the inside, she was tough. In her dealings with others she gave much and took little. I have often reflected on how the ancients likened parental love to the light of springtime. Whenever I was with her, I could feel this light in my body. Even a cat or a chicken in the house could feel it. Now more than thirty-two years have passed since she died. My shortcomings multiply, but when I reflect on my mother, her tenderness and compassion are there to diminish them and give me renewed life. Her spirit has nurtured me, day after day, for eighty years. If these reflections fail to capture one ten-thousandth of the reality that she was in life, neither do they exhaust even one ten-thousandth of what remains of her in my heart. Even if I could succeed in displaying this heart to all the other orphans of this world, so that my heart might no longer be alone, how could I repay Father and Mother in the other world?

Magnificent Heaven, is there a limit to my sorrow?!

Written during six days at Pear Mountain Inn, Martial Wood Farm, and the T'ien-hsiang China Travel Association, and two nights in Hualien, this being the second, at 9:00 P.M. on the anniversary of my birth of seventy-nine years ago (July 30, 1895), by an unfilial son, with profound respect.

V.

The Red Gate Revisited

IN EARLY APRIL 1986 I returned to the red gate in the hills north of Taipei. As I climbed the steps this time my head was filled with conflicting images. I had been to Seven Mansions and I could hear the gentle lapping of the waves against the sides of transport boats on Whistle-and-Swagger Creek. I could feel the earth in the ruins of Five Generations Together Hall under my feet, smell the musty air in the office of the little primary school at the Sea of Caring Charitable Estate, savor the delicate flavors of the local freshwater fishes consumed at the great round table my hosts had moved from the old lineage meeting hall to their home. I had kowtowed at the tomb of Wu Taibo on Hongshan and watched the young craftsman carve the delicate features of Taibo's image in the Taibomiao temple in Meicun, which was being restored. I had felt the spirits of the ancestors by the site of the floating tomb, now a mulberry field; by the dikes at the edge of Goose Lake; in the granaries of the Old Hua Charitable Estate; and at the offices of the Dangkou primary school, where Qian Mu had studied and taught. Beneath this jumble of images rumbled the voices of dozens of local informants in their sixties, seventies, and eighties—teachers, merchants, peasants, musicians, itinerant priests, servants—men and women of the old world who, along with Qian Mu himself, had helped me to make sense of it. But superimposed on these images were the signs of revolutionary upheaval and postrevolutionary development.

Gone are the landlords; gone are the temples; gone are the ancestral tombs. Ancient ginkgo trees stand forlorn in the untended gardens
whose once-sacred buildings have long since been dismantled by peasants in need of bricks. The central canal of Dangkou has become a
road, the Taoist temple a storehouse; the fifteenth-century bridge has
been removed to accommodate traffic. New houses are rapidly replac-
ing the old, as glass fronts appear here and there on shops lining the
main streets, displaying the goods that symbolize the prosperity of the
post-Mao era. Bicycles and motorbikes, radios, cassette players, and
television sets are finding their places alongside manufactured clothing
and canned goods. Across the street in Dangkou a toy factory, a label-
printing factory, and a factory producing heavy wire-pulling machinery for export summon laborers from peasant households in nearby
villages. They stream out from the front gates on their bicycles when
the whistle sounds at 4:00 P.M. and hurry about their marketing before
joining the river of traffic flowing down to the villages. Their new
homes, many times more spacious than the cramped quarters of
China's citydwellers, stand in two-storied rows amid the rice or wheat,
depending on the season. Freshly whitewashed, the housing conveys a
sense of dignity, of rightness, of happiness when compared to the
remaining dilapidated single-story dwellings that are about all that is
left of the old peasant world. On the site of the old Hongsheng charitable estate and spreading far beyond it is a factory producing heavy
cutting machinery. On the site of the Ganlu temple complex, a valve
factory surrounds a little courtyard where the ancient ginkgo trees still
thrive. When I visited in November, the new Hongsheng public audito-
rium was playing host to an eagerly anticipated performance of traditional Shanghai drama by a theatrical group from the big city. The
trucks bearing their heavy industrial loads competed for space with
bicycles on the narrow highway linking the land of streams with Wuxi
City, the railroad, and the world beyond.

Now, once again, I passed up those steps from the high-rise, motor-
ized bustle of Taipei to the serenity of Qian Mu's hillside home, in
search of the spirit of 1911. "Do you believe there is hope for the
mainland?" Qian Mu asked after an hour of conversation about the
changes that had come to Seven Mansions since he last saw it, some
sixty years before. The question ripped through the jumble of images

like a straying rocket. What could it mean? Certainly not hope that the old world might be restored. Certainly not hope that Western-style democracy might suddenly blossom. And the thought that hope is embodied in material wealth is alien to Qian Mu's mind. Qian's hope for China remains the hope of a generation that looked *forward* to the 1911 revolution as a significant turning point in the long decline of Chinese cultural values. The hope was that once the yoke of autocracy was lifted, the Chinese spirit would rise and conquer the bad habits that plagued the people as a result of centuries of political oppression. A strong and unified China would nurture the values that had always produced statesmen and scholars who were humane and selfless in the pursuit of public welfare and national strength.

Qian's "Reminiscences" resonate with the spirit that his revolution would liberate and his new China would nurture. And who could deny its value? Is Qian Mu's question so different from that of any other child of the modern world? To what ends do we strive in the industrial and postindustrial age? What constitutes self-fulfillment and is it or is it not enhanced by self-sacrifice? And commitment to what? For Qian Mu the answers to these questions are conveyed by the spirit that he says is declining in his own body but that he hopes to immortalize in the story of his parents. Does this spirit survive? Is the moral vision of the generation that looked forward to 1911 relevant to the future of China?

The dominant conception of history in China, which is Marxist, rejects the relevance of Qian Mu's vision. The motive force in history is seen as materialistic, and the revolution has changed the material conditions of Chinese culture. For the historian trained in China's new culture, Qian Mu's "spirit" is merely a veil obscuring the truth about social conditions that have disappeared. To this foreign observer, however, the problem is more complex than that. Although it is a fact that changing material conditions render Qian's moral vision increasingly alien, the need to replace it with something more relevant is equally clear.

To borrow Qian Mu's metaphor and alter its meaning, the heart and mind of the old culture are nearly gone now but the heart and mind of the new one have yet to mature. In the meantime, fingers and toes everywhere continue to adapt to the modern environment. Conditions at the local level are changing rapidly as a result of revolution and postrevolutionary development. Yet local practice continues to embody certain moral principles and to legitimize the interests of emergent social groups.

Consider first the changes. In the world around Seven Mansions four tendencies are pronounced: rural industrialization, universal education, the transformation of folk religion, and the growth of a new communications network. In an essay directed at restless students during the war, Qian Mu attributed the peculiar emphasis on filial love in Chinese culture to the nature of north Chinese peasant life in ancient times. It was because Chinese peasants were so sedentary and the land was so stingy that sons were kept at home and the father-son relationship became the standard measure for human love.[1] Elsewhere, in a lecture on "spirit" and "method" in the study of history, he argued that one should study the common people if one wanted to know what the spirit of Chinese history was.[2] We have seen that in 1911 both the peasant households and the gentry lineages in the land of streams were bound to the land, and then, as now, 80 percent of the Chinese population lived in rural villages. The links between Confucian thought, peasant family life, and the structure of power could not be more clear, and these links brought popular morality to bear on the power holders as surely as they brought the power holders' ideology to bear on the people's ways. But the growth of rural industry in the land of streams has changed the rules.[3]

In 1985 fully one-third of the workforce of 12,000 in Hongsheng Township, which includes Seven Mansions, was engaged in wage labor in township and village enterprises.[4] One of the slowest townships to develop the new policies in Wuxi County, Hongsheng's per capita income was nonetheless six times greater than in 1978 (unadjusted). In Dangkou it was nine times greater, and 7,500 of the workforce of 12,000 there worked in factories for a wage. There were thirty-three factories in Dangkou, their gross product reaching 80 million yuan, nearly ten times the gross agricultural product of the township. The figures for Ganlu are similar; Houzhai falls somewhere between Dangkou and Hongsheng. On the other side of the county, where growth has been faster, Qianzhou township employs 82 percent of its workforce in factories, and the single administrative village (formerly brigade) of Xitang, with a gross industrial product of 26 million yuan, employs 1,300 wage earners—more than its own workforce can provide. This startling growth in rural industry is not typical of China as a whole—Xitang is reputed to be the richest village in China, and the poorest in China have nowhere near the wealth of Hongsheng—but the wave of the future has clearly started rolling here. Peasants are becoming industrial wage earners without leaving their villages, and the impact on peasant culture can already be seen.

Peasants no longer count their wealth in land rights. Under the current system the land is publicly owned. About half is entrusted to households on a per capita basis, and the rest is contracted out by the township. Contractors sell a quota of grain to the state and the rest on the free market. A mu of land produces three to four times the rice and four to six times the wheat it did before liberation, the state supports the price of grain, and the free market price is higher than the state's. Townships subsidize contractors with equipment, services, and bonuses, financed by growing industries. And yet virtually no one under the age of forty wants to contract. In Hongsheng, where industrial growth has been relatively slow, only 88 of some 7,000 households contracted for more than five mu, and only 500 were registered as principally engaged in agricultural production for the market. In industry-rich Qianzhou, to encourage agricultural production, contractors are paid 300 yuan per mu in bonuses. Factories close during planting and harvest times to allow the workers to till their land. Whether the land remains public in the future or is given over to private enterprise, the change in peasant attitudes and strategies demands that farming be made more profitable and less exhausting. This means mechanization and farming on a larger scale.

At the moment it is the managers of township enterprises, together with local administrators and party leaders, who determine the value of labor and the distribution of profits. They have, in effect, replaced the landlords, rice merchants, and charitable estate managers in the land of streams; and wages, bonuses and public services have replaced grain sales, rent reduction, and charity. The wage-earning peasant is more dependent than ever on public leaders and less than ever on the family. Whatever inheritance there is to be divided, it does not include land. Both sons and daughters now leave the family with income in hand, perhaps to marry a fellow worker or the relative of one. The currents of obligation and dependency that ran through the old culture have been broken up and redirected in ways that deprive the old symbols of meaning.

In the old culture as Qian Mu describes it, the spirit of the rites was carried from the family to the councils of government by a class of scholar-officials. It was they who determined the content of education in the old China. And the very process of learning to read and write gave the rites meaning. Respect for the teacher, who was living proof of the separation of learning from the sources of wealth, was respect for the ancient sages and former scholars and for the class of people who kept their wisdom alive. But universal education has changed the rules.

The education Qian Mu himself received was that of a member of the scholar-gentry class, for which family instruction, public education, and job preparation were inseparable. Literacy was only a small part of this "learning." The schools that Qian Mu's generation started were an extension of scholar-gentry patronage; its teachers were scholar-gentry sons and daughters. Although Qian Mu felt the impact of the new curriculum in 1920 as the literary language gave place to the vernacular, universal education was still a long way off. Before the 1950s there were still only two lower middle schools in the entire area, and primary schools existed only in the towns. By 1958, however, all children between the ages of six and twelve were in school, and lower middle schools existed in every town. In 1985 nearly all primary school graduates went on to middle school, and about one-fourth of the graduates of lower middle schools went on to upper middle school in their own townships. The best went to target schools in Meicun or the city. Everyone in the new culture spends most of his or her time for nine years—or ten or eleven, depending on the extent of the local kindergarten facilities—in the public school. And everyone sees the chance of spending at least three more.

The ironic result is that literacy—the tool that gave the scholar-gentry class access to power and prestige—has been devalued. Everyone learns the national language and most speak it with less of an accent than Qian Mu and other teachers of his generation. No one has to read classics to gain literacy, and no moral or social status is attached to the ability to read. Higher education, on the other hand, still promises higher status. The difference is that higher education is technical and has nothing to do with the moral values that used to be taught with literacy itself. The local teachers, as poor as ever, have lost the status they used to enjoy.

What, then, of the irrational aspect of the peasant mind which the Confucian spirit used to keep in check? In Qian Mu's view, it was the dominance of Confucian ethical thinking, which was this-worldly and humanistic, that distinguished Chinese culture from those of Europe and South Asia. Neither a political struggle between sacred and secular institutions nor a belief in life after death was central to the course of Chinese history. The culture had disposed of these problems. In "The Ethical Spirit in Chinese History," a lecture he delivered in 1950, Qian defined "the spirit of the culture"—the motive force of history—as a Confucian ethical idea. Central to it are the beliefs that the spirit of a person lives on in the minds of others, and that human nature tends to goodness rather than evil. The road to eternal life is, in the words of an ancient sage, to make one's worth, one's work, and one's words stand up by themselves (*li de, li gong, li yan*). If one can do this, then one's spirit lives on. The guide to success in this endeavor is love and respect for other human beings. Sages great and small have moved Chinese history with their faith in these principles, Qian argued. That's how Chinese civilization spread.

To demonstrate the process, Qian raised the dramatic example of Wu Feng, whose temple stands in a valley in Taiwan where headhunting aborigines once plagued Chinese settlers. Legend has it that Wu Feng was a spokesman for the settlers whose voice could also be heard in high places. For years he mediated disputes between the two cultures and the aborigine chieftain came to trust him. When Wu tried to persuade the chief to give up the custom of headhunting, he was told that the tribe's god demanded a head once each year; failure to provide it would mean death to the tribe. Wu then persuaded the chief to use the heads of several victims of a recent tribal clash—enough to satisfy the tribe's god for several years without more killing—then to rethink the demand. After the years had passed and the victims' heads were used up, the chief informed Wu that the tribe needed a new sacrificial victim. Try as he might, Wu could not persuade the chief to desist. Noting to himself that his own health was failing and that he had already lived seventy years in any case, he decided to sacrifice himself. He told the chief to carry out the deadly ritual, if he must, by sending his warriors to the village that night to take the life of one who wore a red headband. Following Wu's instructions, the chief was shocked to see that the head his warriors brought him was that of his respected friend. The chief was thus converted, the barbarous custom ended, and Wu Feng enshrined as the spirit who brought peace to the valley.

On a national scale, Qian cited the example of Guan Di, the warrior in *Romance of the Three Kingdoms* whose path from unsuccessful general to folk hero to ubiquitous spirit of loyalty left a trail of small temples over the entire Chinese world.[5] We have found Guan Di in the land of streams, but we could easily substitute Lie Di or Wu Taibo. The former absorbed the ritual energies of the community while standing for law and order, and the latter gave shelter to the region's largest Taoist temple, center of the patronage network for local daoren, while standing for the spread of civilization to the south. Countless ancestors were memorialized in shrines and in legend, and stories of ghosts and spirits were given meaning by the layers of Confucian commentary that had infiltrated the oral traditions. The story of the widow in Qian's lineage whose son died in jail is but one example. The Confucian idea humanized, rationalized, and moralized the world of the spirit, opposing it only when human life and public order were at stake. The mandate was, in the words of Confucius, to "respect the spirits but keep them at a distance." Again, science and revolutionary ideology have changed the rules.

Nearly every sign of religious life has disappeared from the land of streams. From the kitchen god to the ancestral shrines, the Buddhist monasteries to the temple of Lie Di, all is void. Cremation has replaced interment and cemetery plots have reverted to cropland. The tombs of the Song Dynasty ancestors of the Qian and Hua clans have been leveled and dug up. The grave of Imperial Tutor Hua was excavated in 1958 and the body exhumed. Observers noted that the head was intact, not replaced by a golden replica, thus debunking another local legend. During the Cultural Revolution of the 1960s even the grave of a Ming Dynasty patriot was destroyed, its stone memorial arch disassembled, and the stones used for a bridge.[6] Charitable estates became granaries or warehouses, genealogies were burned, ancestors denounced, legends forgotten.

The impact of this massive attack on the spiritual forms of the old culture is still uncertain. Sacred ground has a way of remaining sacred, as the history of Ganlu—the town called "sweet dew"—shows. Annual temple fairs have been revived along with the free market economy, appearing spontaneously on the old dates and in the old places, but without the temples or the rituals. The peasants of the village where the Ming patriot's tomb was located have restored it, reclaiming the stones from the bridge and requesting county aid to reconstruct the arch. The tomb of Wu Taibo attracted two hundred thousand visitors at the spring festival in 1985—in the rain—and his temple has been rebuilt, complete with a new icon rising several meters under the Ming roofbeams. More eloquent in their spiritual expression are the complex paper figures representing Taoist heavens that peasant women constructed with their own hands and placed at the shrine to celebrate the opening. More poignant is the tiny makeshift altar covered with candles and incense sticks that graces the wall of the factory built on the site of the old temples of Ganlu. But one thing seems clear: the heavy overlay of the ancestral cult and its rituals are gone forever.

Whether or not a new humanism and a new religious tolerance will eventually serve to soften the effects of Marxist science and the Maoist cultural revolution, the changes in the religious landscape are significant. Just as medical science grew in importance in Qian Mu's descriptions of sickness and death in the "Reminiscences," the role of scientific explanation has grown in the minds of peasants. In 1985 a major investigation of the acoustics of sluice gates in southern Jiangsu province was used to dispel the spreading notion that the sounds emanating from one of them were shamanistic signs.[7] Local color, it seems, has left the spiritual landscape, and the particularistic explanations of Confucian ethics have gone with it. The larger questions of spiritual life and ethics, however, remain.

The role that Qian Mu claimed for "the rites" in the old culture was that of cultural unifier, systematizer of local particulars. It was a language that transcended not only the boundaries of local dialects and ethnic groups but even the boundaries of literacy. But systematizing was a long, slow process, and the distances from peasant kitchens to the centers of power were great. The world in which illiterate women could instruct their scholarly sons and hereditary itinerant ritualists could direct the religious affairs of scholarly households was an isolated one, a world in which a trip to the magistrate's office took an entire day and a boy could learn to read classics before learning the emperor was not Han Chinese. In peasant homes today literate women watch national leaders on the evening news.

Nothing universalizes culture faster than television. In 1985 there were more than two thousand sets in Houzhai, one for every fifteen persons. The daily fare includes Western, Russian, North Korean, Japanese, and Chinese dramas; Peking opera; sports extravaganzas; English lessons; quiz shows; advertisements for household goods; and national and international news. A popular comedy series about a monk with magic powers takes over for Imperial Tutor Hua, and the national language takes over for local dialect. Pop singers whose tunes are hardly distinguishable from those heard in Taiwan and Hong Kong cast their spell from radios and cassette players, as the local folk songs disappear along with the folk memory.

The color television set has become the symbol of arriving in the land of streams. An essential item in the working woman's dowry, it occupies a prominent place in the sitting rooms of the new rural row houses that dominate the landscape. But the TV set is only one sign of the new technology that has changed the nature of communications in this little cosmos. County roads have replaced waterways and hourly buses to Wuxi have replaced hired boats. Townships are directing profits from industry to roads and bridges that central organs cannot afford to build. An airport has appeared south of Meicun, and computerization of the national telephone system has begun. In short, the little cosmos has become a node in a new technological net and the currents flow more and more rapidly to and from Wuxi, Beijing, and beyond.

These are the material changes. How, then, does local practice continue to invoke moral principles consistent with some sort of cultural continuity? From Qian Mu's point of view there is a spiritual vacuum. Nor has the problem escaped the reformers' notice. A brief national campaign against "spiritual pollution," which ran its course in 1983, is generally considered to have been a sign of lingering Maoist influence, something the reformers would rather do without. The half-hearted slogans about "socialist spiritualism" that have succeeded the campaign are blissfully ignored. On the other hand, the material success of the current development policies makes a revival of the old Confucian spirit seem anachronistic. Is there not something even more basic to the process that still links the present to the cultural past?

Even without the shiren and their explanation of values that extend outward from the family as li, the values have tended to renew themselves in the process of change. The story of a woman I will call Deying from a village near Dangkou is a case in point. Born in 1905 to a couple with thirteen mu of surface rights, she was the eldest of five siblings. With a sister four years her junior and three younger brothers, her labor was a great family asset and her parents avoided betrothing her until their eldest son had finished primary school in Dangkou. Betrothed at the age of seventeen, six to nine years later than the norm,

18. *Restoration work at the Taibomiao temple, Meicun, November 1985.*

19. *Artisan carving the image of Wutaibo, Meicun, November 1985.*

20. *The principal of the elementary school in Seven Mansions, with the plaque inscribed by Qian Mu's brother Shengyi, when he founded the school in 1910, with the words "Qian Foundation's Renewal Primary School.*

21. *The author with two surviving members of the Qian lineage and a village cadre at the Qian home in Seven Mansions, November 1985.*

22. *The new Dangkou primary school at the site of the New Hua Charitable Estate and the Guoyu School.*

she worked at home for two more years while her brothers continued their schooling. By that time the value of her labor, much like that of the Yang woman who married the ailing widower in Hongsheng in the eighteenth century, was proven and her father capitalized on it. He got three times the going rate in betrothal gifts as well as the right to use the groom's ox, a deal that was possible only because the two families lived in the same village and their strategies seemed well matched.

The Hua family that took on this hard-working young woman was not poor, but neither was it one for a woman expecting to be looked after. The groom's father had died and his older brother had already married and set up his own household. At home were a younger brother, two sisters, and the widowed mother. All were illiterate. The family lived on rice from the New Hua Charitable Estate and on whatever they could salvage from the harvest on twelve mu of rented land. They also had an ox and three carts which they let others use in exchange for help with planting and harvest. What they needed most was dependable labor, and that is what they got from Deying.

Sixty-two years after her marriage Deying tells her story without a hint of bitterness. She was still too busy to waste much time talking, and her interviewer had to be quick and to the point. As the facts came out, one by one, an educated young cadre who was hearing them for the first time pieced them together and surprised himself with this explanation: her father had used her labor in order to send his sons to school, then he had offered her to the highest bidder. No one had to say so explicitly; it was an obvious example of the way the old society exploited peasant women. And no one had to say that the current life of the village was an obvious example of how the revolution had changed that. Yet even more poignant is Deying's own simple explanation of her late betrothal and marriage, which came naturally with the telling. Her parents had not arranged for her to marry until she was seventeen, she said, because they loved her very much. Because of their love, she was worth more to them in betrothal gifts, and they were able to find her a mate close to home.[8]

Deying also explained the marriage as a healthy alliance between the two families, a pragmatic arrangement that enabled them to share resources. She was too busy to explain that all three brothers took their education to Shanghai, where they became workers, and that her own children, including two daughters, went to school when other village children did not. Her eldest son finished lower middle school and followed her brothers to Shanghai before the Communist victory of 1949. Two granddaughters still in Dangkou are upper middle school graduates with responsible positions in township industries.[9] The key to this whole process was not so much family rites as the expansion of obligations incurred by the beneficiaries of a strategy involving a woman's labor and her love.

Another story that begs for interpretation is that of Yuanlin (not his real name), the son of an educated worker from a village north of Hongshan. Yuanlin was born in 1941 and finished primary school in the mid-1950s. His working class connections enabled him to find a factory job in Wuxi city in 1958, where he married a fellow worker three years later. Once married, the couple returned to his village to raise a family. In 1986 Yuanlin was director of the cloth print factory, a township enterprise. His son, who was also employed there, had just married a fellow worker. The newlyweds, along with his parents, occupied a two-story house newly built for the occasion. The main bedroom and sitting room were filled with two truckloads of dowry goods and other family gifts. The house cost 15,000 yuan, the dowry 4,000 yuan, the betrothal gifts to the bride's family 700 yuan, the groom's wedding party 2,000 yuan.[10] In a township where the annual per capita income is 787 yuan, such are the costs of marriage among successful skilled workers. The display is as grand as anything Seven Mansions saw in the last century, the requirements of face unchanged. But the rites of respect to parents, gods, and ancestors are absent. Will Yuanlin, the returned factory director, be less well remembered because of it?

If, as Qian Mu believes, the spirit of the culture thrives on the efforts of people to make their worth, their works, and their words stand up by themselves, and the belief that people tend to the good, then that spirit still has a chance in the land of streams. But must it be called li; must it bear the weight of a system of kinship and social distinctions that is at odds with the changing world? A consensus is needed about what is good, expressed in a language and in symbols that convey this meaning to all. The problem of consensus is not how to inspire the people with socialist, capitalist, democratic, or Confucian ideals, but how to link the common forms of self-fulfillment and integrity, displayed by the people in their work and in their family life, to changing conditions.

Is there hope for China? That depends on whether a new language that transcends the old culture can give meaning to the values that survive, and on whether a new generation of leaders can use that language to provide some vision for interests that are still on the rise.[11] Hence, in response to Qian Mu's question, I have revised the lesson of 1983.

A LESSON IN CHINESE HISTORY

There is a misconception abroad that the Chinese people are unique in their attachment to family and native place, and that their parochialism makes them susceptible to state control. In fact, the centrality of family and community has always been the Chinese people's defense against the absolutist tendencies of church and state. The strength of the state itself and the breadth of the culture depend upon the people's attachment to place and family. In the past the family taught love and respect and loyalty and shame, demanded much work from its members and an equitable distribution of the fruits of their common labor. It displayed its face to the community and demanded respect in return. The community taught the value of tolerance and unity, fixed the boundaries of status, demanded the orderly settlement of disputes, and directed the diverse spiritual energies of a people constrained by strict customary roles. And from this society in the past emerged the shiren—scholar-officials, literati, leaders and interpreters of value—who mediated between the people and the state.

The culture of the literati unified the peoples of the empire, and the idea it imposed on their communities for this purpose was li—the rites. So long as the customary practices of the people could be explained as consistent with li, they were tolerated and unity was maintained. The degree of tolerance depended on the skill of the literati—both local and national—who had to mediate between the people and the state. In the land of streams, where Qian Mu grew up, the literati managed to integrate Buddhism, Taoism, folk religion, and the ancestral cult. They gave Confucian meaning to the cults of Lie Di and Wu Taibo. They oversaw the transformation of a subsistence economy to a commercial one, and of a patron-client land tenure system to independent farming and permanent tenancy. They invented a system of corporate estate land ownership for financing community projects. The historical process in each community was different, but the explanation was the same—the rites were maintained.

The concept of minzu—the people's descent group—is an extension of the idea of family to the nation and it depends on the acceptance of the idea of li, or of some other idea that links the spirit of family and community to the state. It identifies a people unified by a political structure inspired by the process described above. If the Chinese people are to have a common culture explanations compatible with it must be produced for what is happening in all its local communities, from Seven Mansions to the hills of Taiwan. The explanations must suit both the people and the state.

The *spirit* of Chinese history, or any other history, cannot be distinguished from the *process* of history. If the spirit of the rites has declined, the spirit of the people nonetheless exists in their work. The special historical conditions in China today are the state, which unifies a large region with unique yet diverse cultural traditions, and the rural communities, which have so far survived and which continue to undergo the processes of revolution and industrialization. If we want to understand how history can influence the shape of the modern world, we should try to understand the history of those communities, for the leaders and the spirit of China in the future will come from them.

Recovering from the shock of Qian Mu's question, I thought to tell him of the handicapped girl I had met in Ganlu. Using profits from its growing industries, and in accordance with state policy, the township government in 1983 started up a handicrafts factory that employs handicapped workers. The factory is self-sufficient, with assets of 2,980,000 yuan and profits in 1985 of 590,000. It is also tax exempt. The girl was one of 82 local handicapped in a workforce of 181 at the factory, which manufactures clothing for export along with other light consumer goods. Unable to walk since birth, she works with her hands and lives at the factory weekdays because of her disability. She is a recent graduate of the local upper middle school, which was established in 1968. About one-fourth of the local young people finish the twelve-year course now; the rest, or more than 90 percent, complete nine years of school. But this girl's educational achievement required a special amount of family support. I asked about her interests, and she told me she likes to read, especially English literature, which she is teaching herself. I asked what she did with the income that would seem to allow her some much-needed independence as well as to relieve her family of the burdens of supporting an invalid. The question seemed odd to her. She was, after all, still a member of her family. She paid her nominal room and board at the factory, bought a few necessities, and sent the rest home.[12] Conjuring up her image in his blindness, Qian Mu tapped the table to express his respect.

Whether the story of the handicapped girl meant the same thing to the two of us seemed not to matter. Lie Di did not mean the same thing to everyone either, but the various explanations were able to coexist within a larger cultural consensus. What matters is that whether socialist or capitalist, Confucian or Christian, modern or traditional— whatever one's idea of what is good—there is some measure of goodness here. The process that produced it is uniquely Chinese, and it only makes sense in historical context. This is why, regardless of what one thinks of Qian Mu's view of the world, his lifelong plea to his people to study their past is still timely. In 1950 he argued:

> Tomorrow's world will be a liberated one. We should not be arguing about whether capitalism or communism is the correct way for the future. The conflict between these two sides is a disease that has developed in Western culture and it manifests two opposite abnormal tendencies. This is not to say that Western culture is dying. It ought to have a life ahead of it. But that surely doesn't make it our life! If we want to solve our own problems, we ought to turn around and recognize ourselves.[13]

Qian Mu's recognition of "ourselves" is implicit in his "Reminiscences." His worth, his works, and his words, like those of parents, teachers, and friends, stand up by themselves. The truths thus transmitted are ancient ones, verified again and again by communities like Seven Mansions in the larger context of Chinese culture and politics. Yet if we are to render them meaningful to the rapidly changing present, we must first find the new language that subsumes them and then write the history that shows how they apply. That history will show, as the history of Seven Mansions demonstrates, that in the old China social conditions did change, new interests did emerge, and moral vision as well as leadership evolved along with them. Only when that history is told can the passions and dignity of past lives inspire the present without denying it.

Notes

1 BEHIND THE RED GATE

1. Although Qian Mu was younger than most of those identified by Vera Schwarcz as the generation of 1911, he fits the category otherwise. See her discussion, which distinguishes that generation from those for whom the epoch-making event was the May Fourth movement, 1919, in *The Chinese Enlightenment*, pp. 23–24.

2. Jonathan D. Spence, *The Gate of Heavenly Peace*, pp. 340–45; Qian Mu, "Shiyou zayi" in *Bashi yi shuangqin, Shiyou zayi* (hereafter cited Qian, "Shiyou"), pp. 233–34.

3. Spence, *Gate of Heavenly Peace*, p. 340; Wen Yiduo, *Wen Yiduo quan ji*, vol. 4, p. 13.

4. Qian, "Shiyou," p. 189.

5. Ibid., p. 185.

6. Ibid., pp. 232–33.

7. Ibid., pp. 187–88.

8. Ibid., p. 215.

9. Ibid., p. 210.

10. Ibid., p. 223.

11. Notes on a discussion with Qian Mu, July 7, 1983.

12. The term cultural conservatives refers to a variety of groups that resisted arguments for the replacement of Chinese cultural forms with totally new ones, based on Western models. Most sought to revive some aspect of China's "cultural essence." Qian Mu was not a participant in any of these

movements, but his thinking has been associated with them. For details, see Charlotte Furth, ed., *The Limits of Change*.

13. For a discussion of the conflict between the culturally conservative position that placed "saving the country" first and the "Enlightenment" position that placed intellectual awakening first, see Schwarcz, *Chinese Enlightenment*, esp. p. 87.

2   TO PRACTICE WHEN IT IS TIMELY

1. Qian, "Shiyou," pp. 216–17.

2. Qian Mu, *Bashi yi shuangqin* ("Reminiscences on My Parents at the Age of Eighty," hereafter cited Qian, *Bashi*), p. 7. The classic edition of Sima Qian's *Records* was published with multicolored notes, including those of the sixteenth-century prose master and the eighteenth-century scholar.

3. Qian, *Bashi*, p. 14.

4. The study is Qian Mu's "Liu Xiang, Xin fu zi nianpu."

5. Qian, *Bashi*, p. 13.

6. Luo Guanzhong, *Romance of the Three Kingdoms*, chap. 43.

7. On Qian Bogui and his relationship to Hua Hongmo: Qian Zonglian, ed., *Zongpu beiyao (Qian shi)*, 1922, *shibiao*:1–2; Hua Hongmo, ed., *Hua shi tongsi sanxinggong zongpu*, 1881, 13:67b.

8. Qian, "Shiyou," pp. 33–34.

9. Mary Backus Rankin, *Early Chinese Revolutionaries*, pp. 48–53.

10. Ibid., pp. 56–57.

11. For a summary of the old text/new text controversy, see Hao Chang, *Liang Ch'i-ch'ao and Intellectual Transition in China*, pp. 7–35. Also see Charlotte Furth, "The Sage as Rebel," in her edited volume, *The Limits of Change*, pp. 118–28.

12. Kang Youwei began to advocate a Confucian religion in 1913, and Zhang attacked it explicitly then. See Laurence A. Schneider, *Ku Chieh-hang and China's New History*, pp. 47–48. But the point that Confucius was better understood as a historian whose tradition was maintained in the *Zuo Commentary*, the *Shiji*, and the school of Liu Xin was explicit in Zhang's earlier criticism of Kang's view of Confucius as reformer. For example, see Zhang's "Ding Kong," published in *Qiushu* in 1902, reprinted in *Zhang Taiyan shi wen xuan zhu*, pp. 162–76. Also see Chang, *Liang Ch'i-ch'ao*, pp. 36–57, on Kang Youwei; and Kung-chuan Hsiao, *A Modern China and a New World*, esp. pp. 128–31. More recently Chang Hao has argued that Kang's moral-spiritual mission was an integral part of his thought and not just the ideological means toward reformist political ends in the 1890s, whereas Zhang's view of history emerges in his argument that parliamentary democracy, both in the West and in Japan reflects the legacy of feudalism. See his *Chinese Intellectuals in Crisis*, pp. 48–54, 114–15.

13. The esperanto advocate was Wu Chih-hui, one of the original members of the Chinese Educational Association. See Rankin, *Early Chinese Revolutionar-*

ies, pp. 58–59. Also see Howard Boorman and Richard Howard, eds., *Biographical Dictionary of Republican China,* s.v. Wu Chih-hui.

14. This is the general theme of Zhang's essays in *Qiushu.* See also his letter to Kang Youwei, in which the racist argument and the argument for historical perspective are combined, the point being that one cannot ignore the historical fact of subjugation of the Han race by the Manchus as Kang Youwei does in advocating constitutional reform. *Zhang Taiyan,* pp. 243–305, esp. pp. 255–56.

15. Chang, *Liang Ch'i-ch'ao,* pp. 189–206; Philip A. Kuhn, "Late Ch'ing Views of the Polity."

16. Liang's conclusion that the Chinese were not ready for democracy resulted from a trip to America in the spring of 1903. The American people who listened to Theodore Roosevelt, he learned, were both self-reliant and racist, whereas the American Chinese communities remained as bound to convention as if they had never lived in the United States. See Spence, *Gate of Heavenly Peace,* p. 75.

17. Chang, *Liang Ch'i-ch'ao,* pp. 189–206.

18. Rankin, *Early Chinese Revolutionaries,* pp. 61–64.

19. Zhang, Letter to Kang Youwei, *Zhang Taiyan,* 243–305.

20. Zou Rong, "Geming jun," trans. Chün-tu Hsüeh and Geraldine R. Schiff, in "The Life and Writings of Tsou Jung."

21. See Michael Gasster, *Chinese Intellectuals and the Revolution of 1911,* pp. 27–65, 190–227, on Zhang Binglin.

22. Rankin, *Early Chinese Intellectuals,* pp. 67–69, 76–77, on the agreement.

23. Qian Zonglian, ed., *Zongpu beiyao (Qian shi),* 1922, *shibiao:*1–2; Hua Hongmo, ed., *Hua shi tongsi sanxinggong zongpu,* 1881, 13:67b.

24. Qian, "Shiyou," pp. 36–37.

25. Gui Youguang, *Zhenchuan xiansheng ji,* 2:1.

26. Qian, *Bashi,* pp. 18–21.

27. Qian, "Shiyou," pp. 35–39.

28. See Kuhn's discussion in "Late Ch'ing Views of the Polity," and Chang, *Chinese Intellectuals in Crisis,* pp. 114–15.

29. Spence, *Gate of Heavenly Peace,* p. 88.

30. Qian, "Shiyou," p. 40.

31. Ibid.

32. See Arthur W. Hummel, ed., *Eminent Chinese of the Ch'ing Period,* p. 540. Hua Hengfang was the son of Hua Yilun, the anti-Taiping militia leader described in chapter 3.

33. Qian, "Shiyou," pp. 53–57.

34. Ibid., p. 57.

35. Ibid., p. 59.

36. On Liang's attempt to dissuade Yuan from making himself emperor, see Ernest P. Young, *Presidency of Yuan Shih-k'ai,* pp. 121–22. Zhang Binglin, who had supported the revolution but not representative government, resigned from the token position Yuan offered him in protest against the president's fomenting the "second revolution," the ruse by which he outlawed the

budding nationalist party and abolished the National Assembly. See Schneider, *Ku Chieh-kang*, p. 47.

37. Jerome Grieder, *Intellectuals and the State in Modern China*, p. 218.

38. On Hu Shih, see Jerome B. Grieder, *Hu Shih and the Chinese Renaissance*.

39. Grieder, *Intellectuals and the State in Modern China*, pp. 231–32.

40. Schneider, *Ku Chieh-kang*, pp. 46–50.

41. Qian, "Shiyou," p. 60. See Schneider, *Ku Chieh-kang*, pp. 135, 166.

42. Qian, "Shiyou," p. 60; Schneider, *Ku Chieh-kang*, p. 41.

43. Qian, "Shiyou," p. 81.

44. Ibid., p. 80.

45. Qian Zonglian, ed., *Zongpu beiyao, shibiao:*1–2. Qian Bogui later started up a steamboat transport business, which monopolized the trade between Dangkou and Wuxi. He died relatively young (Hua Zuyao, interview, November 11, 1985; Hou Zhida and others, interview, November 29, 1985).

46. For a general discussion of Dewey's influence, see Barry Keenan, *Dewey Experiment in China*. On Hu Shi's interpretation, see Grieder, *Hu Shih*, esp. pp. 117–20.

47. Qian, "Shiyou," pp. 92–95.

48. Ibid., pp. 97–98.

49. Ibid., p. 96.

50. Ibid., p. 100.

51. Ibid., p. 102.

52. Ibid., p. 117; and Qian Mu, *Guoxue gailun*.

53. Qian, "Shiyou," pp. 117, 215, 244–45, 254–62, describes occasions when he lectured to official groups or otherwise responded to party requests. Charlotte Furth, ed., *The Limits of Change*, pp. 34–36, identifies Qian as a new-style cultural conservative, supportive of the Guomindang because of its culturally conservative ideology, but she cites no evidence of political involvement on his part. In 1949, Mao Zedong labeled Qian Mu, Hu Shi, and Fu Sinian reactionaries for supporting the Guomindang, but Qian, unlike Hu and Fu, neither joined the party nor served the regime. See "Cast Away Illusions, Prepare for Struggle (August 14, 1949)," in Mao Zedong, *Selected Works of Mao Zedong*, 4:427.

54. Qian Mu, "Liu Xiang, Xin fu zi nianpu."

55. See Spence, *Gate of Heavenly Peace*, pp. 185, 277–78; Tsi-an Hsia, "Ch'ü Ch'iu-po;" and Schneider, *Ku Chieh-kang*, pp. 153–87.

56. Schneider, *Ku Chieh-kang*, pp. 106–08, on Hu.

57. Arif Dirlik, *Revolution and History*, describes the debates in detail.

58. Qian, "Shiyou," pp. 158–59.

59. Ibid., pp. 141–42; and his *Zhongguo jin sanbai nian xueshu shi* on Kang Youwei, pp. 633–709. See Kung-chuan Hsiao, *A Modern China and a New World*, pp. 49–51, 415–16, 478, for comments and a partial defense of Kang.

60. Qian, "Shiyou," pp. 147–51.

61. Ibid., pp. 159–60.

62. Ibid., pp. 191–92.

63. Ibid., pp. 193–98.

64. Qian Mu, *Guoshi dagang,* "Introduction."

65. Qian, "Shiyou," p. 198. Qian Weichang, an internationally known aerospace physicist who left the Jet Propulsion Laboratory at California Institute of Technology in 1946 to return to China, is one of the most prominent scientists in the People's Republic. Criticized as a rightist in 1957, he worked as a peasant and factory laborer during the Cultural Revolution, reappeared in 1972 with a scientific delegation to Europe and America, and finally in the 1980s regained his position as an intellectual leader and non-Communist political spokesman. In 1983 in Hong Kong he met Qian Mu, who had tutored him and supervised his early education and whom he followed to Qinghua University in 1930, for the first time since 1949.

66. Qian, "Shiyou," pp. 244–45.

67. Mao, "Cast Away Illusions, Prepare for Struggle," p. 427. On Yan in Canton, see Donald A. Gillin, *Warlord,* pp. 288–91.

3 THE LAND OF STREAMS

1. Between October and December 1985, and again between April and June 1986, I conducted interviews and made observations in the townships of Dangkou, Ganlu, Hongshengli, Anzhen, Meicun, and other places in Wuxi County. Sources are identified in the notes by name, where possible, or by place and date. For the story of the 1911 flood and rice riots: Hua Zuyao, November 20, 1985. On Qian's illness and recovery: Qian, *Bashi,* pp. 21–22.

2. On Qian Bogui and the 1911 revolution: Hua Zuyao, November 20, 1985.

3. On Qian Fenggao and the School: Qian Keyao and others, November 27, 1985. On the school: Hua Ajin, November 28, 1985. On Xicang: Cai Liezu and Shen Boxun, November 30, 1985.

4. On the Lie Di legend and its history, Wu Xi, ed., *Taibo Meili zhi* (1897; hereafter cited as *Taibo*), 5:1–2. On the festivals: Hua Zuyao, November 18, 1985; Qian Keyao and others, November 27, 1985; Zhaojiabang, May 30, 1986.

5. Hou Hongjian, *Xijin xiangtu lishi* (1906), and *Xijin xiangtu dili* (1908–11).

6. Ganlu, December 2, 1985.

7. Hua Hongmo's grandson was Hua Yizhi (1893–1956).

8. On Qian Bogui: Hua Zuyao, November 20, 1985; Hongsheng, November 29, 1985.

9. Tenancy rates varied dramatically across Wuxi County. The figure of 80 percent is based on interviews in Dangkou, Ganlu, and Hongsheng. Farther west tenancy was as low as 40 percent in some places (e.g., Wanxiang, May 22, 1986); landlordism was highest in Dangkou.

10. On rent fixing and the charitable estates: Hua Zuyao, November 18, 1985; Hua Yuzhu, November 19, 1985; Qian Keyao and others, November 27, 1985; Hua Qishu, December 12, 1985; Zhaojiabang, May 28, 1986. On

peasant calculations: Hua Yuzhu, November 19, 1985; Zhaojiabang, May 28, 1986; Lu Ajin and others, November 28, 1985.

11. On charitable estates, see Denis Twitchett, "Fan Clan's Charitable Estate," and Jerry Dennerline, "New Hua Charitable Estate."

12. The figures are estimates based on interviews. Figures for charitable estates are consistent with documentary evidence (cf. Dennerline, "New Hua Charitable Estate"), but documents for pre–land reform holdings were not available. It was generally agreed that about 80 percent of the subsoil was owned by landlords before land reform. There are currently 58,955 mu under cultivation in the three townships, so the amount controlled by landlords must have been about 47,000. After the 15,000 mu of charitable estate land came the estates of Zhang Yongbin in Ganlu (3,000), Hua Yizhi in Dangkou (2,000), Qian Fenggao in Qifangqiao (2,000), and Cai Guichu in Xicang (1,600). Several others had more than 300 mu, but the norm was said to have been fewer than 50.

13. Hua Zuyao, November 16, 1985.

14. The standard discounted rent was 45 kilograms per mu (the Chinese measurements are in *shi*, or piculs: 1 shi = 150 *jin* = 75 kg), so that the rent on 30–40 mu would be 1,350–1,800 kilograms. Peasants in Zhaojiabang claim that rents in the 1930s rarely exceeded 30 kilograms per mu, but the land belonged mostly to Hua charitable estates, not small landlords (Zhaojiabang, May 28, 1986).

15. On the cost of a manager: Hua Zuyao, November 16, 1985; Hua Qishu, December 3, 1985. According to Fei Xiaotong, peasant households reckoned on 225 kilograms of rice per person in 1936, although working adults, small children, the elderly, men, and women received varying amounts. In 1962 the figure was up to 365 kilograms, which is seen as sufficient. See Fei, *Chinese Village Closeup*, pp. 29, 200.

16. Dangkou maids had their own network in Shanghai, apart from the brokers who placed women from other towns. A popular ditty in nearby Anzhen ridiculed them: "Hongshan has eighteen famous sites; first is the big feet of the Dangkou girls.... " Hua Fuxing and Hua Yuzhu, November 19, 1985; Zhang Zuliang and others, May 15, 1986.

17. Cai Liezu, November 30, 1985.

18. Hua Yilun, *Liyuxuan wenji, xu:*1:3.

19. Hua Zuyao and others, November 20, 1985.

20. The current combined population of the three townships is 68,400. In 1981 Fei Xiaotong found that the population of Kaixiangong in nearby Wujiang had increased by 60 percent since 1936. If the increase is roughly similar for the whole area, then the population of the area now included in the three townships was around 42,000 in 1911. On the other hand, it is quite clear that the populations of the towns of Dangkou and Ganlu and the landlord villages of Xicang and Qifangqiao were larger in the late Qing than they are now. These figures represent only the peasant population and are rough estimates.

21. Lu Ajin, November 28, 1985.

22. Hua Ajin, November 28, 1985.

23. Shao Genrong, November 29, 1985; Qian Keyao and others, November 27, 1985.

24. Lu Ajin and others, November 28, 1985.

25. Shao Genrong and Hou Zhida, November 29, 1985.

26. Ding Ajin, November 28, 1985; Hua Zuyao, November 18, 1985.

27. Shen Jusheng, November 28, 1985.

28. *Taibo*, 4:9b-10.

29. Hua Yuzhu, November 19, 1985.

30. Hua Zuyao, November 19, 1985. The origins of the Sea of Learning Academy, now lost to the folk memory, are described in *Taibo*, 5:8b-10. It was attached to a shrine commemorating three officials who had used their influence to reform the tax system and carry out a land survey, erected by Hua Ch'a (Imperial Tutor Hua) in 1557. The Taoist temple was also attached, just as a Taoist temple had been attached to the Taibomiao in Meicun, but by the twentieth century the intentions of its builder had long since been forgotten. In 1986 a granary occupied the site of the shrine. A stone inscription dated 1830 describes the history and the last restoration of the shrine, and a standard for the measure used in the survey is also preserved in stone.

31. Hua Hengfang, "Chen shi mutian ji," in *Xingsuxuan wencun*, 18.

32. Qian Keyao and others, November 27, 1985.

33. Shen Jusheng, November 28, 1985.

34. Qian Keyao and others, November 27, 1985; Hua Zuyao, November 18, 1985; Shao Zhishan and others, December 3, 1985; Zhaojiabang, May 30, 1986. As explained below, Lie Di's festivals were given a Confucian interpretation by the local scholar-gentry. The villages of Qianze, Zhongze, and Houze, north of Hongshan, where the descendants of another Ming scholar-gentry clan named An lived, were excluded when the local peasant god, who was not Confucianized, made his rounds. The Ans claim they did not participate because they were Confucianists and, therefore, not superstitious. On the other hand, the Ans supported a large Guandi temple and a temple to the town god in Anzhen.

35. Arthur Waley, trans., *Book of Songs*, no. 159 (Mao no. 154).

36. Folksong in Wu dialect from Wuxi, in *Wu Ge*, pp. 30–31.

37. *Taibo*, 5:1–2.

38. Hua Zuyao, November 18, 1985; Qian Keyao and others, November 27, 1985.

39. *Taibo*, 1:8. Shao Zhishan and others, December 2, 1985.

40. *Taibo*, 5:1.

41. Hua Zuyao, November 18, 1985.

42. This version of the story was told by Hua Zuyao, (November 16, 1985), whose branch descended from the eldest son, who had built the tomb. It is virtually the same as one recorded in the Wuxi county gazetteer, 1690:10:9 and 1881:12:45. A different version is told by the sons of Hua Yizhi, descendants of Hua Hongmo and a different branch.

43. The figure of thirty to forty rice merchants is Hua Zuyao's.

44. Hua Yuzhu and Hua Fuxing, November 19, 1985; Tang Jinhu, November 21, 1985.

45. Two stone horses were all that remained at the site in December 1985.

46. I have heard many versions of the story, some of which replace the essential ingredient of Dongting beancurd with dumplings or other items not unique to Dongting. The geomancy expert appeared in the version told by Mr. Huang, former school principal in Dangkou, November 19, 1985.

47. *Wuxi-Jingui xianzhi* (1881), 22:11b-12, 37:5b-9b, 40:17 (Hereafter cited *Wuxi* 1881); Hua Ziheng, ed., *Hua shi chuanfangji* (1743), 5:44; *Taibo*, 3:8–9b, 5:8b-11b and 13–15, 6:16b, 7:11b-14, 8:18b, 19b, 34b, 36.

48. On the local silk industry, see Lynda Schafer Bell, "Merchants, Peasants and the State."

49. Wang Atu, December 3, 1985.

50. Hua Qishu, December 3, 1985; Jiaoshang, November, 20, 1985. According to the stone inscription, dated 1844, the charitable estate provided for descendants of three branches that were outside the lineages that originated with Leqin's sons; cf. *Wuxi* 1881:30:13b, where the estate is listed as *Hua shi Yongxizhi yizhuang* (charitable estate of the Yongxi branch of the Hua).

51. Qian Keyao and others, November 27, 1985. Xinmei was identified as the first local ancestor in the lineage shrine, which has been destroyed; cf. Qian, *Bashi*, pp. 1–2. Qian Mu left Qifangqiao in his youth and never saw the genealogical record or the tablets in the shrine.

52. *Qian shi hutou zongpu* 1892, *xia:*72:6–8 (hereafter cited *Qian shi* 1892). Xinmei's given name was Laihuang and he occupies the seventh position in generation twenty-two of the Qifangqiao genealogy. Descendants of the other *fang* lived elsewhere. According to local legend, he was "the seventh fang" but no one knows how many fang there were or the relationship among them (Qian Keyao and others, November 27, 1985). Hence the name Qifangqiao. Although there were seven branches living in the village, they were not numbered consecutively and no one knows their origins. They were the old sixth, new sixth, seventh, ninth, old eighth, new third, and *sheng*. Five Generations Together Hall, Qian Mu's branch, was the old sixth fang. Compare Qian, *Bashi*, pp. 3–4.

53. *Qian shi* 1892, *xia:*3–13. For details on the history of the Qian clan, see Jerry Dennerline, "Marriage, Adoption, and Charity."

54. *Qian shi* 1892, *xia:*72, *shang:*8: maps of gravesites of Qian Xinmei and Qian Huifu.

55. Dennerline, "Marriage, Adoption, and Charity."

56. A copy of the imperial proclamation is in *Qian shi* 1892, *shang:*6.

57. Qian, *Bashi*, pp. 2–3; Qian Keyao and others, November 27, 1985; Qian Axing and others, November 29, 1985.

58. *Wuxi* 1881, 37:7–7b.

59. Ibid., 2–3b.

60. Ye Xian'en and Tan Tihua, "Lun Zhujiang sanjiaozhou di zutian," p. 26.

61. *Qian shi* 1892, *xia:*72. Details are in Dennerline, "Marriage, Adoption, and Charity."

62. The history of the founding and early growth of the estate is described and documented in Hua Hongmo, ed., *Hua shi xin yizhuang shilüe*, (hereafter, *Hua shi* 1901). Details are in Dennerline, "New Hua Charitable Estate."

63. Hua Yilun, "Zuzu Moting fujun zhuan," in *Liyuxuan wenji*, 4:15. Hua Fenyuan was Hongmo's grandfather.

64. Hua Zhan'en, *Xijin zhiwai*, 5:1–14, describes and documents the case. Hua Zhan'en, who also compiled and published a set of maps of the tax districts of Jingui (eastern Wuxi) County, was a descendant of the "old" Hua charitable estate's founder. It is interesting to note that the problem of monopolization of tax collection by tax farmers nonetheless continued to plague the area in the 1930s. Weng Zushan, describes the case of nine owners of a total of 55 mu who paid tax farmers three times the amount assessed simply because the tax farmers had paid the collector for them ("Wuxi dongnan xiang nongminde tianfu fudan," p. 190).

65. Shi Jianlie, "Ji (Wuxi) xiancheng shishou kefu benmo," pp. 253-54; Arthur W. Hummel, ed., *Eminent Chinese of the Ch'ing Period*, p. 540.

66. *Hua shi* 1901, 2:16, on the building of the shrine. In his introduction to *Hua shi tongsi sanxing gong zhi zongpu* (hereafter, *Hua shi* 1911), Hua Hongmo noted that of the twelve main branches in the Tongsi line (originating with a thirteenth-century ancestor), the two with charitable estates had compiled their own genealogies. With the exception of three whose main branches resided outside the county, the rest had compiled genealogies with the support of the estate he managed, all between 1899 and 1908. The 1911 genealogy was a revision of his own line's, which he first compiled in 1881.

67. *Hua shi* 1901, 1:5, 2:1, list the two warehouses. The first such warehousing concern was built in 1862. Hua's first was built in 1871 and his second in 1894. Between them they could hold about 23,000 metric tons (220,000 *dan*) of husked rice. "Wuxi mishi diaocha," *Liangshi diaocha* 8 (1935), excerpted in *Wuxi difang ziliao huibian*, pp. 95–96.

68. *Hua shi* 1901, 1:58–59b, 2:1; *Hua shi* 1911, preface, 13:98; Hua Zuyao, November 20, 1985.

69. Feng Guifen, *Jiaobin lu kangyi*.

70. Zou Jingheng later studied silk manufacturing in Japan and developed the technologies in Wuxi factories. He has also published extensively on the history of silk technology in China; see his *Cansang sizhi zakao*. Much of the information here on Houzhai was obtained in interviews with Zou Jingheng in Taipei during the summer of 1983.

71. Zou Jingheng, "Jing shu xian sao Hua Ruizhen nüshi zhijie."

72. See *I Ching* (The Book of Changes), "Xici" (The Great Commentary), part 1. The terms *gang* and *rou* are often translated "strong" and "weak" in this context, as they apply to the unbroken and broken lines in the hexagrams. The former connotes forms that are hard, unbending, hard to melt, etc., while the latter connotes their opposites. The imagery is also sexual.

73. I encountered several cases in 1985 and 1986. One village north of

Hongshan had a reputation for producing many daughters and few sons, and some families' property had devolved on daughters for three generations in a row. Houze, May 13, 1986. In other villages surveyed, this type of marriage and devolution seemed to run between 5 and 10 percent before liberation.

74. *Qian shi* 1892, *xia:*14, 18.

75. The rituals were, as Qian Mu pointed out, essentially the same all over China. Variations in the towns and villages surveyed in Wuxi in 1985 and 1986 reflected differences of wealth and educational heritage, but not of ritual form or religious belief. Wealthier or better-educated families spent more money for finer quality dowry goods, but the goods were of the same kind. The number of guests and quality of the food served at wedding parties varied, but not the timing or the types of food. And the status of the persons serving as formal witnesses depended on the status of the groom's family, but the functions were the same.

76. Hua Zonghua, *Hua Zhengu xiansheng Lüdeji,* 3:6.

77. D. C. Lau, trans., *Lao Tzu,* Book 28, and Book 78, verses 186–87.

78. *Qian shi* 1892, *shang:*6, *xia:*55:41ff., *xia:*18; Qian Zonglian, ed., *Zongpu beiyao,* pp. 4–6.

79. *Qian shi* 1892, *xia:*72:73, 88.

4   "REMINISCENCES ON MY PARENTS AT THE AGE OF EIGHTY"

1. Qian Mu, *Guoshi dagang.* The arguments presented here are found in the original author's preface, dated 1939.

2. An interesting analysis of *An Outline History of the Nation,* comparing the approach to that of the German historicists, is found in Hu Ch'ang-chih, "Ch'ien Mu ti *Kuo shih ta kang* yü Te-kuo li-shih-chu-i."

3. Qian Mu's "Bashi yi shuangqin" was originally published serially in several places in Hong Kong and Taiwan. The first complete edition was published by New Asia College as the first in a projected series entitled Xiaocongshu. The revised edition used here was published together with "Shiyou zayi" in Taipei in 1983.

4. Qian, "Shiyou," in *Bashi,* p. 39.

5   THE RED GATE REVISITED

1. Qian Mu, "Zhongguo wenhua yu zhongguo qingnian" (October 15, 1941), in *Wenhua yu jiaoyu,* p. 7.

2. Qian Mu, "Shixue jingshen yu shixue fangfa" (Spring 1951), in *Zhongguo lishi jingshen,* p. 17.

3. The collective rural industry that is thriving in the lower Yangzi region is not typical of China as a whole, but neither was the old literati culture. That culture was nonetheless extremely influential, and the pattern of rural devel-

opment described here is still considered one of two model forms, the other being the private farming enterprises currently booming further south along the coast.

4. The statistics here, unless otherwise noted, were obtained in interviews with township and village officials in autumn 1985 and spring 1986. The interpretation is my own.

5. Qian Mu, "Zhongguo lishishangde daode jingshen" (Spring 1951), in *Zhongguo lishi jingshen*, pp. 113–28.

6. The tomb was that of Gu Xiancheng, leader of the Donglin Academy movement that opposed the last Ming emperors and tried to shore up the polity while the Manchus were confederating.

7. *Renminribao* (The people's daily), June 1985.

8. Wuxi, May 30, 1986.

9. Family records from village survey (1986), cases 11.0030–32.

10. Wuxi, May 12, 1986.

11. The current relaxation of ideological demands along with the massive recruitment of young people to manage reforms are signs that the new generation is emerging despite the setbacks of 1987. On the recruitment of young people, see Hong Yung Lee, "The Implications of Reform for Ideology, State and Society in China," pp. 78–79. Of 126 new provincial-level cadres appointed in 1982–83, 63 percent were under the age of fifty and 80 percent had college-level education. According to *Jiushi niandai* (The nineties), September 1985, over a million new cadres have been recruited to implement reforms. My own impressions of the ages and educational levels of cadres and factory managers in Wuxi are consistent with these figures.

12. Ganlu fuli gongchang (Ganlu factory for the handicapped), December 2, 1985.

13. Qian Mu, "Shixue jingshen yu shixue fangfa," in *Zhongguo lishi jingshen*, pp. 16–17.

Selected Bibliography

Alitto, Guy S. *The Last Confucian: Liang Shu-ming and the Chinese Dilemma of Modernity.* Berkeley and Los Angeles: University of California Press, 1979.

Ayers, William. *Chang Chih-tung and Educational Reform in China.* Cambridge: Harvard University Press, 1971.

Bays, Daniel H. *China Enters the Twentieth Century: Chang Chih-tung and the Issues of a New Age, 1895–1909.* Ann Arbor: University of Michigan Press, 1978.

Bell, Lynda Schafer. "Merchants, Peasants and the State: The Organization and Politics of Chinese Silk Production, Wuxi County, 1870–1937." Ph.D. diss., History, U.C.L.A., 1985.

Biggerstaff, Knight. *The Earliest Modern Government Schools in China.* Ithaca: Cornell University Press, 1961.

Boorman, Howard, and Richard Howard, eds. *Biographical Dictionary of Republican China.* New York: Columbia University Press, 1967.

Chang, Hao. *Chinese Intellectuals in Crisis: Search for Order and Meaning (1890–1911).* Berkeley and Los Angeles: University of California Press, 1987.

——— . *Liang Ch'i-ch'ao and Intellectual Transition in China, 1890–1907.* Cambridge, Mass.: Harvard University Press, 1971.

Ch'ien, Chung-shu. *Fortress Besieged.* Trans. Jeanne Kelly and Nathan K. Mao. Bloomington: Indiana University Press, 1979.

Chu, Samuel C. *Reformer in Modern China: Chang Chien, 1853–1926.* New York: Columbia University Press, 1965.

Cohen, Paul A. *China and Christianity: The Missionary Movement and the Growth of Chinese Antiforeignism, 1860–1870.* Cambridge: Harvard University Press, 1963.

Dennerline, Jerry. "Marriage, Adoption, and Charity in the Development of Lineages in Wu-hsi from Sung to Ch'ing." In *Kinship Organization in Late Imperial China, 1000–1940.* Ed. Patricia Buckley Ebrey and James L. Watson. Berkeley and Los Angeles: University of California Press, 1986. Pp. 170–209.

————. "The New Hua Charitable Estate and Local Level Leadership in Wuxi County at the End of the Qing." In *Select Papers from the Center for Far Eastern Studies, no. 4, 1979–80.* Ed. Tang Tsou. Chicago: University of Chicago, 1981. Pp. 19–70.

Dewey, John. *Lectures in China, 1919–1920.* Trans. and ed. Robert W. Clopton and Tsuin-chen Ou. Honolulu: University Press of Hawaii, 1973.

Dirlik, Arif. *Revolution and History: The Origins of Marxist Historiography in China, 1919–1937.* Berkeley and Los Angeles: University of California Press, 1978.

————. "T'ao Hsi-sheng: The Social Limits of Change." In *The Limits of Change: Essays on Conservative Alternatives in Republican China.* Ed. Charlotte Furth. Cambridge: Harvard University Press. Pp. 305–331.

Fei, Hsiao-t'ung (Fei Xiaotong). *Chinese Village Closeup.* Beijing: New World Press, 1983.

Feng, Guifen. *Jiaobin lu kangyi* (Protests from the study of Jiaobin). 1897. Reprint, Taipei, 1967.

Feuerwerker, Albert. *China's Early Industrialization: Sheng Hsuan-huai (1844–1916) and Mandarin Enterprise.* Cambridge: Harvard University Press, 1958.

Feuerwerker, Albert, Rhoads Murphey, and Mary C. Wright, eds. *Approaches to Modern Chinese History.* Berkeley and Los Angeles: University of California Press, 1967.

Furth, Charlotte. "Culture and Politics in Modern Chinese Conservatism." In *The Limits of Change: Essays on Conservative Alternatives in Republican China.* Ed. Charlotte Furth. Cambridge: Harvard University Press, 1976. Pp. 22–53.

————. "The Sage as Rebel: The Inner World of Chang Ping-lin." In *The Limits of Change: Essays on Conservative Alternatives in Republican China.* Ed. Charlotte Furth. Cambridge: Harvard University Press, 1976. Pp. 113–50.

Gasster, Michael. *Chinese Intellectuals and the Revolution of 1911: The Birth of Modern Chinese Radicalism.* Seattle: University of Washington Press, 1969.

Gillin, Donald A. *Warlord: Yen Hsi-shan in Shansi Province, 1911–1949.* Princeton: Princeton University Press, 1967.

Grieder, Jerome B. *Hu Shih and the Chinese Renaissance: Liberalism in the Chinese Revolution, 1917–1937.* Cambridge: Harvard University Press, 1970.

————. *Intellectuals and the State in Modern China: A Narrative History.* New York: Free Press, 1981.

Gui Youguang. *Zhenchuan xiansheng ji* (Writings of Master Zhenchuan). Sibu beiyao, 1927–35.

Hou, Hongjian. *Xijin xiangtu dili* (A geography of rural Wuxi-jingui). Wuxi, 1908–11.

————. *Xijin xiangtu lishi* (A history of rural Wuxi-jingui). Wuxi, 1906.

Hsia, C. T. *A History of Modern Chinese Fiction, 1917–1957.* New Haven and London: Yale University Press, 1961.

Hsia, Tsi-an. "Ch'ü Ch'iu-po: The Making and Destruction of a Tender-hearted Communist." *China Quarterly* (1966), 3–54. Reprinted in his *The Gate of Darkness: Studies on the Leftist Literary Movement in China.* Seattle: University of Washington Press, 1968.

Hsiao, Kung-chuan. *A Modern China and a New World: K'ang Yu-wei, Reformer and Utopian, 1858–1927.* Seattle: University of Washington Press, 1975.

Hsüeh, Chün-tu. *Huang Hsing and the Chinese Revolution.* Stanford: Stanford University Press, 1961.

Hsüeh, Chün-tu, and Geraldine R. Schiff. "The Life and Writings of Tsou Jung." In *Revolutionary Leaders of Modern China.* Ed. Chün-tu Hsüeh. Oxford: Oxford University Press, 1971. Pp. 153–209.

Hu, Ch'ang-chih. "Ch'ien Mu ti *Kuo shih ta kang* yü Te-kuo li-shih-chu-i (Ch'ien Mu's *Outline history of the nation* and German historicism)." *Shih-hsüeh p'ing-lun* (Historical criticism), 6 (September 1983).

Hu, Shih. *The Chinese Renaissance.* Chicago: University of Chicago Press, 1934. Reprint, New York: Paragon, 1963.

Hua, Hengfang. *Xingsuxuan wencun* (A posthumous collection of writings from the study of Xingsu). Wuxi, n.d.

Hua, Hongmo, ed. *Hua shi xin yizhuang shilüe* (A documentary account of the new Hua charitable estate). Wuxi, 1901.

————. *Hua shi tongsi sanxinggong zhi zongpu* (Genealogy of the Tongsi sanxinggong branch of the Hua). Wuxi, 1881, 1911.

Hua, Yilun. *Liyuxuan wenji* (Collected writings from the study of Liyu). Wuxi, 1883.

Hua, Zhan'en. *Xijin zhiwai* (An unofficial gazetteer of Wuxi-jingui). Wuxi, 1846. Reprint, Taipei: Wuxi T'ung-hsiang hui, 1976.

Hua, Ziheng. *Hua shi chuanfangji* (A collection of writings from the glorious traditions of the Hua). Wuxi, 1743.

Hua, Zonghua. *Hua Zhengu xiansheng Lüdeji* (The contemplations of Master Hua Zhengu). Preface by Qian Zhongyi, 1398; printed by Sun Congzhi, Wuxi, 1532.

Hummel, Arthur W., ed. *Eminent Chinese of the Ch'ing Period*. Washington, D.C.: U.S. Government Printing Office, 1943.

Huters, Theodore. *Qian Zhongshu*. Boston: Twayne, 1982.

Inoue, Kiyoshi. *Nihon no Rekishi*. Tokyo: Iwanami Shinshū, 1966.

Kamachi, Noriko. *Reform in China: Huang Ts'un-hsien and the Japanese Model*. Cambridge: Harvard University Press, 1981.

Keenan, Barry. *The Dewey Experiment in China: Educational Reform and Political Power in the Early Republic*. Cambridge: Harvard University Press, 1977.

Kuhn, Philip A. "Late Ch'ing Views of the Polity." In *Select Papers from the Center for Far Eastern Studies, no. 4, 1979–80*. Ed. Tang Tsou. Chicago: University of Chicago, 1981. Pp. 1–18.

Kuo, Thomas C. *Ch'en Tu-hsiu (1879–1942) and the Chinese Communist Movement*. South Orange, N.J.: Seton Hall University Press, 1975.

Kwok, D. W. Y. *Scientism in Chinese Thought, 1900–1905*. New Haven and London: Yale University Press, 1965.

Lau, D. C., trans. *Lao Tzu: Tao Te Ching*. Baltimore: Penguin, 1963.

———. *Mencius*. Baltimore: Penguin, 1970.

Lee, Hong Yung, "The Implications of Reform for Ideology, State and Society in China." *Journal of International Affairs* 39:2 (Winter 1986).

Levenson, Joseph R. *Confucian China and Its Modern Fate: A Trilogy*. Berkeley and Los Angeles: University of California Press, 1968.

Lewis, Charlton. *Prologue to the Chinese Revolution: The Transformation of Ideas and Institutions in Hunan Province, 1891–1907*. Cambridge: Harvard University Press, 1976.

Li, Yu-ning. *The Introduction of Socialism into China*. New York: Columbia University Press, 1971.

Liew, K. S. *Struggle for Democracy: Sung Chiao-jen and the 1911 Chinese Revolution*. Berkeley and Los Angeles: University of California Press, 1971.

Liu, Kwang-ching. "Li Hung-chang in Chihli: The Emergence of a Policy, 1870–1875." In *Approaches to Modern Chinese History*. Ed. Albert Feuerwerker, Rhoads Murphey, and Mary C. Wright. Berkeley and Los Angeles: University of California Press, 1967.

Luo, Guanzhong. Excerpt (chaps. 43–50) from *Romance of the Three Kingdoms*. Trans. Yang Xianyi and Gladys Yang. In *Excerpts from Three Classical Chinese Novels*. Beijing: Panda Books, 1981. Pp. 7–122.

Mao, Zedong. *Selected Works of Mao Zedong*. 4 vols. Beijing: Foreign Languages Press, 1961.

Peake, Cyrus H. *Nationalism and Education in Modern China*. New York: Columbia University Press, 1932. Reprint, New York: Howard Fertig, 1970.

Qian, Mu. *Bashi yi shuangqin, Shiyou zayi* (Reminiscences on my parents at the age of eighty, Memories of teachers and friends). (Ch'ien Mu. *Pa-shih i shuang-ch'in, Shih-yu tsa-i: ho-k'an*.) Taipei: Tung Ta T'u-shu, 1983.

———. *Guoshi dagang* (Outline history of the nation). Shanghai: Shangwu, 1940. Rev. ed., Taipei: Shang-wu, 1982.

———. *Guoxue gailun* (A Survey of national studies). Shanghai: Shangwu, 1931.

———. "Liu Xiang, Xin fu zi nianpu (Chronological record of Liu Xiang and Xin, father and son)." *Yanjing xuebao*, 7 (vol. 6 of the series *Gu shi bian* [Critiques of ancient history], ed. Gu Jiegang), 1930.

———. *Wenhua yu jiaoyu* (Culture and education). Taipei: Tung-ta, 1976.

———. *Xianqin zhu zi xi nian*. (Chronological studies of the pre-Qin philosophers). Shanghai: Shangwu, 1935.

———. *Zhongguo jin sanbai nian xueshu shi* (A history of Chinese scholarship of the last three centuries). Shanghai: Shangwu, 1937.

———. *Zhongguo lishi jingshen* (The spirit of Chinese history). Taipei: Tung-ta, 1976.

Qian, Shibing, ed. *Qian shi hutou zongpu* (Genealogy of the Qian of Hutou). Wuxi, 1887–92.

Qian, Zonglian, ed. *Zongpu beiyao (Qian shi)* (Draft genealogy of the Qian). Wuxi, 1922.

Rankin, Mary Backus. *Early Chinese Revolutionaries: Radical Intellectuals in Shanghai and Chekiang, 1902–1911*. Cambridge: Harvard University Press, 1971.

Rawski, Evelyn Sakakida. *Education and Popular Literacy in Ch'ing China*. Ann Arbor: University of Michigan Press, 1979.

Schiffrin, Harold Z. *Sun Yat-sen: Reluctant Revolutionary*. Boston: Little, Brown, 1980.

Schneider, Laurence A. *Ku Chieh-kang and China's New History*. Berkeley and Los Angeles: University of California Press, 1971.

Schoppa, R. Keith. *Chinese Elites and Political Change: Zhejiang Province in the Early Twentieth Century.* Cambridge: Harvard University Press, 1982.

Schwarcz, Vera. *The Chinese Enlightenment: Intellectuals and the Legacy of the May Fourth Movement of 1919.* Berkeley and Los Angeles: University of California Press, 1986.

Schwartz, Benjamin. *In Search of Wealth and Power: Yen Fu and the West.* Cambridge: Harvard University Press, 1964.

Shi, Jianlie. "Ji (Wuxi) xiancheng shishou kefu benmo (A record of the loss and recovery of Wuxi)." In *Taiping Tianguo* (The Taiping heavenly kingdom). Ed. Xiang Da. Shanghai, 1952.

Spence, Jonathan D. *The Gate of Heavenly Peace: The Chinese and Their Revolution, 1985–1980.* New York and Middlesex: Penguin Books, 1981.

Twitchett, Denis. "Documents on Clan Administration, Part 1: The Rules of Administration of the Charitable Estate of the Fan Clan." *Asia Major* 8 (1960–61): 1–35.

———. "The Fan Clan's Charitable Estate, 1050–1760." In *Confucianism in Action.* Ed. D. S. Nivison and A. F. Wright. Stanford: Stanford University Press, 1959.

Waley, Arthur, trans. *The Book of Songs.* New York: Grove Press, 1960.

Wen, Yiduo. *Wen Yiduo quan ji.* 4 vols. Hong Kong: Yuandong tushu, 1968.

Weng, Zushan. "Wuxi dongnan xiang nongminde tianfu fudan (The burdens of tax payment on the peasants of southeastern Wuxi county)." *Nongcun shenghua congtan* (Village life forum), May 1937.

Wu Ge (Songs of Wu). Ed. Suzhou shi wenxue yishu jie lianhe hui. Beijing: Zhongguo minjian wenyi chubanshe, 1984.

Wu Xi, ed. *Taibo Meili zhi.* Wuxi, 1897. Reprint Taipei: Wuxi t'ung-hsiang hui, 1981.

Wuxi difang ziliao huibian (Selected local documents on Wuxi). Vol. 1. Wuxi, 1984.

Wuxi-Jingui xianzhi (Wuxi-jingui gazetteer). Wuxi, 1881.

Ye, Xian'en, and Tan Tihua. "Lun Zhujiang sanjiaozhou di zutian (On lineage-owned land in the Pearl River delta)." In *Ming-Qing Guangdong shehui jingji xingtai yanjiu* (Studies of social and economic conditions in Guangdong in the Ming-Qing period). Ed. Guangdong lishi xuehui. Guangzhou: Guangdong renmin chubanshe, 1985.

Young, Ernest P. *The Presidency of Yuan Shih-k'ai: Liberalism and Dictatorship in Early Republican China.* Ann Arbor: University of Michigan Press, 1977.

Zhang, Taiyan. *Zhang Taiyan shi wen xuan zhu* (Selected and annotated prose and poetry of Zhang Binglin [Taiyan]). Ed. Zhang Taiyan zhuzuo bianzhu zu. Shanghai renmin chuban she, 1976.

Zou, Jingheng (Tsou Ching-heng). "Jing shu xian sao Hua Ruizhen nüshi zhijie (In commemoration of my sister-in-law Hua Ruizhen's commitment to chaste widowhood)." Unpublished manuscript, 1981.

———. *Cansang sizhi zakao* (Studies of sericulture). Taipei: San-min shu-chü, 1981.

Index